Redefining Information Security

Redefining Information Security

How to build a security-driven organization

Brian Wagner

KoganPage

First published in Great Britain and the United States in 2025 by Kogan Page Limited

Kogan Page

Kogan Page Ltd, 2nd Floor, 45 Gee Street, London EC1V 3RS, United Kingdom
Kogan Page Inc, 8 W 38th Street, Suite 902, New York, NY 10018, USA
www.koganpage.com

EU Representative (GPSR)

Authorised Rep Compliance Ltd, Ground Floor, 71 Baggot Street Lower, Dublin D02 P593, Ireland
www.arccompliance.com

Kogan Page books are printed on paper from sustainable forests.

ISBNs

Hardback	978 1 3986 2003 2
Paperback	978 1 3986 2001 8
Ebook	978 1 3986 2002 5

British Library Cataloguing-in-Publication Data

A CIP record for this book is available from the British Library.

Library of Congress Control Number

2025935621

Typeset by Integra Software Services, Pondicherry
Print production managed by Jellyfish
Printed and bound by CPI Group (UK) Ltd, Croydon CR0 4YY

CONTENTS

PREFACE

I wrote my first production application when I was 16 years old using Microsoft Access 2000. It was basically a back-office system that ran the clinical side of a healthcare company; it managed patients, facilities, doctors, vendors and even the billing side. For almost five years it ran the business I wrote it for, before it was replaced with a more comprehensive solution that was purpose built for the industry. Back then, the network was a few large switches and a handful of towers in the IT manager's office under his desk. My biggest challenge at the time was concurrent user access: what happens when two users on two different workstations access the same information at the same time? Cybersecurity had not entered my world yet, as I was relying on the safety of a closed system. However, the application did have user role management to be sure that access was scoped appropriately, so I was already doing some primitive risk management before I knew what that was.

Having been successful with that project, I launched into the next project, then another one after that. By the time I was 20 years old, I had collected a lot of experience with some big projects for global automotive manufacturers, and I even started outsourcing some of my lower-level contracts to friends of mine pursuing the same field. I learned a lot about building software and employing engineers during those days, but nothing about cybersecurity. During my tenth year as a professional software engineer for hire, I had to get what my mortgage advisor called a 'real job'; it was 2009 in the United States, just one year after the big housing market crash. Banks were reluctant to give mortgages to young 20-somethings who had been self-employed for the last 10 years, so I traded my professional independence for my first house outside of Research Triangle Park just outside of Raleigh, North Carolina.

My first experience as a full-time Senior Systems Analyst was in the financial services industry. This was a departure from my usual work around the Detroit area where I grew up: if you didn't work directly for an automotive company, you worked for a supplier. Financial services is a different animal. For the first time, I found that there were websites that I was prevented from visiting, and applications I was not allowed to install (I had to get sign-off and a special visit from desk side support just to install Python on my Windows workstation). My username had to be exactly eight characters long to appease the mainframe, and my password had to be rotated every 90 days. It was exhausting, but I quickly fell in line... although I didn't understand the 'why' behind it. The code base for many of the applications was VB6 (Visual Basic version 6) which was already about 6–8 years out of date, even then. I only did as much VB6 patching as I had to and instead focused much of my time building .NET applications in C#. These were mainly internal web-based applications, which were fun and exciting, but the change process seemed to take forever. Once I was done with my work, I would put the code in our repository and tag it for deployment. It was at this point entirely a black box to me. I would eventually get some sort of automated message containing the logs which were cryptic and nonsensical, so I usually just scrolled to the bottom to see the output looking for good news.

I had a knack for finding new ways to play by old rules, for example, I found out from port scanning the mainframe that it had an FTP function (port 21 was open and accepting network traffic) which I shimmed a primitive event system into by giving it tab-separated data files, then writing Job Control Language (JCL) to parse and load it. It really felt like I was going backwards from VB6 rather than forwards, but this was an investment of my time to work on more interesting projects. When the data loading was complete, I had the JCL write an empty file in the same FTP directory, as there was a process running on the network polling the FTP for the existence of that file. Once the file was picked up, we were able to perform some downstream ETL (Extract–Transform–Load) work in more modern tools like Powershell. I got so good at stitching together disparate systems, that it led the company to invest in some enterprise scheduling software which orchestrated these steps in a more sophisticated way, complete with error handling and retry logic.

Even after all that creative engineering, I felt pigeon-holed. As many technical people can relate to, I was getting calls and emails from recruiters on a weekly basis, looking for a C# or a .NET developer (or worse: Java). Those requests bothered me, not because I wasn't interested, but I just could not live with the idea that .NET solves every problem, and I had proof of that. I view technology as a toolbox: sometimes you need a saw, sometimes you need a spanner, sometimes you need a drill. You select the best tool for the task at hand. This principle is what led me to master a multitude of programming languages, having written production code in four or five by that time. It is the same principle that kept my ear to the ground for the right sort of company that felt the same way I did; I couldn't shake the feeling that technology was passing me by – that I just wasn't moving fast enough, or that I didn't have enough exposure to the world which I have been a part of for over 10 years already.

In 2010, I had been daydreaming of riding the wave of modern technology, making magic happen once again for a multitude of customers across various industries. 2010 is when Microsoft Azure was launched, and AWS as well as Google Cloud Platform were gaining some popularity. I would lazily peruse the job boards for these providers, and one day there was an opening for AWS local to me at the time; it was the only of those three providers with a local opening relevant to my skillset, so I applied for a Solutions Architect role. It didn't take long to get my rejection letter, but it was hand-written citing specific feedback (which I will paraphrase): 'not enough technical breadth'. I was right. The technical world was passing me by – I had been living in a bubble. I would then spend many of my waking hours pulling apart my CV trying to visualize my strengths and weaknesses to figure out what part of technology systems I lacked experience in. It made me think about what was on the other side of that black box, the one that comes after I tag my commit for deployment. It led me to making friends with the Ops team and the Security team who explained a lot about the how and why.

Those things were useful to know, but that was more about depth rather than breadth, and then it dawned on me: I knew nothing about networking. My entire development life to that point was mostly centred around closed systems accessed internally within the same network, but what about the internet at large? How did that work? It must be important because cloud is becoming 'a thing' and that is entirely over the network. If that is the future, I had to know more, so I managed to find my way into Cisco Systems which is more or less responsible for the proliferation of enterprise routing; they played a pivotal role in the development and commercialization of Ethernet switching in the 1990s which eventually became the foundation of modern local area networks (LANs).

I worked for Cisco rebuilding their performance analytics suite of tools for the Enterprise Router division. That means, before new enterprise routers were going to market, we would first get them into our lab and run a battery of tests on them to ensure that new software features did not degrade router performance by more than an acceptable (and thin) margin. The old system was built over 10 years prior and would fail once it hit 20,000 data points. These modern routers were multicore and multiprotocol which allowed for features such as Quality of Service (QoS) routing, Border Gateway Patrol (BGP) features, and encryption on the fly, and 20,000 data points was only a fraction of the telemetry we would collect. It was here that I learned about firewalls, the Open Systems Interconnection (OSI) model, authentication and asymmetric encryption, as my automation software would have to test these features on big enterprise routers. Those were exciting times, as I was putting all of my skills earned up to that point into something new and learning every single day. It didn't take long before I was back on the job boards for those cloud providers, but this time, I wasn't daydreaming: I was determined to make my move from software to architecture.

In addition to my disciplinary change, I was also motivated to move abroad. From my home in North Carolina, I applied to hundreds of jobs all over Europe. So many that I stopped keeping track of every single application and would instead just react to the responses I got (and instantly forgot about any that never got back to me at all). I knew it was a long shot from the start, especially because I had no other spoken language apart from English (but that itself is an asset, globally). I was applying to jobs faster than new ones were being posted, which meant that eventually the frequency of applications inevitably slowed. A few months into the pursuit, I had a few nibbles, but nothing materialized. Then, during a trip back to Michigan, I received an invitation for an interview for a job at AWS in Berlin, Germany. The reply was pretty basic and only referenced the job by some sort of identifier that meant nothing to me; I had applied for several roles in several locations across Europe for AWS, so I had no idea which one of these it was. I made the arrangements and found myself moving to Berlin within 60 days of accepting my offer as a Solutions Architect. And that is where my cybersecurity journey really began.

In October 2013, there was an all-German office offsite where all the technical resources across the region gathered to discuss strategy and share knowledge. We had a guest visitor from the offices in London, Dob, who I learned was the only named security specialist in all of Europe, and I was fascinated with his segment when he shared with the wider team. I didn't know anyone there yet, so approaching him was just as easy as approaching anyone else, but I did so at the first opportunity and asked him to be my mentor. From that day onward, I had access to one of the most influential people in my career. Over the years, more specialists like Dob either came forward with their previous experience as security specialists or were hired in from the outside. They also played a pivotal role in my cyber-security education, particularly Dave and Bertram, and I really had unobstructed access to decades of deep security knowledge at my fingertips by the generosity of my mentors. They helped spread the word internally and externally that I too was a security professional, and I quickly gained the respect of my peers and colleagues. I went on to other roles within AWS such as Senior Security Consultant and Head of Compliance for Financial Services in EMEA.

Since my time at AWS, I've combined my technical skills with my security skills and have held positions such as Director of Cloud and

Security at a Silicon Valley analytics company, CTO of a cybersecurity firm, and CTO of a Y Combinator fintech building products fit for the financial services industry's strict security requirements. It might only be after all of my career achievements that my friends and family have started to pay attention to the importance of security by enabling multi-factor authentication on their messaging apps, and swapping the same password they use for every single account for a password wallet ('SpottyDog123!' is just not a good enough password). This book is my chance to share my experience with more than just my immediate circles. It is my chance to promote the goodness of security to the masses in hopes that it will reach the same products and services that my family and friends use, making the digital world a little bit safer from cybercrime.

1

Introduction

The drumbeat of cybersecurity threats is impossible to ignore. Ransomware attacks, data breaches and digital disruptions regularly make front-page news, serving as a constant reminder of the escalating risks facing organizations and their customers. Yet, for many businesses, the traditional approach to security remains mired in a mindset that views it as a mere cost centre – a necessary box-ticking function that imposes obstacles which constrain innovation and progress. *Redefining Information Security* presents a transformative philosophy that challenges this outdated paradigm. This book positions security not as a burden, but as a strategic enabler for organizational growth and success by shifting the narrative from a culture of 'no' to one of 'yes' within the realm of cybersecurity and empowering security professionals to become facilitators of progress and catalysts for innovation.

In an era where digital threats continue to proliferate, the time to move beyond a reactive and restrictive security mindset is now. This book offers a modern approach, offering a comprehensive roadmap for organizations seeking to transform their security posture from a necessary constraint to a competitive advantage. Underpinning this transformative vision is the recognition that security is not just a defensive necessity, but a strategic asset capable of unlocking new opportunities. Rather than simply shielding themselves from risks, organizations that adopt a proactive security stance can actively leverage those very risks to fuel progress and growth. The book explores strategies for balancing risk and security investments, empowering leaders to make informed decisions that prioritize both security and strategic advancement.

Traditionally, security teams have been perceived as the gatekeepers and naysayers, often seen as obstacles to the organization's forward momentum. *Redefining Information Security* challenges this perception, offering a holistic approach that integrates security seamlessly into the fabric of operations, rather than treating it as an afterthought. The book recognizes that successful security strategies must go beyond technical aspects, considering organizational culture, leadership and human factors as integral components. Drawing on real-world examples, this book provides a framework for cultivating a security-driven culture, where security professionals collaborate with their counterparts in engineering, product development and business strategy to drive innovation and growth. Readers will discover how to empower security teams to become facilitators of progress, shedding their traditional role as the 'department of no' and embracing a new identity as catalysts for change. Importantly, *Redefining Information Security* goes beyond current best practices, offering a forward-looking perspective on how security can evolve to meet the challenges of tomorrow's challenges. The book delves into emerging trends, technologies and security challenges, equipping readers with the knowledge and foresight to future-proof their security strategies.

This book sounds a rallying cry for a fundamental shift in organizational mindsets around security. It challenges the entrenched status quo, empowering both business leaders and security professionals to reconceive security's role. No longer should it be viewed as a necessary constraint, but rather as a catalyst capable of propelling progress and growth. Through embracing the principles laid out here, organizations can unlock the true strategic potential of security, harnessing it as a powerful asset to drive sustainable success.

The evolution of cybersecurity

Cybersecurity – well, cyber*crime* – is really a consequence of progress in the technical world: modern technology systems in enterprise landscapes have created a sub-industry of opportunistic cybercrime, which, in turn, has created the need for cybersecurity.

Early beginnings

The earliest known computer virus long pre-dates the internet, even in business technology systems. The 'Creeper' virus was both created and discovered in 1971 by Bob Thomas who was a computer programmer working for Raytheon BBN.[1] Bob wrote the virus as an experiment to test a theory that was developed five years prior in 1966 by John von Neumann in an article titled 'Theory of self-reproducing automata'.[2] The article itself is based on lectures that he gave at the University of Illinois about 'Theory and Organization of Complicated Automata' dating back to 1949. Considering that the World Wide Web was first available in 1989, and that businesses did not start using networking regularly until the 1990s, viruses and worms had already been prevalent for over 20 years.

In 1971, Bob Thomas wrote the Creeper virus to spread across ARPANET (which preceded the internet as we know it today) which means it was effectively a worm. A worm is a type of virus that replicates itself and spreads to infect connected systems – something that became easier to do once we had computer networks. Creeper was more or less innocuous and was created to prove a theory. Its only symptom was a message to the logged-in user which read 'I'm the creeper, catch me if you can!' Creeper's 'blast radius' (more on that later) was a maximum of 28 machines, as it only infected DEC PDP-10 mainframe computers running the TENEX operating system, and there were exactly 28 machines which matched that profile connected to ARPANET at that time.[3] Later that year, Bob Thomas's colleague – Ray Tomlinson – created 'Reaper' which navigated the ARPANET network, detected Creeper, and removed it.[4] Creeper and Reaper are still considered to be the first virus and antivirus (respectively). Later that year, a graduate student named Alan Davis at the University of Illinois at Urbana-Champaign created a process on a PDP-11 mainframe that would replicate itself if it first detected that it was not running on the host system. Once running, it would create a file the size of the remaining disk space on the host (which all users of the system shared!). What's more, it would repeat this process over and over; when a user saved a file, the system advised them that the disk was full and that they needed to delete existing files. Once they deleted a file, the process would immediately fill the free disk space with another file, thus crippling the system. At that point, the user would inform the system administrator to investigate, who would discover the malicious process and delete it. However, due to its cyclical nature, it would have started again and create a copy of itself moments later. Only a reboot of the machine would break the cycle. In 1974, the work of Alan Davis seems to have inspired the 'Wabbit' virus. The Wabbit virus would make multiple copies of itself on a single computer rather quickly (hence the name 'rabbit') until it completely disabled and crashed the system.

A year later, in 1975, John Walker, who would later co-found Autodesk (a pioneer in Computer Aided Design), wrote the ANIMAL Trojan. Unlike the previous viruses and worms, ANIMAL was not a self-replicating program. Instead, it was a Trojan horse – a seemingly benign application that concealed malicious code. ANIMAL was distributed as a simple guessing game, where the program would 'think' of an animal and the user would try to guess what it was by asking yes-or-no questions. However, behind the scenes, ANIMAL was surreptitiously copying itself into the system's startup files, ensuring that it would run automatically every time the computer was booted up. Once installed, ANIMAL would slowly degrade the system's performance, consuming more and more memory and CPU cycles over time. This 'creeping' effect was designed to avoid detection, unlike the more dramatic system crashes caused by the earlier 'Wabbit' virus.[5] ANIMAL's insidious nature earned it the nickname the 'Trojan Horse'.[6]

The ANIMAL Trojan highlighted a new frontier in the evolving world of cybersecurity threats. Unlike the previous generation of self-replicating viruses, ANIMAL demonstrated how malicious code could be hidden within ostensibly harmless programs, making it much harder for system administrators to detect and remove. This foreshadowed the rise of increasingly sophisticated social engineering attacks that would plague computer users in the decades to come.

Cybercrime emerges

The dawn of the 1980s ushered in an evolution of cybercrime, as attackers deployed increasingly sophisticated techniques to target computer systems for financial gain and political motives. The success of the ANIMAL Trojan had demonstrated the power of social engineering and deception in breaching computer defences, providing a blueprint that cybercriminals quickly adapted. They created a new generation of Trojan horses and other malware designed to infiltrate systems under the guise of legitimate software. These technical exploits exposed the vulnerabilities of softly defended computer networks, inspiring a new breed of cybercriminals to push the boundaries even further.

Alongside the proliferation of malware, groups like the notorious '414 Gang' emerged, leveraging their technical prowess to gain unauthorized access to sensitive systems through brute-force tactics like systematically probing dial-up connections. This showcased how the growing sophistication of cybercrime was also fuelling more opportunistic, low-tech attacks – foreshadowing the diversity of cyber threats to come.

From state-sponsored hacking for espionage to financially motivated assaults on critical infrastructure, the 1980s saw the cybercrime landscape expand rapidly, forcing governments, businesses and the public to grapple with the escalating dangers posed by malicious actors in the new digital frontier.

414 Gang

One of the earliest high-profile cases was the '414 Gang' in 1983. A group of Milwaukee-area teenagers, all under the age of 18, gained unauthorized access to a number of computer systems, including those belonging to Los Alamos National Laboratory, Memorial Sloan-Kettering Cancer Center and Security Pacific National Bank.[7]

According to reports, the 414 Gang primarily used their access to explore and navigate the computer systems they had breached, rather than attempting to cause direct damage or financial harm. They would often leave behind calling cards or messages to taunt the system administrators, such as displaying the group's name '414' on login screens. In some cases, the 414 Gang went further, demonstrating their ability to manipulate the compromised systems. For example, they were able to access sensitive files and databases belonging to the Los Alamos National Laboratory, which was conducting nuclear research at the time.[8] While they did not appear to have stolen or tampered with any classified information, their mere presence on these sensitive systems was deeply concerning. The 414 Gang also gained access to the computer systems of Memorial Sloan-Kettering Cancer Center in New York. Here, they were able to view patient records and medical information, raising serious privacy and security concerns. Again, there was no evidence that the group had misused or leaked any of this sensitive data. Perhaps most alarmingly, the 414 Gang managed to breach the computer network of Security Pacific National Bank. While they did not directly steal any funds, their ability to access the bank's systems highlighted the potential for cybercriminals to target financial institutions for financial gain – a threat that would only grow in the years to come.[9]

The activities of the 414 Gang, while not overtly destructive, demonstrated the ease with which technically skilled individuals could infiltrate supposedly secure computer systems, even at the highest levels of government and industry. This early case served as a harbinger of the more sophisticated and damaging cyber-attacks that would emerge in the latter half of the 1980s and beyond. Their exploits prompted increased scrutiny of computer security practices and led to the passage of the first major federal computer crime law, the Comprehensive Crime Control Act of 1984.

Comprehensive Crime Control Act of 1984

The Comprehensive Crime Control Act of 1984 was a landmark piece of legislation in the United States that addressed the growing threat of computer-related crimes. The Act contained several key provisions to combat the emerging challenge of cybercrime. It criminalized unauthorized access to computer systems and the theft or destruction of data, establishing hacking and malicious code creation as federal crimes and providing law enforcement with the legal tools to prosecute these activities.

Additionally, the Act increased the penalties for computer-related offences, reflecting the growing recognition of the potential harm that could be caused by these crimes. The legislation also authorized the seizure of computer equipment used in criminal activities, giving law enforcement the ability to disrupt the operations of cybercriminals.[10] The Comprehensive Crime Control Act of 1984 marked a significant step forward in the legal framework for addressing cybercrime, recognizing that the advancement of computer technology had created new avenues for criminal activity that required dedicated legislation and enforcement mechanisms.

Morris worm

The emergence of the Morris worm in 1988 marked a significant turning point in the evolution of cybercrime and the growing threat it posed to computer systems worldwide. Developed by Robert Tappan Morris, a graduate student at Cornell University, the Morris worm was not designed to be overtly destructive. Rather, it was an experiment intended to gauge the size of the nascent internet. However, a programming flaw caused the worm to replicate itself at an exponential rate, quickly overwhelming and crashing thousands of computers across the United States.[11]

The worm's growth rate can be described by the common equation for exponential growth over time:

$$N(t)=N_0 \times 2^{t/T}$$

where $N(t)$ is the number of infected systems at time t, N_0 is the initial number of infected systems, and T is the time constant for the worm's replication. The Morris worm's blast radius was staggering, infecting an estimated 6,000 to 60,000 computers – a significant portion of the internet at the time. This unprecedented scale of disruption brought the issue of cybersecurity into focus, as governments and corporations scrambled to understand and mitigate the threat.[12]

The aftermath of the Morris worm incident led to the creation of the Computer Emergency Response Team (CERT) at Carnegie Mellon University, one of the first dedicated organizations tasked with coordinating the response to major cyber incidents.[13] It also prompted the passage of the Computer Fraud and Abuse Act, which criminalized unauthorized access to computer systems and the creation of malicious code.[14]

The Morris worm demonstrated that even a relatively unsophisticated piece of malware, if left unchecked, could wreak havoc on a global scale, and set the stage for the emergence of increasingly complex and destructive cyber threats in the decades to come.

AIDS Trojan

A particularly notorious example of a technically sophisticated attack was the AIDS Trojan. Discovered in 1989, it was a malicious program that foreshadowed the rise of a new and particularly insidious form of cybercrime: ransomware. The AIDS Trojan was distributed on floppy disks that purported to contain information about the AIDS virus, a topic that was generating significant public concern and media attention at the time. Unsuspecting users who inserted these disks into their computers were met with a sinister surprise – the Trojan would immediately begin encrypting the files on the victim's hard drive, rendering them inaccessible.[15] Once the encryption process was complete, the user would be confronted with a demand for a ransom payment, typically in the range of $189, in order to regain access to their data. The Trojan's creators claimed that the payment would provide the user with a 'software key' that could decrypt the locked files. In reality, there was no guarantee that the decryption key would be provided, even if the ransom was paid.[16]

The AIDS Trojan represented a significant shift in the motivations of cybercriminals. Unlike earlier viruses and worms, which were often created out of technical curiosity or as ideological statements, the Trojan was designed solely for financial gain. Its creators recognized the growing reliance on computers and digital data in both personal and professional settings, and they sought to exploit this vulnerability for their own profit.

The impact of the AIDS Trojan was widespread and devastating. Thousands of individuals and organizations fell victim to the attack, with many losing critical files and data that were essential to their daily operations. The ransom demands placed a significant financial burden on those affected, and the emotional toll of having one's data held hostage was equally damaging.

The response to the AIDS Trojan was swift, with law enforcement agencies and cybersecurity experts working tirelessly to identify the perpetrators and mitigate the damage. However, the Trojan's success highlighted the growing sophistication of cybercriminals and the need for stronger security measures to protect against these attacks and others to come. In the aftermath of the AIDS Trojan incident, the cybersecurity community began to recognize the emerging threat of ransomware. This new form of malware, which encrypts victims' data and demands a ransom payment for its release, would go on to become one of the most prevalent and damaging types of cybercrime, even over 30 years later.

The World Wide Web

As the 1980s gave way to the 1990s, the world witnessed a technological revolution that would forever change the landscape of cybercrime: the emergence of the World Wide Web.[17] This new global network, built upon the foundations of the earlier ARPANET and other computer networks, opened up a vast and interconnected digital frontier, offering unprecedented opportunities for communication, collaboration and the exchange of information. However, this new world of the internet also presented a tantalizing target for cybercriminals, who quickly recognized the potential to exploit the inherent vulnerabilities of this rapidly expanding digital ecosystem.

In the early days of the World Wide Web, the infrastructure and security protocols were still in their infancy, leaving many entry points for malicious actors to infiltrate and wreak havoc. The widespread adoption of web browsers, such as Mosaic and Netscape Navigator, provided cybercriminals with new avenues to distribute their malware, often disguising it as legitimate software or web content.

One of the first high-profile examples of this new breed of internet-based cybercrime was the 'ILOVEYOU' virus, which emerged in 2000. Masquerading as a love letter, the ILOVEYOU virus spread rapidly through email, exploiting the inherent trust that users placed in messages from their contacts. Once activated, the virus would not only infect the victim's computer but also send copies of itself to everyone in the user's address book, exponentially increasing its reach.[18] The virus caused widespread disruption, infecting millions of computers worldwide and causing an estimated $15 billion in damages.[19] This incident highlighted the ease with which cybercriminals could leverage the global connectivity of the internet to launch attacks on an unprecedented scale, far surpassing the localized impact of earlier viruses and worms.

As the World Wide Web continued to grow and evolve, so too did the tactics and sophistication of cybercriminals. The development of web-based technologies, such as dynamic content, scripting languages, and interactive applications, provided new avenues for exploitation. Cybercriminals began to target vulnerabilities in web browsers, web servers and web-based applications, using techniques like cross-site scripting (XSS) and SQL injection to gain unauthorized access to sensitive data and systems. The rise of e-commerce and online banking in the 1990s also presented a tempting target for financially motivated cybercriminals. Phishing attacks, in which fraudsters would create fake websites and emails to trick users into divulging their login credentials or financial information, became increasingly prevalent. These scams often leveraged the anonymity and global reach of the internet to target victims across borders, making it challenging for law enforcement to effectively respond.

As the 1990s progressed, the cybercrime landscape continued to evolve, with the emergence of even more sophisticated and targeted attacks. State-sponsored hacking groups, motivated by geopolitical agendas, began to leverage the internet to conduct espionage, disrupt critical infrastructure, and sow discord. The 1998 'Solar Sunrise' incident, in which a group of hackers with suspected ties to the Middle East gained unauthorized access to US military computer systems including the Department of Defense (DOD),[20] was a stark reminder of the growing threat of cyber warfare. The then-Deputy Secretary of Defense John Hamre called it 'the most organized and systematic [cyber] attack the Pentagon has seen to date'.[21] In response to these escalating threats, governments and the private sector began to invest heavily in cybersecurity measures, developing new technologies, policies and legal frameworks to combat the rising tide of cybercrime. The establishment of specialized law enforcement units, such as the FBI's Cyber Division, and the enactment of legislation like the Cybercrime Convention of 2001 were important steps in this ongoing battle.

The World Wide Web also enabled the emergence of online black markets, where cybercriminals could buy and sell stolen data, malware and other illicit goods. The anonymity provided by the internet, coupled with the use of cryptocurrencies, made these underground marketplaces difficult to disrupt, further fuelling the growth of cybercrime. Chief among these was Silk Road, a hidden website that leveraged the anonymity of the dark web to facilitate the sale of a wide range of illegal goods and services. Launched in 2011, Silk Road was accessible only through the Tor network, which obscured the identities and locations of its users. Here, buyers and sellers could engage in transactions for everything from narcotics and firearms to forged documents and hacking tools, all while evading the scrutiny of law enforcement.[22] The site's use of the cryptocurrency Bitcoin further shielded these activities from traditional financial oversight.

Stuxnet

Alongside the proliferation of online black markets, malware and financial scams, a new and more ominous threat began to emerge – the rise of state-sponsored cyber-attacks. One of the most sophisticated and impactful examples of this new era of cyber warfare was the Stuxnet worm, which was discovered in 2010.[23] Stuxnet represented a significant departure from the cybercrime activities that had dominated the preceding decades, showcasing the potential for nation-states to leverage digital tools and techniques to target critical infrastructure and achieve strategic objectives.

Stuxnet's origins can be traced back to the growing tensions between the West and Iran over the latter's nuclear programme. Concerned about Iran's pursuit of nuclear weapons, the United States and its allies sought to find ways to disrupt and delay the country's progress. Enter Stuxnet – a highly complex piece of malware that was specifically designed to target and sabotage the industrial control systems used in Iran's uranium enrichment facilities. Unlike the financially motivated cybercrime activities that had come before, Stuxnet was not interested in stealing data or holding systems for ransom. Instead, its primary objective was to cause physical damage to the centrifuges used in Iran's nuclear facilities, effectively sabotaging the country's nuclear ambitions from the inside.[24] To achieve this, Stuxnet employed a multi-pronged attack strategy that combined several innovative and highly sophisticated techniques. The worm was engineered to exploit previously unknown vulnerabilities in the Windows operating system, allowing it to infiltrate targeted systems without detection.[25] It then used specialized code to manipulate the programmable logic controllers that governed the operation of the centrifuges, instructing them to spin at speeds that would cause the equipment to fail.

Stuxnet's success in disrupting Iran's nuclear programme was a watershed moment in the evolution of cyber warfare. It demonstrated that nation-states had the capability to develop and deploy highly targeted, precision-guided malware capable of causing real-world, physical damage – a capability that had previously been the stuff of science fiction. Stuxnet highlighted the vulnerability of critical infrastructure systems, which were often reliant on outdated or poorly secured industrial control technologies. It also raised concerns about the potential for cyber-attacks to be used as a new form of asymmetric warfare, where smaller, technologically advanced nations could potentially level the playing field against larger, more conventional military powers.

Stuxnet's success inspired other nation-states to invest heavily in the development of their own cyber warfare capabilities. As the 2010s progressed, a new era of digital conflict began to emerge, with countries like China, Russia and North Korea all suspected of launching increasingly sophisticated cyber-attacks against their adversaries. The rise of state-sponsored cyber threats, exemplified by Stuxnet, also had a profound impact on the cybersecurity landscape more broadly. Governments and private sector organizations were forced to reevaluate their defensive strategies, investing in new technologies and techniques to detect and mitigate the growing risk of advanced persistent threats – highly targeted, stealthy cyber-attacks often backed by nation-state resources.

The legacy of Stuxnet continues to reverberate to this day. The worm's code has been analysed and reverse-engineered by security researchers, providing valuable insights into the evolving tactics and capabilities of cyber adversaries. The incident has sparked a global debate about the ethical and legal implications of using digital weapons, and the need for international cooperation and governance to prevent the escalation of cyber conflicts.

Diversifying threats

The inherent adaptability and resourcefulness of cybercriminals ensured that they continued to stay one step ahead. As new security measures were implemented, they found innovative ways to circumvent them, often exploiting the very technologies and platforms that were designed to protect against their activities. The creation of the World Wide Web marked a pivotal moment in the evolution of cybercrime, ushering in an era of unprecedented scale, sophistication and global impact. The internet's boundless potential for connectivity and information-sharing also enabled the growth of a vast and ever-changing digital underworld, where cybercriminals could operate with increasing impunity.

As the 21st century dawned, the cybercrime landscape continued to diversify and expand, with new threats emerging at pace. Ransomware, for instance, became a scourge of the digital age, with attackers leveraging the internet to rapidly distribute malware that could encrypt victims' data and hold it for ransom. The WannaCry and NotPetya attacks of the 2010s demonstrated the devastating potential of these extortion-based schemes, causing billions of dollars in damages worldwide. Alongside the rise of ransomware, the internet also facilitated the growth of other lucrative cybercrime enterprises, such as online fraud and identity theft. The ubiquity of e-commerce, social media and cloud-based services provided cybercriminals with a wealth of personal and financial data to exploit, often through sophisticated phishing campaigns and data breaches. The interconnectedness of the modern digital landscape also enabled the emergence of botnets – networks of compromised computers that could be controlled remotely by cybercriminals. These botnets were used to launch distributed denial-of-service (colloquially known as DDoS) attacks, flood inboxes with spam and even mine cryptocurrency, all while concealing the true identities of the perpetrators.

As the scale and complexity of cybercrime continued to escalate, the need for robust international cooperation and coordination became increasingly apparent. Cybercriminals were able to exploit the borderless nature of the internet, often operating across multiple jurisdictions to evade law enforcement. This challenge was compounded by the rapid pace of technological change, which often outpaced the ability of legal and regulatory frameworks to keep up. In response, governments and the private sector have invested heavily in developing new strategies and tools to combat the growing threat of cybercrime. This has included the establishment of specialized cybersecurity agencies, the enactment of comprehensive data protection laws and the deployment of advanced threat detection and mitigation technologies. Yet, despite these efforts, the cybercrime landscape remains a constantly shifting and elusive target. As new vulnerabilities are discovered and exploited, and as cybercriminals continue to adapt their tactics, the battle to secure the digital frontier remains an ongoing and ever-evolving challenge.

Cybersecurity as a profession

With the threat of cybercrime escalating in the late 20th century, the need for dedicated professionals to protect against emerging threats became increasingly apparent. The 1990s marked the emergence of cybersecurity as a distinct and rapidly growing field, driven by the recognition that the security of computer systems, networks, and digital assets required specialized expertise and a proactive approach. One of the key drivers behind the rise of cybersecurity as a profession was the establishment of government agencies and regulatory bodies tasked with addressing the challenges posed by cybercrime. In the United States, the National Security Agency (NSA) and the National Institute of Standards and Technology (NIST) played significant roles in shaping the modern cybersecurity landscape.[26]

Established in 1901, the National Institute of Standards and Technology (NIST), originally known as the National Bureau of Standards, had a focus on developing standards and measurements for physical and industrial technologies in its early decades.[27] However, NIST's role in cybersecurity and securing digital systems emerged much later, in the 1990s and beyond. It was not until the 1990s, as the digital revolution and the growth of the internet gained momentum, that NIST's mission expanded to include the development of standards and guidelines for securing digital systems and infrastructure. In the 1990s and 2000s, NIST began publishing influential cybersecurity-related publications, such as the NIST Cybersecurity Framework and the NIST Special Publication 800 series, which have become essential references for organizations seeking to enhance their cybersecurity posture.[28]

The NSA, originally founded in 1952 as a cryptographic agency, expanded its mandate in the 1990s to include the protection of critical national infrastructure from cyber threats. The agency's expertise in cryptography, signals intelligence and information security proved invaluable as it worked to develop and implement robust security protocols and standards for government and military systems.[29] The NSA's efforts to train and certify cybersecurity professionals, through programmes such as the National Centers of Academic Excellence in Cybersecurity,[30] helped to establish a pipeline of skilled practitioners to meet the growing demand.

As the cybersecurity field gained momentum, academic institutions also responded to the growing demand for specialized education and training. Universities and colleges began to offer dedicated degree programmes and certifications in areas such as information security, network administration and digital forensics. These programmes not only provided students with the technical skills required to protect against cyber threats but also instilled a deeper understanding of the legal, ethical and policy implications of cybersecurity. The private sector, too, played a crucial role in the evolution of cybersecurity as a profession. As businesses increasingly relied on digital technologies and faced the risk of data breaches, cyber-attacks and other cyber-related incidents, the demand for skilled cybersecurity professionals skyrocketed. Companies began to establish dedicated cybersecurity teams, often led by Chief Information Security Officers (CISOs) or Chief Security Officers (CSOs), responsible for developing and implementing comprehensive security strategies (which will be addressed in the next chapter).

The rise of cybersecurity as a profession also coincided with the emergence of specialized cybersecurity firms and consultancies. These organizations provide a range of services, from vulnerability assessments and penetration testing to incident response and security operations centre (SOC) management. The growth of these specialized service providers not only supported the needs of businesses but also created new career paths for cybersecurity professionals.

As the cybersecurity field continued to evolve, the need for standardized certifications and professional development opportunities became increasingly important. Industry-recognized certifications, such as the Certified Information Systems Security Professional (CISSP), the Certified Ethical Hacker (CEH) and the CompTIA Security+, have become highly sought-after credentials, demonstrating an individual's expertise and commitment to the field.

The cybersecurity profession has become increasingly diverse, attracting individuals from a wide range of backgrounds, including computer science, engineering, law enforcement and even military and intelligence services. This diversity has enriched the field, bringing together a range of perspectives and skill sets to tackle the evolving challenges of securing systems in our digital age. Today, cybersecurity professionals play a critical role in protecting individuals, organizations and nations from the growing threat of cyber-attacks. They work to identify and mitigate vulnerabilities, implement robust security controls and respond to security incidents. As the expansion continues and the tactics of cybercriminals become more sophisticated, the demand for skilled cybersecurity professionals is expected to remain high, with the Bureau of Labor Statistics projecting a 33 per cent growth in employment in the field between 2020 and 2030. The profession has come a long way since its emergence in the 1990s, and it continues to evolve and adapt to the changing technological landscape. As our society becomes increasingly interconnected and interdependent, the role of cybersecurity professionals in safeguarding the digital frontier has become more crucial than ever before.

Increasing complexity and scale of cyber threats

As our world becomes more interconnected, the attack surface for cybercriminals has expanded exponentially. The proliferation of the Internet of Things (IoT) has introduced a vast array of new entry points for malicious actors, with everyday devices like smart home appliances, security cameras and industrial control systems becoming potential targets. These IoT devices often lack robust security measures, making them vulnerable to exploitation and the creation of botnets – networks of compromised devices that can be used to launch large-scale attacks.

REAL-WORLD EXAMPLE

The Mirai botnet was a large network of compromised IoT devices, such as security cameras, routers and digital video recorders, that were used to launch a series of devastating DDoS attacks in 2016. The Mirai malware was designed to scan the internet for IoT devices that used default or weak login credentials, and then infect them, adding them to the botnet. Once a device was part of the Mirai botnet, the attackers could use it to generate massive amounts of traffic, overwhelming the targeted websites and services.[31]

One of the most notable attacks carried out by the Mirai botnet was the assault on the website of cybersecurity journalist Brian Krebs, which reached a peak of 620 Gbps, making it one of the largest DDoS attacks ever recorded at the time. The Mirai botnet was also used to target the infrastructure of the French web hosting company OVH, as well as the domain name system (DNS) provider Dyn, which resulted in widespread internet outages across the eastern United States.[32]

The Mirai botnet highlighted the significant security vulnerabilities present in many IoT devices, which often come with default or easily guessable login credentials and lack of proper security updates and patches. This incident underscored the need for IoT device manufacturers to prioritize security and for users to change default passwords and keep their devices up-to-date to prevent them from being hijacked and used in large-scale cyber-attacks.

The shift towards cloud computing has further eroded the traditional security perimeter, blurring the boundaries between internal and external networks. While the cloud has brought numerous benefits, such as increased scalability and flexibility, it has also moved many security challenges downstream, requiring cybersecurity professionals to adapt their strategies and tools to protect data and systems that are no longer confined within a physical network. Engineers who once built software for a closed network then become tasked with things outside of their skillset such as access management, routing and networking, and even encryption. As I once was this kind of engineer, I too would not have been able to cope with these changes overnight.

As the tactics of cybercriminals become more sophisticated, the scale of cyber threats has also grown exponentially. Ransomware attacks, for instance, have evolved from targeting individual users to crippling entire organizations, with the potential to disrupt critical infrastructure and services. The rise of advanced persistent threats and state-sponsored cyber espionage campaigns has further heightened the complexity of the cybersecurity landscape, as these actors often employ highly targeted and persistent methods to infiltrate and maintain access to sensitive systems, like Stuxnet.

Traditional security

Risk is a limit (in mathematics) which forever approaches x, where x is always increasing. Therefore, to continuously address your cyber risk, you must also continuously address your approach to security within your organization. A popular analogy that I have re-used in my career is about an individual who is a motorcycle enthusiast who deeply understands the need for safety. They buy all of the gear: the right helmet, protective jacket, trousers, boots and gloves. They enrol themselves in motorcycle safety courses, always drive at the speed limit, and whilst they do not have control over the actions of other drivers on the road, they take all of the precautions available to them to stay as safe as possible. Then, one day, they buy a car. As a cautious person about to drive their car for the first time, they put on their helmet, protective jacket, trousers, boots and gloves, just as they did with the motorcycle. They don't need things like seatbelts and airbags because they have the gear that has lovingly protected them up to this point, so why risk it?

Hopefully the flaw in their logic is obvious: those things that protected them when they were riding a motorcycle are not suitable for protecting them in the car. You could argue that a helmet serves as protection against a head injury, but you could also argue that a seat-belt and airbag combination make the helmet unnecessary, and possibly even that it is a hindrance to peripheral vision and sound awareness. This same logic applies to securing IT systems as time goes on, but in a much more gradual way; we aren't going from motorcycle to car one day, but with every new vendor, with every new service or workload, we are potentially – even if only slightly – changing the parameters, and the approach to security must change with it.

Traditionally speaking, protecting data, applications and entire systems began with the four walls of the data centre: keep the servers under lock and key to prevent unauthorized access, and have strict access procedures otherwise to ensure minimal exposure. Of course, intra-company systems will need access to that data over the internal network, so access to that network is also protected against outsiders getting in, because once they are into the network, they could have access to the data on those servers inside the data centre (of course, limited by the access of a particular user or network account). In the early days of cyber threats, getting into the network was the most difficult part, but once there, an attacker found it much easier to move around laterally throughout the network and do reconnaissance, inspect user behaviour or steal information. This is called 'the perimeter' and it is both physical and virtual.

In the data centre, physical security is used to protect physical assets. These often include CCTV, locks, strong doors, alarms, mantraps, second factors of authentication such as biometrics or a PIN code and badged access. Visitors will be logged and escorted, and nobody has standing access. Logical access to digital assets is controlled at the network level, protected by firewalls which are configured to allow only specific subnets of a network access to specific applications and data; the accounting department has a particular block of 1024 IP addresses which are permitted to access relevant financial data sets and prevented from access to the database control plane (for example). Requests for additional access will undergo a review by the security and network team, and exceptions in the rules are created and documented, all to capture and assess risk to the assets in question.

On the business side, security often comes in the form of anti-virus; the machines with network access (permitted by the firewall) must also be safe from external threats or user negligence; you wouldn't want an infection spreading across the network. Virus scanning, intrusion detection, data extraction prevention – any endpoint security feature – is means to protect the end-user computer device from poisoning the system because, in traditional security, once you are 'in', you're in. In those days, it was assumed that if a device *could* connect to its destination, that it was meant to be there; it was 'trusted'. That is why password complexity, second factors of authentication (such as RSA fobs) and smart cards were introduced in the enterprise: companies needed to be sure it was you logging in and not a threat actor.

Depending on what era you started your technical career in, that may sound ridiculous. Credentials (e.g. passwords) are not all that hard to come by. Sure, a second factor adds some complexity, but not all organizations use a second factor of authentication which makes them a target. Regardless, how is a firewall supposed to know the difference between an authorized user and a threat actor who is impersonating said user? Even more challenging: how is **anything** supposed to know the difference between an authorized user and an authorized user with bad intentions (insider threat)?

REAL-WORLD EXAMPLE

In November 2014, Sony Pictures Entertainment fell victim to a breach orchestrated by a hacking group known as the 'Guardians of Peace' (GOP), who exposed the company's vulnerabilities and the ease with which determined attackers can navigate a compromised network. The breach began with the exploitation of expired credentials, a common security flaw that often goes unnoticed. The hackers were able to gain initial access to Sony's network by using a set of login credentials that had been forgotten and left active long after the associated employee had departed the company. This initial foothold allowed the attackers to bypass the organization's perimeter defences and infiltrate the internal systems.[33]

Once inside the network, the hackers were able to move freely and access a vast trove of sensitive data, including employee information, unreleased films and internal communications. The ease with which the attackers navigated the system highlighted the limitations of traditional security approaches that focus primarily on securing the network's perimeter, rather than addressing the potential vulnerabilities within.

The stolen data was subsequently released to the public, causing significant embarrassment and reputational damage for Sony. The incident also led to the cancellation of the release of the film *The Interview*, further compounding the financial and operational impact on the company.

Limitations of traditional security approaches

The increasing complexity and scale of cyber threats have exposed the limitations of traditional security approaches. Risk, in the context of cybersecurity, is a constantly moving target, as new vulnerabilities and attack vectors emerge with the rapid pace of technological change. Just as organizations work to address one set of threats, cybercriminals adapt and develop new tactics to circumvent existing security measures.

Risk is a fundamental concept in cybersecurity, as it represents the potential for harm or loss resulting from the exploitation of vulnerabilities by cyber threats. Threats can take many forms, from malware and phishing attacks to advanced persistent threats and nation-state-sponsored cyber espionage. These threats can compromise the confidentiality, integrity and availability of an organization's critical data and systems, leading to financial losses, reputational damage and regulatory penalties. Understanding and managing risk is crucial for organizations to protect themselves. Assessing risk involves identifying, analysing and evaluating the potential risks an organization faces, taking into account the likelihood of an event occurring and the potential impact it could have. This information is then used to develop and implement appropriate security controls and mitigation strategies to reduce the overall risk to an acceptable level.

Effective risk management requires a holistic approach that considers not only technical factors but also organizational, human and operational elements. This includes implementing strong security policies, training employees on cybersecurity best practices, and regularly reviewing and updating security measures to address emerging threats.

Move to cloud

Interestingly enough, the primitives of cybersecurity really haven't changed much, in principle. However, much like the motorcycle rider who now drives a car, the practical application of the same principles needs to be adapted. The nature of traditional cybersecurity and technical infrastructure meant that security was left to the security team. If you were an engineer at that time, you wrote the code to solve the problem. It would then likely go through a security review which might do checks in the code for any privileged operations, calls to external systems, or vulnerabilities from libraries or software development kits (SDKs) being used as part of the solution before finally being gently rolled into the production environment. In that world, information is siloed. The engineers write the code, the security team does the security and operations does the deployment.

That siloed way of thinking does not translate well in the modern technology environment because we have been breaking down the walls between these functions. Most organizations are building solutions using some flavour of DevOps – you build it, you run it. That means the solution now includes things like networking, credentials management, authentication and cybersecurity. The modern engineer is a multi-disciplined jack of many trades who finds themselves responsible for the success and safety of their entire application. With cloud being more or less a household concept to even the largest and most conservative technical departments, and a wide adoption of service-based tools, even end users find themselves much closer to the safety of data than ever before.

The need for a proactive and adaptive approach

The changing nature of technology and the blurring of traditional boundaries means that a reactive, siloed approach to security is no longer sufficient: by the time a security team identifies and responds to one issue, several more have likely already arisen. This reactive model is inherently flawed – it is always playing catch-up, struggling to keep up with evolving threats.

What is needed is a more proactive stance, where security is baked into the entire technology ecosystem from the ground up. Engineers must think about security as a core design principle, not an after-thought. Secure coding practices, robust access controls, and comprehensive monitoring and alerting need to be integrated throughout the development lifecycle. This proactive security mind-set needs to permeate the entire organization, from developers to operations to end-users. But even a proactive approach is not enough on its own. The pace of change is so rapid that static, rigid security measures will quickly become outdated and ineffective. An adaptive, flexible security posture is essential. Security controls, policies and processes must be continuously evaluated and updated to address new and emerging threats. Automation and machine learning can play a key role here, helping to rapidly identify anomalies, adapt defences and respond to incidents in real-time.

Crucially, this adaptive approach must extend beyond just the technical implementation. Organizational structures, roles and responsibilities, and communication channels also need to be designed for agility. Security can no longer be siloed – it must be a shared responsibility, with clear lines of accountability and mechanisms for cross-functional collaboration. Security teams must work closely with engineering, operations and business stakeholders to ensure a cohesive, organization-wide security strategy. Even the end-user must also take an adaptive approach. As technology is now most-often distributed, end-users often find themselves on the front lines of security, whether managing cloud services, handling sensitive data or defending against phishing attacks. Security awareness, training and empowerment of end-users is crucial to creating a truly resilient security posture.

Embracing a zero trust security model

With the proliferation of cloud services, remote work and distributed architectures, the concept of a well-defined network perimeter has become increasingly obsolete. In this new reality, a fundamentally different security approach is required – one that embraces the principle of zero trust. At the core of zero trust security is the fundamental assumption that all communications, both internal and external, should be treated as inherently hostile. Gone are the days of implicitly trusting anything that originates from within the corporate firewall. Instead, every request, every connection, every transaction must be thoroughly authenticated and authorized before being granted access. This shift in mindset is critical. By abandoning the notion of a trusted internal network, zero trust security forces organizations to rethink their entire security architecture. Rather than relying on perimeter defences, the focus shifts to granular, application-level controls. An API layer is established between services, with each interaction subjected to rigorous authentication and authorization checks. Even internal communications are encrypted by default, reducing the potential blast radius of a breach.

This zero trust approach empowers application owners and developers to take a more active role in securing their own systems. Rather than deferring to a centralized security team, engineers are given the tools and autonomy to implement strong access controls, data encryption and monitoring within their own applications. This distributed security model not only improves responsiveness and agility, but also fosters a stronger security culture throughout the organization.

Implementing a true zero trust security posture requires a fundamental rethinking of network architecture, identity management and access control policies. Legacy systems and siloed data stores must be modernized and integrated. Automation and machine learning play a crucial role in continuously verifying user and device identities, detecting anomalies and adapting security controls in real-time. Organizations which treat all communications as hostile and verify every request can significantly reduce their attack surface and the potential impact of a breach. If a single credential is compromised or a rogue actor gains access, their ability to move laterally and cause widespread damage is severely limited. The blast radius is contained, and the organization's most critical assets remain protected.

The zero trust model also aligns well with the shift towards cloud-native, microservices-based architectures. As applications become more distributed and interdependent, the need for granular, application-level security controls becomes paramount. Zero trust provides a scalable framework for securing complex, dynamic environments.

Leveraging emerging technologies

The emergence of transformative technologies has opened up new frontiers in the fight against digital threats. Among the most promising of these innovations is the rise of artificial intelligence (AI), which has the potential to fundamentally reshape the way organizations approach security challenges. AI's unique capabilities make it a particularly compelling tool for cybersecurity applications. Its ability to process and analyse vast amounts of data at lightning speed, coupled with its capacity for pattern recognition and anomaly detection, make it well-suited for tasks such as threat detection, incident response and data leakage prevention. Unlike traditional rule-based security systems, AI-powered solutions can identify subtle indicators of compromise and respond to emerging threats in near real-time. AI can uncover anomalies and potential attack vectors that might otherwise go unnoticed by human analysts by sifting through the deluge of security logs, network traffic and user activity data. This atomic-level visibility, combined with the speed and scale of AI processing, can significantly enhance an organization's ability to detect and mitigate cyber threats.

However, it's important to note that AI is not a drop-in replacement for human expertise and decision-making. Recently, the US military conducted a dogfight simulation between an AI system and a human pilot. While the AI system was able to outmanoeuvre the human in the simulated environment, taking risks that a human would not or could not, the real-world outcome of a similar confrontation remains undisclosed. In the end, the human pilot did not even need to take control of the aircraft, underscoring the need for a balanced, collaborative approach between AI and human security professionals.

The true value of AI in cybersecurity lies in its ability to augment and empower human analysts, not to replace them entirely. By automating repetitive tasks, analysing massive datasets and providing real-time alerts, AI can free up security teams to focus on the more complex, strategic aspects of threat mitigation. The applications of AI in cybersecurity are wide-ranging and continue to expand. From threat detection and incident response to data leakage prevention and distributed denial-of-service mitigation, AI-powered solutions are proving their worth in safeguarding organizations against a diverse array of cyber threats. Ultimately, the key to leveraging emerging technologies like AI in cybersecurity lies in striking the right balance between human expertise and machine intelligence.

Importance of collaboration and information sharing

The notion of security as a fixed, static subject matter is no longer tenable. Security is inherently contextual, deeply intertwined with the specific workloads, architectures and technologies that organizations employ. Those who own, operate and build these systems possess the most intimate knowledge of their inner workings – a tribal knowledge that is essential for effective security (more on that in Chapter 6).

However, the importance of collaboration and information sharing extends far beyond the boundaries of any single organization. The cybersecurity field as a whole must come together, pooling their collective expertise and experiences, to address the complex and ever-changing threat landscape. Examples of this collaborative approach can already be seen in initiatives like information sharing and analysis centres (ISACs), where industry peers share threat intelligence and best practices. Similarly, bug bounty programs and vulnerability disclosure frameworks encourage security researchers to work hand-in-hand with organizations to identify and mitigate vulnerabilities which will be discussed in Chapter 8.

Democratizing security knowledge and fostering a culture of collaboration can build a more resilient, adaptive and effective security posture for any organization. No longer can security be the domain of a select few; it must be a shared responsibility, with everyone from developers to operations to end-users playing a role. Only through this collective effort can we hope to stay one step ahead of the looming cyber threats that challenge us all.

Vision: security as an enabler

Organizations have focused on building fortified perimeters, deploying signature-based detection tools and ensuring adherence to a rigid set of security standards. While these measures have their place, they often come at the expense of agility, flexibility and user experience. Employees find themselves frustrated by cumbersome access controls and convoluted approval processes, while IT teams struggle to keep up with the relentless pace of technological change; we will deep dive into the human element in Chapter 8.

But what if security could be reimagined as a strategic business enabler – a competitive advantage that empowers organizations to innovate, adapt and thrive in the digital age? This vision of security as an enabler is not merely a theoretical construct; it is a reality that forward-thinking organizations are already embracing.

At the heart of this transformative approach is a fundamental shift in mindset. Security is no longer viewed as a siloed function, but rather as a core design principle that is seamlessly integrated into every aspect of the technology ecosystem. Engineers, architects and business stakeholders work in close collaboration to embed security controls and processes directly into the fabric of applications, infrastructure and workflows. This proactive, security-by-design approach not only enhances the overall security posture, but also streamlines operations, improves user experience and accelerates time-to-market. Organizations can unlock a wealth of benefits by aligning security with business objectives and empowering employees to be active participants in the security process. Secure-by-default cloud services, for example, can enable rapid innovation and experimentation, while robust identity and access management solutions can facilitate seamless collaboration both within and across organizational boundaries. Automated threat detection and incident response capabilities can free up security teams to focus on strategic initiatives, rather than firefighting tactical issues.

This vision of security as an enabler also fosters a culture of shared responsibility and continuous improvement. Security becomes a collective effort, with everyone from developers to end-users playing a role in safeguarding the organization. This distributed security model not only enhances resilience, but also empowers individuals to take ownership of their own security practices, driving a more proactive and adaptive security posture.

Notes

1 Manish Sahay. The history of the first computer virus on Windows, Mac, and Linux, PCInsider, 26 June 2024. www.thepcinsider.com/history-of-computer-virus/ (archived at https://perma.cc/B6AP-DNC7)

2 bart. The origins of computer viruses: a journey through time, Safe-connect, 18 July 2024. https://safe-connect.com/the-origins-of-computer-viruses-a-journey-through-time/ (archived at https://perma.cc/XR5D-9YLR)

3 history tools. The first computer virus of Bob Thomas, History Tools, 24 March 2024. www.historytools.org/inventions/the-first-computer-virus-of-bob-thomas (archived at https://perma.cc/69ZE-6FBT)

4 bart. The origins of computer viruses: a journey through time, Safe-connect, 18 July 2024. https://safe-connect.com/the-origins-of-computer-viruses-a-journey-through-time/ (archived at https://perma.cc/M9AW-6CPK)

5 Joey Dupont. A history of major computer viruses from the 1970s to the present, The Devolutions Blog, 30 April 2019. https://blog.devolutions.net/2019/04/a-history-of-major-computer-viruses-from-the-1970s-to-the-present/ (archived at https://perma.cc/YUD9-4HN6)

6 S Makhija. Year 1975: the first trojan horse- 'ANIMAL', Chaintech, 11 March 2024. www.chaintech.network/blog/year-1975-the-first-trojan-horse-animal/ (archived at https://perma.cc/B7RN-24XC)

7 Alex Orlando. The story of the 414s: the Milwaukee teenagers who became hacking pioneers, Discover Magazine, 10 October 2024. www.discovermagazine.com/technology/the-story-of-the-414s-the-milwaukee-teenagers-who-became-hacking-pioneers (archived at https://perma.cc/Q3UY-FRNG)

8 A Makhija. Year 1982: the saga of Group '414'- Milwaukee Teenage Hackers, Chaintech, 2 April 2024. www.chaintech.network/blog/year-1982-the-saga-of-group-414-milwaukee-teenage-hackers/ (archived at https://perma.cc/9X8U-EAK7)

9 The story of a group of 414 – Milwaukee teenagers who pioneered the hacking, Clever Geek Handbook, 2015. https://tech-en.netlify.app/articles/en532384/ (archived at https://perma.cc/E27F-K6G5)

10 Congress.gov (2019) S.1762 - 98th Congress (1983–1984): Comprehensive Crime Control Act of 1984. www.congress.gov/bill/98th-congress/senate-bill/1762 (archived at https://perma.cc/H3EJ-XDZR)

11 Federal Bureau of Investigation. Morris worm, Federal Bureau of Investigation, 2019. www.fbi.gov/history/famous-cases/morris-worm (archived at https://perma.cc/YFS7-WKL7)

12 Adithyaa Sivamal. Deep dive: understanding the Morris Worm, contemporary defenses, and exploits, Threat Treks, 11 June 2024. https://threattreks.wordpress.com/2024/06/11/deep-dive-understanding-the-morris-worm-contemporary-defenses-and-exploits/ (archived at https://perma.cc/EKX3-TQG8)

13 Meghan Holahan. As the Morris worm turned, The Link, 2009. www.cs.cmu.edu/link/morris-worm-turned (archived at https://perma.cc/SUL9-GHEP)

14 Federal Bureau of Investigation. Morris worm, Federal Bureau of Investigation, 2019. www.fbi.gov/history/famous-cases/morris-worm (archived at https://perma.cc/4D2A-63N5)

15 Victor Poitevin. Ransomware history: emergence and evolution, Stormshield, 12 June 2022. www.stormshield.com/news/a-short-history-of-ransomware/ (archived at https://perma.cc/X2J3-52KQ)

16 Kieran Laffan. A brief history of ransomware, Varonis, 9 June 2023. www.varonis.com/blog/a-brief-history-of-ransomware (archived at https://perma.cc/XTM4-DLZW)

17 History Tools. The complete guide to ARPANet: The groundbreaking computer network that led to the internet, History Tools, 19 November 2023. www.historytools.org/concepts/arpanet-complete-guide (archived at https://perma.cc/PP5P-AQJ2)

18 Hope Trampski. The ILOVEYOU worm, a global crisis, cyberTap, Purdue.edu, 20 August 2024. https://cyber.tap.purdue.edu/blog/articles/the-iloveyou-worm-a-global-crisis/ (archived at https://perma.cc/4KGC-TQSV)

19 Iloveyou virus, Damage, 2025. https://iloveyouvirus.weebly.com/damage.html (archived at https://perma.cc/7GWF-G9U4)

20 Bipin Damodaran. Biggest cyber attacks in history (from 1988 to 2021), Scriptonet Journal, 26 January 2024. www.scriptonet.com/journal/biggest-cyber-attacks-in-history/ (archived at https://perma.cc/6B5B-P8YE)

21 National Security Archive. SOLAR SUNRISE after 25 years: are we 25 years wiser? National Security Archive, 28 February 2023. https://nsarchive.gwu.edu/briefing-book/cyber-vault/2023-02-28/solar-sunrise-after-25-years-are-we-25-years-wiser (archived at https://perma.cc/2FAK-GCKR)

22 Bitstamp Learn. Silk Road: the first crypto-powered black market. 1 November 2024. www.bitstamp.net/learn/company-profiles/what-is-silk-road/ (archived at https://perma.cc/39HS-V58W)

23 Wikipedia. Stuxnet (2019). https://en.wikipedia.org/wiki/Stuxnet (archived at https://perma.cc/97VA-LHJ2)

24 Lorenzo Franceschi-Bicchierai. The history of Stuxnet: the world's first true cyberweapon, VICE, 9 August 2016. www.vice.com/en/article/the-history-of-stuxnet-the-worlds-first-true-cyberweapon-5886b74d80d84e45e7bd22ee/ (archived at https://perma.cc/8AGV-QREL)

25 Threat Analyst. Unveiling Stuxnet: a deep dive into the pioneering cyber weapon targeting industrial control systems, TIR, 17 July 2020. www.threatintelreport.com/2020/07/17/incident_reports/stuxnet/ (archived at https://perma.cc/6R4B-4RH3)

26 Computer Systems Laboratory Bulletin. Computer security roles of NIST and NSA, February 1991. https://csrc.nist.gov/files/pubs/shared/itlb/cslbul1991-02.txt (archived at https://perma.cc/3VRD-SWG7)

27 robin.materese@nist.gov (2019) NIST History, NIST. www.nist.gov/history (archived at https://perma.cc/VZC6-95XF)

28 csrc.nist.gov (n.d.) Search | CSRC. https://csrc.nist.gov/publications/search (archived at https://perma.cc/SWH8-2789)

29 nsa.gov. National Security Agency/Central Security Service > Helpful Links > NSA FOIA > Declassification & Transparency Initiatives > Historical Releases > NSA 60th Timeline, 2025. www.nsa.gov/Helpful-Links/NSA-FOIA/Declassification-Transparency-Initiatives/Historical-Releases/NSA-60th-Timeline/ (archived at https://perma.cc/2JGV-HM29)

30 www.nsa.gov (n.d.) National Centers of Academic Excellence. www.nsa.gov/Academics/Centers-of-Academic-Excellence/ (archived at https://perma.cc/33Y9-5CJS)

31 Radware. What is the Mirai botnet? Radware, n.d. www.radware.com/security/ddos-knowledge-center/ddospedia/mirai/ (archived at https://perma.cc/8EZH-HQBY)

32 nj.gov. Mirai | NJCCIC, 2024. www.cyber.nj.gov/threat-landscape/malware/botnets/mirai (archived at https://perma.cc/DB4R-WHGD)

33 Samuele De Tomas Colatin. Sony Pictures Entertainment attack (2014) – international cyber law: interactive toolkit. cyberlaw.ccdcoe.org, 2021. https://cyberlaw.ccdcoe.org/wiki/Sony_Pictures_Entertainment_attack_(2014) (archived at https://perma.cc/5PMY-WPBA)

2

Rethinking security culture

From 'no' to 'yes': transforming mindsets

The security profession has long been characterized by a certain tribal mentality, where practitioners often adopt an adversarial stance towards one another. When security professionals gather, there is a palpable sense of sizing each other up, a ritualistic dance of proving their expertise and asserting their domain. This dynamic, while understandable given the highly specialized nature of the field, can inadvertently perpetuate a culture of exclusivity and resistance to change.

Historically, security has been viewed as the exclusive domain of a select few, the 'experts' who possess the specialized knowledge and skills required to safeguard an organization's assets. This perception has contributed to a security mindset that is often characterized by a culture of 'no' – a restrictive approach that sees security as a necessary evil, a barrier to progress and innovation.

However, as the IT landscape evolves rapidly, the reality is that security is no longer the sole purview of the security professionals. Every employee, every user within an organization, now interacts with security concepts on a daily basis, whether they are aware of it or not. If you've ever had to scan your badge to gain access to a facility, locked your computer screen when you stepped away from your desk, or even shredded a document, then you have been practising secure behavior without realizing it. This shift presents a unique opportunity to transform the security culture from one of exclusivity and resistance to one of inclusivity and enablement where employees actively participate in and contribute to the security posture of the organization.

By recognizing that security is not just the domain of the experts, but rather a shared responsibility across the organization, we can begin to break down the silos and foster a more collaborative, 'yes-oriented' security culture. Simple education and awareness initiatives (discussed below) can go a long way in empowering employees to understand the importance of security and their role in upholding it.

Moreover, the traditional adversarial dynamic between security professionals can be reframed as an opportunity for alliance and collaboration through widely used formats such as forums, town halls or 'lunch and learn' sessions. Regardless of the 'how', the common theme is to normalize security practices through open and frequent communication. By embracing a mindset of shared expertise and mutual understanding, security practitioners can move beyond the ritual of proving themselves and instead focus on leveraging their collective knowledge to drive positive outcomes for the organization.

This transformation from a culture of 'no' to a culture of 'yes' is not merely a semantic shift; it represents a fundamental change in the way security is perceived and integrated within the broader organizational context. By reframing security as an enabler of innovation and growth, rather than a constraint, we can unlock the true potential of security investments and position it as a strategic asset in the face of evolving digital threats.

Security is everybody's job

Transforming security culture is as much about fostering a sense of democratic security within the organization as it is about technical expertise. It is a common misconception that security is the exclusive domain of the specialists and enthusiasts. The reality is that in today's digital landscape, every individual within an organization, regardless of their role or technical acumen, will inevitably interact with security-related concepts on a daily basis.

Rather than viewing this ubiquity of security touchpoints as a burden or a bottleneck, organizations can embrace it as an opportunity to empower and engage the entire workforce in strengthening the overall security posture. A healthy security culture is one that actively shares information and knowledge, empowering every employee to become a security stakeholder and contributor. While it is true that traditional security training sessions may not always rank high on the list of employees' favourite activities, there are creative and engaging ways to educate users about security best practices. The days of dry, lecture-style training sessions are giving way to more interactive and contextual approaches that resonate better with the workforce. For example, incremental security awareness campaigns, such as simulated phishing exercises, can be an effective way to raise user vigilance and reinforce security concepts in a real-world, relevant manner. When employees who fall for these simulated attacks are provided with immediate feedback and education, they are more likely to remember the lessons learned and apply them in their day-to-day interactions.

By modifying behaviour and raising security awareness through these innovative approaches, organizations can empower every individual to become an active participant in the security journey. Rather than viewing security as a necessary evil or a bottleneck to productivity, employees can be empowered to see themselves as integral components of the organization's security posture, actively contributing to its progress and resilience.

This shift from a culture of exclusivity to one of inclusivity and shared responsibility is a critical step in transforming the security landscape. By democratizing security and fostering a sense of ownership and engagement among all employees, organizations can unlock the true potential of their security investments and position security as a strategic enabler of innovation and growth.

My career involved a time spent at Amazon Web Services. Amazon is well known for its methodology of working backwards in order to solve a problem. When applied to the topic at hand, transforming the security mindset from a stereotypical 'no' culture to a more positive and progressive 'yes' orientation, a compelling framework for approaching this critical shift in organizational dynamics emerges. At the heart of this transformation lies the recognition that a simplistic 'yes' approach is just as problematic as the entrenched 'no' mentality. The key is to move the dialogue from a flat-out rejection – 'no' – to a more constructive 'how' mindset. This can be done by not simply rejecting ideas or proposals but instead asking probing questions that uncover the underlying needs, concerns or constraints. The goal should be to have a dialogue that explores the 'how', such as 'How can we address the core issue you're trying to solve?' or 'What are the specific challenges or risks we need to work through?' This 'how' mindset encourages collaboration and problem-solving and involves actively listening to understand the motivations and goals and then working together to find viable solutions. Ultimately, it builds trust, and can lead to better, more sustainable outcomes for the organization. By adopting this nuanced perspective, security professionals can work collaboratively with their counterparts across the organization to find solutions that address the underlying concerns while still enabling the progress and innovation so vital to the enterprise's success.

This shift in approach is not merely an exercise in word choice; it denotes a deep-rooted change in the organization's underlying attitudes and actions. Transforming the security culture is inextricably linked to transforming the behaviours of those who operate within it. The catalyst for this behavioural change is education – a critical component in empowering the workforce to become active participants in strengthening the organization's security posture. Much like their counterparts in the healthcare sector, security professionals are often exposed to the darker, more unsavoury aspects of the digital landscape on a daily basis. This constant immersion in the 'ugly side' of technology can understandably foster a sense of pessimism and a tendency towards fearmongering. However, such fear-based tactics are rarely effective in driving the desired outcomes. Rather than scaring people into compliance, security leaders must focus on empowering and educating their colleagues, fostering a shared understanding of the risks and the proactive measures that can be taken to mitigate them. By shifting the narrative from doom and gloom to a more constructive, solution-oriented approach, security professionals can position themselves as strategic partners in the organization's growth and innovation efforts.

Ultimately, the transformation of security culture from 'no' to 'yes' is not merely a superficial change in language or tone. It represents a holistic, organization-wide shift that requires a concerted effort to reshape mindsets, behaviours and the very way security is perceived and integrated within the enterprise. It is a journey that demands strong leadership, cross-functional collaboration and a relentless commitment to empowering every employee to become a security stakeholder and contributor. Only through this comprehensive approach can organizations unlock the true potential of their security investments and position security as a critical enabler of progress and innovation.

The evolving role of the modern CISO

Hiring the right Chief Information Security Officer (CISO) is a crucial component of this comprehensive approach. The CISO is the senior-level executive responsible for establishing and maintaining an organization's security vision, strategy and programme to ensure information assets and technologies are adequately protected. As the guardian of an organization's digital assets and reputation, the CISO must blend technical expertise with strategic business acumen to lead the enterprise-wide transformation of security culture. Gone are the days when the CISO was solely responsible for implementing security controls and mitigating technical threats. Today's CISO must be a multifaceted leader, capable of navigating the complex interplay between technology, risk management and organizational dynamics. At the core of this transformation is the need for the CISO to be a skilled communicator and a savvy business partner, capable of selling the importance of cybersecurity to the entire organization.

One of the primitive functions of a CISO is navigating the ever-evolving threat landscape. Cybersecurity threats are becoming increasingly sophisticated, with cybercriminals, nation-state actors and other malicious entities constantly developing new tactics and techniques to breach an organization's defences. To effectively protect the organization, the CISO must maintain a deep understanding of the latest threat trends, vulnerabilities and attack vectors by staying abreast of industry intelligence, collaborating with security researchers and law enforcement agencies, and continuously assessing the organization's risk profile. Additionally, the CISO must be able to translate this technical knowledge into actionable security strategies that align with the organization's business objectives.

This involves prioritizing risks, allocating resources and implementing security controls that not only mitigate threats but also enable the organization to operate securely and efficiently. The successful implementation of security controls is discussed more in Chapter 3. As the role of the CISO continues to evolve, the required skillset has also expanded beyond the traditional technical expertise.

One of the primary challenges facing the modern CISO is the need to position cybersecurity as a strategic imperative, rather than a mere cost centre. In many organizations, security is still viewed as a necessary evil – a burden that detracts from the core business objectives. The CISO must, therefore, become a skilled salesperson, adept at articulating the value of security investments in a language that resonates with the C-suite and the board of directors. This requires the CISO to possess a deep understanding of the organization's business model, its strategic priorities, an awareness of emerging technologies and the evolving threat landscape. By framing security as an enabler of innovation, growth and customer trust, the CISO can effectively position cybersecurity as a strategic asset rather than a hindrance. This shift in perspective is crucial, as it empowers the CISO to secure the necessary resources, budget and executive-level support to implement robust security measures.

To be an effective salesperson for security, the modern CISO therefore must be allowed to step out of the traditional IT silo so that they can develop a comprehensive understanding of the organization's core functions, decision-making processes and the competitive landscape. By understanding the business's strategic objectives, the CISO can align security initiatives with the organization's overall goals, ensuring that cybersecurity investments directly support the company's growth and profitability. This business acumen also enables the CISO to anticipate and address the security implications of new technologies, products or services, allowing the organization to innovate with confidence. Moreover, the CISO must maintain a keen awareness of nascent technologies and industry trends, constantly scanning the horizon for potential threats and opportunities. This technological awareness allows the CISO to proactively identify and mitigate emerging risks, while also exploring innovative security solutions that can provide a competitive edge.

Today's CISO must be a strategic thinker, a skilled communicator and a business-savvy leader. In addition to their deep understanding of cybersecurity technologies and best practices, the modern CISO must possess strong analytical and problem-solving skills. They must be able to interpret complex data, identify patterns and make data-driven decisions that align with the organization's risk appetite and strategic objectives. Effective communication skills are also essential, as the CISO must be able to translate technical jargon into language that resonates with executives, board members and other stakeholders. This includes the ability to present security metrics, risk assessments and incident response plans in a clear and compelling manner. Furthermore, the CISO must be a skilled negotiator and influencer, capable of securing the necessary resources, budget and executive-level support to implement robust security measures. This requires the CISO to possess strong business acumen, emotional intelligence and the ability to build trust and collaborate with cross-functional teams. Organizations must recognize the importance of investing in the development and retention of these highly skilled professionals. By empowering the CISO with the necessary resources, authority and strategic influence, organizations can position themselves to navigate the complex and ever-changing cybersecurity landscape with confidence and resilience.

An often-overlooked influential factor in the success of a CISO at a given organization is their positioning within the organizational structure. The placement of the CISO in the org chart can have a significant impact on their ability to influence decision-making and integrate security into the fabric of the organization. Ideally, the CISO should report directly to the CEO or the CIO, ensuring that security concerns are elevated to the highest levels of the organization. When the CISO is relegated to a lower-level position, they often face an uphill battle in gaining the necessary visibility, resources and executive-level support to implement effective security measures. This can lead to a siloed approach to security, where the CISO is viewed as an auditor or gatekeeper, rather than a strategic business partner.

Building relationships and earning trust

To overcome these challenges, the CISO must cultivate strong relationships with other members of the executive team, fostering a collaborative and transparent approach to risk management. By engaging with stakeholders across the organization, the CISO can ensure that security is not an afterthought, but rather an integral component of the company's overall strategy. This collaborative approach also extends to the CISO's interactions with the board of directors. The CISO must be able to effectively communicate the organization's cybersecurity posture, the evolving threat landscape and the potential impact of security incidents. To ensure that a CISO is empowered, executive leadership needs to view and treat security as a strategic element of the business; they must view cyber risks as strategic risks. Collaboration with the security function of the business should ideally be supported and encouraged within all departments. In order to gain the confidence and support of leadership outside of the security function, the CISO should demonstrate a deep understanding of the organization's business objectives and priorities, and how security initiatives can directly support and enable those goals. The CISO should also be able to effectively communicate the value of security investments in terms that resonate with business leaders, such as risk mitigation, cost savings and competitive advantage. Be sure to read Chapter 6 for more details on communicating effectively.

When it comes to managing up, the CISO needs to engage with the board on a regular basis. Board members would ideally seek the opinions and advice from their security leadership and even request brief educational sessions; however, that is rarely the case. This is because the board is deliberately comprised of a variety of representation from across the business and often lacks the technical understanding of security risks and mitigation strategies. As such, they may not know what to ask for, or may even feel uncomfortable or out of depth to engage with the CISO on complex topics. Therefore, the security function must take the initiative to engage with other business units and demonstrate the value that security can bring to the organization; they must ultimately 'cross the aisle' to more-or-less invite themselves to the table, then educate. Board directors need to understand why leadership has chosen a particular course of action and how a particular plan will be evaluated for efficacy: a CISO is to technology risk what a CFO (Chief Financial Officer) is to financial risk. The goal is to be treated more as a business partner than an auditor – the various lines of business should engage with security and be upfront and honest about the risks involved with the strategic growth initiatives set forth by senior leadership. This can be achieved with several board-appropriate activities such as security briefings, tabletop exercises, industry benchmarking, awareness training, threat briefings, regulatory and compliance updates, and security roadmaps.

A security briefing is a critical component of board education on the organization's cybersecurity posture, risks and mitigation strategies. The primary purpose of these presentations is to increase the board's awareness of the current threat landscape, help them understand the potential business impact of security incidents and cyber-attacks, and ensure they have a clear grasp of the organization's cybersecurity risks and vulnerabilities. By demonstrating the security team's efforts to detect, respond to and recover from security incidents, as well as the organization's compliance with relevant regulations and industry standards, the CISO can help the board appreciate the effectiveness of the security programme. Importantly, the security briefing should also align the security strategy and initiatives with the organization's over-all business goals and risk management priorities, explaining the rationale behind security-related decisions and resource allocation. Typical metrics and outputs included in the briefing cover risk management, incident response and resilience, security programme effectiveness, security investment and budget, and regulatory and compliance considerations. The goal is to provide the board with a clear, concise and actionable understanding of the organization's security posture, enabling them to make informed decisions that support the organization's long-term success in the face of evolving cyber threats. Tabletop exercises are a highly effective way for the security leadership to engage the board of directors in a hands-on, interactive learning experience around cybersecurity. These exercises simulate various cyber-attack scenarios, walking the board through the decision-making process and potential impacts on the organization. These exercises help educate board members to better understand the real-world implications of a security incident and the organization's incident response capabilities.

First, the interactive nature of the exercises helps board members develop a deeper understanding of the complex and dynamic nature of cyber threats, allowing them to experience firsthand the challenges faced by the security team and executive leadership in responding to an evolving cyber crisis. Second, the tabletop exercises enable the board to assess the organization's incident response plan, communication protocols, and the roles and responsibilities of key stakeholders, which helps identify gaps or areas for improvement in the organization's preparedness. Third, the exercises provide a safe environment for the board to engage in strategic discussions around risk appetite, resource allocation and the overall cybersecurity strategy, leading to more informed decision-making and better alignment between the board and security leadership. Finally, the tabletop exercises often involve participants from various departments, encouraging cross-functional collaboration and a shared understanding of the organization's security posture. The format of these exercises can vary, ranging from simple, scenario-based discussions to more complex, multi-stage simulations, but they should always be tailored to the board's level of technical understanding and focus on the strategic implications of the cyber threats being addressed.

Providing the board with industry benchmarks and peer comparisons on key security metrics is another useful way to help the directors assess the organization's security posture relative to its industry counterparts. This type of industry benchmarking demonstrates where the organization stands in terms of security spending, a critical indicator of the resources dedicated to protecting the business. By comparing the organization's security investments to industry averages and peer companies, the board can gain insights into whether the security function is adequately funded and resourced. The benchmarking data can shed light on the organization's incident response capabilities, such as breach detection and containment times. Knowing how the company's performance in these areas stacks up against industry peers allows the board to evaluate the effectiveness of the security programme and identify areas for improvement. Industry benchmarks on security metrics like vulnerability management and compliance status can increase the credibility of the organization's overall security maturity and risk profile compared to its competitors. This information can inform strategic decision-making around security priorities and investments. Benchmarking data serves as a valuable point of reference, enabling the board to have more informed discussions with the CISO about the organization's security posture and the rationale behind security-related initiatives.

Broad-level security awareness training can be an effective component of a CISO's efforts to educate the board on cybersecurity. This training helps board members understand their own role in maintaining the organization's security, covering topics such as phishing, social engineering and the importance of strong access controls and password hygiene. The training helps the board develop a deeper appreciation for the human element of cybersecurity, recognizing that even the most sophisticated technical controls can be undermined by a single employee falling victim to a social engineering attack. They can also provide the board with practical knowledge and skills to identify and mitigate common cyber threats, empowering them to be more vigilant and proactive in their own security practices (which is especially important as their level of seniority is often the target of cybersecurity attacks). The interactive nature of the training fosters a shared understanding between the board and the security team, strengthening the collaborative relationship and ensuring the board is better equipped to support the organization's overall cybersecurity strategy. Ultimately, by incorporating security awareness training into the board's education programme, the CISO can help the directors become more security-conscious leaders, setting the tone for a strong security culture throughout the organization.

Reporting on up-to-date intelligence on emerging cyber threats is another way to keep leadership informed and prepared. Threat briefings help the board stay abreast of the evolving threat landscape, ensuring they have a clear understanding of the latest attack vectors, tactics and techniques being employed by cybercriminals, nation-state actors and other malicious entities. Awareness into these emerging threats can help them comprehend the dynamic nature of the cybersecurity challenges facing the organization. An effective threat briefing should outline how the organization is preparing to address these new and evolving threats which involves discussing the security controls, processes and technologies being implemented to detect, prevent and respond to these threats, as well as the potential business impact if the organization fails to adequately mitigate them. By demonstrating the security team's proactive approach, the CISO can assure the board that the organization is taking the necessary steps to stay ahead of the curve. Additionally, the threat briefings provide an opportunity for the board to engage in strategic discussions around the organization's risk appetite and the allocation of resources to address the most critical threats. This collaborative dialogue helps ensure that the security strategy and investments are aligned with the board's overall risk management priorities and the organization's long-term business objectives. Regularly incorporating threat briefings into the board's cybersecurity education programme can help the directors develop a comprehensive understanding of the threat landscape and the organization's preparedness, ultimately empowering them to make more informed decisions that strengthen the company's cybersecurity resilience.

Another angle to educate leadership on security posture is regulatory and compliance requirements that impact the organization's products and services. First and foremost, these requirements help the board understand the legal and regulatory landscape in which the organization operates, and how they might apply to new initiatives and existing offerings. Regulatory and compliance updates demonstrate the organization's commitment to maintaining a robust security programme that meets or exceeds the required standards. Highlighting the security controls, processes and certifications in place to address these regulatory requirements can assure the board that the organization is taking the necessary steps to mitigate legal and reputational risks. When done correctly, these updates can also serve as a catalyst for strategic discussions between the CISO and the board as they provide valuable insights and guidance on how to navigate the evolving regulatory landscape, while the CISO can explain the potential impact of new or changing regulations on the organization's security strategy and resource allocation. This approach must be well-researched and will ultimately scale with the size of the business, as different markets have different compliance requirements, which can impact different parts of the business. For example, a bank that operates in the United States, Singapore and the European Union would need to implement security measures that meet region-specific regulatory requirements such as Gramm-Leach-Bliley Act (GLBA), General Data Protection Regulation (GDPR) and Personal Data Protection Act (PDPA), all three regulations which address data privacy and security. Scoping this education to the most relevant markets is essential in building and earning trust, so that you continue to be invited back to the table!

Lastly, a strategic security roadmap which outlines the organization's planned security initiatives, investments and the expected benefits and return on investment, is a direct way to show the board a comprehensive view of the security function's strategic direction. The roadmap helps the board understand the long-term vision and priorities for the organization's security programme which is essential for them to assess whether the security strategy is aligned with the company's overall business goals and risk management priorities. It also demonstrates the CISO's commitment to continuous improvement and the organization's willingness to invest in strengthening its cybersecurity posture. By detailing the planned security initiatives and the associated resource allocation, the CISO can give the board confidence that the security function is proactively addressing the evolving threat landscape and the organization's changing risk profile; the roadmap should provide a framework for evaluating the effectiveness and impact of the security programme. By regularly presenting the board with a comprehensive security roadmap, the CISO can foster a collaborative and transparent relationship, ensuring the board has a clear understanding of the security function's strategic direction and the rationale behind the security-related decisions and resource allocation.

The CISO's responsibility to educate the board of directors on cybersecurity encompasses a diverse approach, leveraging a range of techniques to ensure the board has a comprehensive understanding of the company's security standing and the dynamic threat environment. Ultimately, the CISO, the rest of the executives and the board should develop an approach to reporting and discussing cyber risks that fits the organization and its risk profile. Anything measurable and quantifiable, such as metrics, dashboards and reports, are going to be useful for decision-makers to consume this otherwise obscure, cryptic information.

A business that marginalizes their security function, most commonly by placing it within the IT function, will eventually find themselves inadequately prepared to deal with modern cyber risks and, therefore, unable to take on new projects that could advance and benefit the business as a whole. In the modern technology stack, where much of the services and functions that used to be within our own data centres are now outsourced and service-based, it is risky business to undervalue a CISO.

The pivotal role of a CISO

For too long, security has been perceived as a hindrance to productivity and innovation within the workplace. However, by reframing the narrative, security leaders can position their function as a strategic enabler that drives business value and growth. The key is to communicate security in a way that resonates with executives and other stakeholders (especially cross-functionally), focusing on the positive outcomes it can deliver. When presenting security initiatives, it is essential to ground them in the context of the organization's overarching business objectives.

Highlighting how security measures can protect critical assets, ensure business continuity and unlock new opportunities for the enterprise is a great way to earn trust. It is important to show how security plays a vital role in safeguarding an organization's most valuable and sensitive assets, such as intellectual property, customer data, financial information and trade secrets. With the implementation of robust security controls, organizations can mitigate the risk of data breaches, cyber-attacks and other threats that could compromise these critical assets. This protection helps maintain the integrity and confidentiality of the information, preserving the organization's competitive advantage and reputation, which is something that any leader across any of the business units within can easily agree on. Operationally speaking, the ability to maintain operations and recover quickly from disruptions is paramount. Security measures, such as incident response plans, disaster recovery strategies and redundancy systems, can help withstand and recover from unexpected events, such as natural disasters, system failures or cyber incidents, which can be a competitive advantage in the product landscape because ensuring business continuity and security enables the organization to minimize downtime, maintain customer trust and avoid costly disruptions to its operations.

Far from being a hindrance, security can actually unlock new commercial opportunities for growth and innovation. When security is integrated into the design and development of new products, services or business models, it can enable organizations to confidently explore and capitalize on emerging market trends and customer demands. For example, robust security measures can facilitate the secure adoption of cloud computing, the Internet of Things, artificial intelligence and other transformative technologies, empowering the organization to stay ahead of the competition and deliver enhanced value to its customers. By highlighting these tangible benefits, security leaders can demonstrate how security is not just a necessary cost centre, but a strategic enabler that protects the organization's most valuable assets, ensures business continuity and unlocks new avenues for progress. This shift in perspective can help cultivate a more positive and collaborative security culture within the enterprise.

Showcasing real-world success stories and using cases where security has enabled the organization to innovate, expand into new markets or enhance the customer experience is another way to communicate security as a force multiplier. For example, you could find and share a case study of how a robust security framework allowed the organization to safely experiment with new technologies without compromising data protection or compliance. Demonstrating how security can be an enabler of innovation can position the security function as a strategic partner in the organization's growth and transformation efforts. Security can also play a crucial role in enabling expansion into new geographic markets or industry verticals. Providing examples of how security measures have helped an organization navigate complex regulatory environments, address local data privacy concerns or build trust with new customer segments can illustrate how security is a key enabler of global expansion and market diversification. This can be particularly impactful when communicating with executives who are focused on driving the organization's international growth and market share. In today's digital landscape, customers are increasingly concerned about the security and privacy of their data. Furnishing use cases where security has directly improved the customer experience, you can demonstrate the business value of security investments. For instance, you could point out that the implementation of advanced authentication methods, such as biometrics or multi-factor authentication, has reduced friction in the customer journey while also enhancing the protection of sensitive customer information. This type of success story can help position security as a strategic differentiator that builds customer trust and loyalty.

When security leaders can point to real-world examples of how security has driven positive business outcomes, it helps to shift the perception from security as a necessary cost to security as a strategic enabler. Fostering open dialogues and feedback loops between security teams and other departments is also crucial. Encourage cross-functional collaboration, where security professionals work closely with their counterparts in IT, operations and product development to understand their needs and pain points. This collaborative approach not only helps to build trust and buy-in but also ensures that security solutions are tailored to the specific requirements of the business. Additionally, make a concerted effort to translate technical security concepts into accessible, business-oriented language that resonates with non-technical stakeholders.

Ultimately, the CISO, the rest of the executives and the board should develop an approach to reporting and discussing cyber risks that fits the organization and its risk profile. Anything measurable and quantifiable is going to be useful for decision-makers to consume this otherwise obscure, cryptic information.

KEY TAKEAWAYS

- In a security context, aim to change 'no' to 'yes' by asking and answering the question 'how?'
- Turn specialty knowledge into common knowledge by communicating in a way that suits your audience.
- Security is a team sport so get as many people involved as possible.
- The modern CISO is a good listener with a sharp business acumen.
- A CISO should be as close to the board as possible.

3

Security and innovation

Historically, the relationship between security and innovation has often been characterized by tension and conflict. As organizations have sought to drive growth and agility through the adoption of new technologies and business models, security has frequently been perceived as a barrier, slowing down progress and stifling creativity. In the early days of the digital revolution, the primary focus of security was on building robust perimeter defences to keep threats out. Firewalls, antivirus software and access controls were the order of the day, with the goal of creating a secure, controlled environment. This approach was well-suited to the relatively static, on-premises IT infrastructures of the time, but it quickly became a hindrance as the pace of technological change accelerated. The rise of the internet, the proliferation of mobile devices and the emergence of cloud computing all challenged the traditional security paradigm. Organizations were under pressure to embrace these new technologies to remain competitive, but security teams struggled to keep up. Rigid security policies and cumbersome approval processes often delayed the deployment of innovative solutions, frustrating business leaders who were eager to capitalize on the potential of these technologies.

This tension was particularly acute in the early 2000s, as the dot-com boom gave way to a series of high-profile security breaches and cyber-attacks, such as the SQL Slammer worm which emerged in January 2003. The worm exploited a vulnerability in Microsoft's SQL Server database software, allowing it to spread rapidly across the internet and infect hundreds of thousands of systems within the first 10 minutes of its release. The SQL Slammer worm caused widespread disruption, with many organizations experiencing network outages, system crashes and the loss of critical data.

Another significant attack was the Blaster worm, which appeared in August 2003. This targeted a vulnerability in Microsoft's Windows operating system, allowing it to spread quickly and infect millions of computers worldwide. The worm caused significant disruption, with many organizations struggling to contain the outbreak and restore their systems to normal operation.

In 2004, the Sasser worm emerged, exploiting a vulnerability in the Local Security Authority Subsystem Service in Microsoft Windows. The worm was particularly problematic, as it could cause infected systems to crash or become unstable, leading to widespread service disruptions and downtime for many organizations.

Organizations that had prioritized speed and agility over security found themselves facing the consequences, with data breaches, reputational damage and significant financial losses. The fallout from these incidents led to a renewed focus on security, but it also reinforced the perception that it was a necessary evil: a cost centre that stood in the way of innovation and growth.

The advent of cloud computing further exacerbated the divide between security and innovation. As organizations migrated their IT infrastructure to the cloud, security teams were faced with a new set of challenges. Traditional security controls and processes were often ill-suited to the dynamic, distributed nature of cloud environments, and security teams struggled to keep pace with the rapid deployment of new cloud services and applications. Similarly, the security teams tasked with safeguarding their organizations' cloud-based infrastructure found themselves in a similar predicament. The traditional security controls and processes that had served them well in the past were suddenly ill-equipped to handle the dynamic, distributed nature of the cloud. Considering the analogy presented in Chapter 1, just as the motorcycle rider's protective gear would have been ill-suited to the car's safety systems, the legacy security measures that had once provided a reliable defence against threats were now struggling to keep pace with the rapid deployment of new cloud services and applications. It was a mismatch that increased the growing divide between security and innovation. As organizations rushed to embrace the agility and growth promised by the cloud, their security teams were left scrambling to adapt their strategies, adopting new tools and techniques to navigate the shifting sands of the cloud landscape.

The road ahead was anything but clear, and the security professionals tasked with safeguarding these emerging technologies found themselves caught in a delicate balancing act – torn between the imperative for innovation and the imperative for robust security and risk management.

This tension was particularly acute in the early days of cloud adoption, when security concerns were often cited as a major barrier to cloud migration. Organizations were hesitant to entrust their sensitive data and critical systems to third-party cloud providers, fearing the loss of control and the potential for data breaches. Organizations were accustomed to having complete oversight and management of their IT infrastructure, which allowed them to implement robust security measures and maintain a tight grip on their sensitive information. The prospect of handing over this control to a third-party cloud provider was a significant source of anxiety as well as the potential for data breaches and the associated reputational and financial consequences. Organizations held a deep-seated belief that their own on-premises data centres were inherently more secure than the cloud, as they could physically control and monitor the infrastructure. The idea of storing sensitive data on servers owned and managed by a third-party raised concerns about the cloud provider's security practices, the potential for data leaks and the ability to respond effectively to security incidents. Many industries and sectors are subject to strict regulations and standards, such as the General Data Protection Regulation (GDPR) in the European Union (as well as the jurisdictions around the world that wrote similar legislation inspired by it). Organizations were unsure whether cloud providers could guarantee the appropriate level of data protection and compliance, particularly when data was stored in geographically dispersed data centres. The lack of visibility and control over the cloud infrastructure was also a significant barrier. Security teams were accustomed to having detailed information about the underlying systems, network configurations and security controls. The perceived 'black box' nature of cloud services made it challenging for them to assess and manage the risks, leading to a reluctance to embrace cloud technologies.

Over time, however, the relationship between security and innovation has begun to evolve, as organizations have recognized the need to strike a balance between the two. The rise of development, security and operations (DevSecOps), for example, has sought to integrate security into the software development lifecycle, ensuring that security is a key consideration from the outset, rather than an afterthought. Similarly, the emergence of cloud-native security solutions and the adoption of a 'security-by-design' approach have helped to bridge the gap between security and innovation. By embedding security into the fabric of new technologies and business models, organizations have been able to unlock the benefits of innovation while mitigating the associated risks.

The increasing sophistication and complexity of cyber threats have highlighted the need for a more proactive and strategic approach to security. Organizations that have embraced security as a strategic enabler, rather than a necessary evil, have been able to unlock new opportunities for growth and expansion, leveraging their security posture as a competitive advantage. For example, organizations that have built a reputation for robust security and data privacy have been able to enter new markets and partner with high-risk vendors, secure in the knowledge that their security controls can withstand the scrutiny of regulators and customers. Similarly, organizations that have invested in security-enabled innovation, such as secure-by-design software or secure-by-default cloud services, have been able to differentiate themselves in the market and attract new customers.

In this way, the relationship between security and innovation has evolved significantly over the past two decades. What was once characterized by tension and conflict, with security perceived as a barrier to agility and growth, has now transformed into a strategic alignment where organizations recognize the value of security as a key enabler. Organizations now view a strong security posture not as a roadblock, but as a competitive advantage that can drive differentiation, build customer trust and position the enterprise for long-term success in an increasingly complex and dynamic business environment. This shift in mindset has allowed organizations to embrace security as a core component of their innovation strategy, rather than seeing it as a constraint to be overcome.

Security as a driver of innovation

In highly regulated industries such as finance, healthcare and government, robust security controls are not just a nice-to-have, but a fundamental requirement for doing business – table stakes. These sectors are subject to stringent regulations and standards around data privacy, risk management and compliance. Organizations that have invested in building a mature security posture are often better positioned to navigate these complex regulatory environments and potentially secure lucrative contracts.

In addition to unlocking new market opportunities, a strong security posture can also enable organizations to pursue mergers and acquisitions with greater confidence. In today's business landscape, mergers and acquisition activity is often driven by the need to acquire new technologies, talent or market share. However, these transactions can also introduce significant security risks, as organizations seek to integrate disparate systems, data and processes. Organizations that have a robust security culture and a well-developed security programme are often better equipped to navigate the complexities of mergers and acquisitions, mitigating the risks of data breaches, system failures and regulatory non-compliance. By conducting thorough security assessments, implementing secure integration processes and ensuring that security is a key consideration throughout the mergers and acquisitions lifecycle, these organizations can unlock new opportunities for growth and expansion, while minimizing the associated risks.

A strong security posture can also serve as a source of competitive differentiation, helping organizations to attract and retain customers, partners and investors. In an increasingly digital and interconnected world, customers are becoming more discerning about the security and privacy practices of the organizations they do business with. Organizations that can demonstrate a commitment to security and data protection, and can offer secure and reliable services, may be able to gain a competitive edge in the market. For example, a cloud service provider that has implemented robust security controls, such as end-to-end encryption, multi-factor authentication, and comprehensive logging and monitoring, may be able to attract customers who are seeking a secure and reliable platform for their data and applications. Similarly, a retail organization that has invested in secure-by-design e-commerce solutions and has a proven track record of protecting customer data may be able to differentiate itself from its competitors and build customer loyalty.

In addition to customer-facing benefits, a strong security posture can also help organizations to attract and retain top talent. In today's competitive job market, skilled cybersecurity professionals are in high demand, and organizations that can demonstrate a commitment to security and innovation may be better positioned to attract and retain these valuable employees. By fostering a security-conscious culture, providing opportunities for professional development and growth, and showcasing the strategic value of security, organizations can position themselves as attractive employers, helping to build a strong and resilient security team that can support the organization's growth and innovation efforts.

Financial services

In the financial services industry, a firm that has implemented stringent security controls around data protection, access management and transaction monitoring may be able to expand into new markets or partner with fintech startups that are seeking a secure and compliant platform to build their services on. By demonstrating their ability to meet the rigorous security and compliance requirements of the financial sector, these organizations can differentiate themselves from their competitors and open up new revenue streams. For example, a financial services firm that is considering acquiring a fintech startup may conduct a detailed security audit to ensure that the startup's systems and data are secure and compliant with industry regulations. Conversely, a fintech startup that is seeking to partner with or be acquired by a larger financial institution may proactively invest in strengthening its security posture.

The fintech startup can position itself as an attractive and low-risk partner by demonstrating robust security controls, data protection measures and compliance with relevant regulations, thus increasing its chances of securing a lucrative deal. In this scenario, the fintech startup recognizes that its security capabilities are not just a defensive measure, but a strategic asset that can unlock new business opportunities. By aligning its security practices with the expectations of the financial services industry, the fintech startup can differentiate itself from competitors, build trust with potential partners and ultimately accelerate its growth and expansion plans. The financial services firm, in turn, can leverage the fintech startup's security capabilities to enhance its own offerings, expand into new markets and stay ahead of the competition. This mutually beneficial relationship highlights how a strong security posture can serve as a catalyst for mergers and acquisitions, enabling organizations to pursue growth and expansion strategies with greater confidence and reduced risk. By presenting security as a key consideration throughout the deal-making process, both parties can unlock new opportunities and create lasting value for their respective businesses.

Healthcare

A provider in the healthcare industry that has invested in secure-by-design medical devices and telemedicine solutions may be able to expand its reach and offer its services to a wider range of patients and healthcare providers. Robust security measures, such as end-to-end encryption for data transmission, secure data storage with advanced access controls, and comprehensive identity and access management systems, are crucial in the healthcare sector, where the protection of sensitive patient information is of paramount importance. Implementing these security-centric design principles will establish that its medical devices and telemedicine solutions are inherently secure, minimizing the risk of data breaches, unauthorized access and system vulnerabilities. This not only safeguards patient privacy but also demonstrates the organization's commitment to compliance with industry regulations, such as the Health Insurance Portability and Accountability Act (HIPAA) in the United States or the General Data Protection Regulation (GDPR) in the European Union.

Healthcare organizations that can showcase a strong security posture and their ability to protect patient data can position themselves as trusted partners, potentially leading to securing lucrative contracts with government agencies responsible for public health initiatives, insurance providers seeking secure platforms for telemedicine services or large healthcare networks looking to expand their reach and capabilities. These healthcare providers can differentiate themselves from competitors by leveraging their security expertise and at the same time expand their market share, and even solidify their reputation as industry leaders in secure and innovative healthcare solutions.

A healthcare organization that is looking to expand its reach through the acquisition of a smaller provider may prioritize the assessment of the target's medical devices, telemedicine solutions and data protection measures. The acquiring organization can identify potential vulnerabilities, compliance gaps and security weaknesses that could pose a risk to the combined entity by conducting a thorough security audit of the target's systems and processes. This comprehensive security assessment allows the acquiring organization to develop a detailed integration plan that addresses these security concerns upfront. For example, the acquirer may implement secure data migration protocols to ensure the seamless and secure transfer of patient records, implement unified access control policies across the combined organization and establish incident response and disaster recovery procedures to maintain the continuity of critical healthcare services. By ensuring that the acquired organization's security posture aligns with industry standards and regulatory requirements, the acquiring healthcare provider can confidently integrate the new assets and services, while maintaining the trust of patients, healthcare providers and regulatory bodies. This not only mitigates the risks associated with the merger but also enables the combined organization to leverage the security capabilities of both entities, further strengthening its position as a trusted and secure healthcare provider.

Government

Consider the government sector, where the safeguarding of sensitive national security information and the protection of critical infrastructure are of significant importance: security is not just a consideration, but an essential prerequisite for doing business. Organizations seeking to engage with government agencies must demonstrate an unwavering commitment to the highest standards of information security and operational resilience, and – in many cases – be certified to a relevant standard. Those that have successfully navigated the stringent security requirements of government clients, such as compliance with rigorous data classification protocols and the implementation of secure communication channels, are often rewarded with high-value contract opportunities. These can range from the provision of mission-critical IT services, the development of cutting-edge cybersecurity solutions or even the design and deployment of systems that underpin the nation's strategic capabilities.

A technology firm that has proven its ability to handle classified data in accordance with government guidelines, maintain secure enclaves for sensitive workloads and implement robust access controls may be entrusted with the development of a secure communications platform for military operations. Similarly, a cybersecurity specialist that has demonstrated its expertise in protecting government networks from advanced persistent threats may be awarded a contract to deploy its threat detection and incident response solutions across various government agencies. The government's reliance on trusted partners with impeccable security credentials creates a significant barrier to entry for organizations that have not invested in building a comprehensive security programme. However, for those that have made security a strategic priority, the potential rewards can be substantial. Not only do these contracts provide a reliable revenue stream, but they also serve as a testament to the organization's security capabilities, potentially opening doors to new commercial opportunities in the private sector as well.

Positioning security as a core competency and aligning their practices with the government's stringent requirements allow organizations to differentiate themselves from competitors, solidify their reputation as trusted security providers and unlock a wealth of growth prospects within the public sector.

Innovations fuelled by security

Security is not just a defensive measure, but a strategic driver for business growth and innovation. This is exemplified by several prominent case studies, including Apple Pay's approach to tokenization, Netflix's bug bounty program and JPMorgan Chase's investment in security following a major breach in 2014. These examples demonstrate how organizations can leverage security practices and technologies to enhance their products, services and overall competitiveness in the market.

Apple Pay

One shining example of how innovative security practices can drive business success is the case of Apple Pay, the mobile payment solution introduced by Apple in October 2014. This was a significant market disruptor, especially considering that it was not the first of its kind (for example, Google Wallet was launched three years before Apple Pay), but its rate of adoption eclipsed their competition. Within the first 72 hours of its launch, over one million credit cards were activated on Apple Pay.[1] By the end of 2014 when Apple Pay was only a few months old, they had already partnered with over

500 US banks and credit unions[2] which totalled around 90 per cent of the US credit card market.[3] By the end of 2015, Apple Pay had facilitated $10 billion in transactions, and had already expanded to the UK, Canada and Australia,[4] collecting over 2,500 institutions worldwide[5] – a remarkable achievement, especially considering (in context of the subject matter of this book) that each of these markets has disparate regulatory requirements.

Apple Pay's rapid adoption and widespread success can be attributed (at least, in part) to its groundbreaking approach to security, which centred around three key pillars: tokenization, encryption and authentication.

At the heart of Apple Pay's security strategy was the use of tokenization, a process that replaced sensitive payment information, such as credit and debit card numbers, with unique digital identifiers known as tokens. These tokens have no intrinsic value and cannot be reversed or mathematically predictable which makes them useless to attackers even if intercepted. This innovative approach addressed a critical concern that had long plagued traditional payment methods: the risk of data breaches and the subsequent exposure of customers' financial information. When a user adds a payment card to Apple Pay, the actual card number is not stored on the device or on Apple's servers. Instead, a unique token is generated and securely stored on the device's dedicated hardware component, the Secure Element. This token is then used to authorize transactions, effectively shielding the real card number from merchants and payment networks.

As a security innovation in its own right, the Secure Element is a hardware-based tamper-resistant component embedded in Apple's iPhone which provides an extra layer of security for sensitive data and operations. It is a dedicated, secure chip separate from the main processor which has been designed to resist physical and logical attacks to protect sensitive data even if the device itself is compromised.[6]

The beauty of this secure tokenization process lies in its ability to minimize the attack surface and reduce the risk of data compromise. Even if a merchant's systems were to be breached, the stolen tokens would be useless, as they do not contain the actual card information.

This innovative approach to data protection not only enhanced the security of Apple Pay transactions but also instilled a sense of trust and confidence in users, a critical factor in the widespread adoption of the mobile payment solution.

Complementing the tokenization strategy, Apple Pay also leveraged encryption techniques to ensure the security of data in transit. When a user initiates a payment, the transaction data, including the token and a one-time security code (which is unique per transaction), is encrypted before being transmitted from the device to the payment terminal. This end-to-end encryption ensures that the sensitive information remains protected throughout the entire transaction process, even if it is intercepted by malicious actors. The data is encrypted at the source (the Secure Element on the device) and remains encrypted until it reaches the intended recipient (the payment network or merchant), providing a layer of security that further reinforced the trustworthiness of Apple Pay.[7]

The encryption used in Apple Pay is not just any standard encryption; it is the same advanced encryption algorithms and protocols employed by the financial industry to secure high-value transactions. Apple demonstrated its commitment to the highest standards of security by adopting these industry-leading encryption practices which resonated with both consumers and merchants, ultimately contributing to the success of Apple Pay.

The third pillar of Apple Pay's security strategy was its innovative approach to authentication. Rather than relying on traditional methods, such as PINs or passwords, Apple Pay leveraged the power of biometric authentication, specifically Touch ID (for older devices) and Face ID (for newer devices).[8] When making a payment with Apple Pay, users are required to authenticate the transaction using their fingerprint or facial features. This biometric authentication not only provided a secure way to verify the user's identity but also offered a seamless and convenient user experience, as it eliminated the need to enter a PIN or password. Importantly, the biometric authentication in Apple Pay was not directly linked to the user's actual card information. Instead, it was used to authorize the use of the tokenized payment data stored on the device in the Secure

Element. This meant that the user's biometric data was never shared with the merchant or the payment network, further enhancing the security and privacy of the transaction. The integration of biometric authentication into the Apple Pay workflow was a game-changer, as it addressed a common pain point in traditional payment methods – the need to remember and enter complex credentials. Through providing a frictionless authentication process, Apple Pay made the payment experience more intuitive and user-friendly, driving increased adoption and acceptance among both consumers and merchants.

The combination of tokenization, encryption and biometric authentication created a synergistic effect that was instrumental in the success of Apple Pay. By addressing the key security concerns that had long plagued traditional payment methods, Apple was able to build trust and confidence among both consumers and merchants, paving the way for widespread adoption. Consumers, who had grown increasingly wary of the risks associated with sharing their sensitive financial information, were reassured by the robust security measures implemented in Apple Pay. The use of tokenization ensured that their card numbers were never exposed, while the encryption and biometric authentication provided an additional layer of protection against fraud and unauthorized access. This heightened sense of security resonated strongly with users, who were eager to embrace a payment solution that prioritized the safeguarding of their personal and financial data. The seamless and convenient authentication process, enabled by Touch ID and Face ID, further reinforced the user-centric approach of Apple Pay, making it an attractive alternative to traditional payment methods.

Merchants, on the other hand, were equally impressed by the security features of Apple Pay. The tokenization process effectively eliminated the risk of data breaches, as merchants never had access to the actual card numbers. This was a significant advantage, as it shielded them from the reputational and financial consequences of a security breach, which had become all too common in the payment industry. The encryption used in Apple Pay transactions also provided an additional layer of protection, ensuring that the payment data remained secure even during the transmission process. This gave merchants the confidence to adopt Apple Pay, knowing that their customers' sensitive information was being safeguarded to the highest standards.

The synergistic effect of these security innovations was further amplified by the broader ecosystem that Apple had built around its mobile devices and services. Apple was able to leverage the trust and loyalty that its customers had already established with the brand from integrating Apple Pay into the iOS ecosystem. This holistic approach, where security was not just an afterthought but a core component of the user experience, was a key differentiator for Apple. It allowed the company to position security as a strategic advantage, rather than a mere compliance requirement or a cost centre.

As a result, Apple Pay quickly gained traction in the mobile payments market, outpacing its competitors and becoming the de facto standard for secure and convenient digital transactions. The success of Apple Pay has not only solidified Apple's position as a leader in the payments industry but has also set a new benchmark for how enterprises can leverage security innovations to drive business growth and expansion.

Netflix

Another story of security-fuelled innovation comes from Netflix. Cybersecurity has always been important to Netflix, even before it began streaming video online. The company's initial business model involved mailing DVDs to customers, but even then, it needed to protect its customer data and intellectual property. In the early days of the company, Netflix collected sensitive customer information such as names, addresses and payment details in-house, likely on-premises. As they were disrupting the traditional (and physical) video rental business, protecting this information was critical to building customer trust and avoiding data breaches that could have resulted in significant damage to the brand.

As the company moved into digital streaming, the importance of cybersecurity only increased. Streaming video requires the transmission of large amounts of data over the internet, making it a prime target for cybercriminals. In addition, the company's systems and infrastructure became more complex, increasing the potential attack surface and the number of vulnerabilities that needed to be identified and addressed. Netflix recognized the importance of cybersecurity early on and invested in building a strong security posture from the outset. The company established a dedicated security team and implemented a range of security measures to protect its systems and customer data. These measures included firewalls, intrusion detection systems and vulnerability scanning tools, as well as employee training and awareness programmes.

At the heart of Netflix's security strategy was its bug bounty program, which was launched in 2013. This initiative was spearheaded by the company's security team, who recognized the value of tapping into the collective expertise of the global security community to identify and address vulnerabilities in Netflix's systems and applications. A bug bounty program is a crowdsourced approach to cybersecurity, where organizations invite security researchers and ethical hackers to find and report vulnerabilities in exchange for financial rewards, or 'bounties'. The charter of Netflix's bug bounty program was to incentivize security researchers to scrutinize the company's digital assets, from its streaming platform to its internal systems, and uncover any weaknesses that could be exploited by malicious actors.

The benefits of a well-designed bug bounty program are numerous. Firstly, it allows organizations to leverage the skills and knowledge of a vast network of security experts, who are often able to identify vulnerabilities that may have been overlooked by the company's internal security team. This is particularly valuable for enterprises like Netflix, which operate complex, large-scale digital ecosystems that are constantly evolving and expanding. Secondly, bug bounty programs foster a collaborative and mutually beneficial relationship between organizations and the security community. By rewarding researchers for their contributions, companies demonstrate their commitment to security and their willingness to work with external partners to enhance their defences. This, in turn, helps to build trust and goodwill, making it easier for the organization to attract and retain top security talent. Bug bounty programs can be a cost-effective way for companies to improve their security posture. Rather than investing in a large, in-house security team, organizations can leverage the expertise of the global security community on an as-needed basis, paying only for the vulnerabilities that are successfully identified and reported. This allows companies to focus their resources on other strategic priorities, while still maintaining a robust and proactive security stance.

For Netflix, the launch of its bug bounty program in 2013 was a pivotal moment in the company's security journey. Netflix was able to uncover and address a wide range of vulnerabilities via the expertise of security researchers around the world. This, in turn, helped to maintain the integrity and reliability of the company's streaming platform, which was crucial as it rapidly expanded its user base both domestically and internationally.

The impact of the bug bounty program on Netflix's growth and success cannot be overstated. As word of Netflix's commitment to security spread, it began to attract a growing number of security-conscious customers who were drawn to the company's reputation for safeguarding their personal data and viewing habits. The program served as a powerful marketing tool for Netflix, positioning the company as a leader in the field of cybersecurity. Through public acknowledgement and rewarding the contributions of security researchers, Netflix demonstrated its willingness to collaborate with the broader security community, further enhancing its reputation and attracting top talent to its ranks.

The financial benefits of the bug bounty program were also significant. Outsourcing the discovery and remediation of security vulnerabilities to a global network of researchers enabled Netflix to avoid the costly and time-consuming process of building and maintaining an in-house security team capable of identifying and addressing every potential threat. Instead, the company could focus its resources on developing and refining its core product offerings, confident that its security posture was being actively monitored and maintained by a dedicated community of security experts.

As Netflix's user base continued to grow, the company's commitment to security only intensified. The bug bounty program was expanded to include a wider range of assets, including its mobile applications, content delivery network and even its internal systems. This holistic approach to security ensured that every aspect of the Netflix ecosystem was subject to rigorous scrutiny and testing, further bolstering the company's reputation as a trusted and secure platform.

The success of Netflix's bug bounty program has not gone unnoticed by other enterprises. Many companies, across a variety of industries, have since followed suit, launching their own bug bounty initiatives in an effort to tap into the expertise of the global security community and enhance their security posture. Apple, Uber, Airbnb and Tesla (to name a few) are well known for their bug bounty programs as well. This trend has not only raised the bar for security standards across the business landscape but has also created new opportunities for security researchers and ethical hackers to contribute to the greater good while being fairly compensated for their efforts.

The company's focus on cybersecurity has paid off, with Netflix experiencing relatively few security incidents over the years. This has helped to build trust with customers and partners, who have come to rely on the company's secure and reliable streaming service, which is supported by an estimated volume of 15 per cent of downstream internet traffic globally during peak hours attributed exclusively to Netflix.[9]

JPMorgan Chase

For years, organizations in the financial services industry have grappled with the challenge of balancing the need for robust security measures with the demands for seamless customer experiences and rapid innovation. This delicate balance was put to the test in 2014 when JPMorgan Chase, one of the largest and most prominent financial institutions in the United States, experienced a devastating security breach that compromised the personal information of millions of its customers. The events leading up to the 2014 breach painted a familiar picture for the industry. As technology advanced and customer expectations shifted, many organizations struggled to keep pace with a rapidly changing technical landscape which contributed to an underinvestment in security infrastructure, outdated protocols and a reactive approach to emerging threats.

JPMorgan Chase was no exception. Prior to the 2014 breach, the organization was grappling with an average of 12 significant cybersecurity incidents per year, and its security processes were largely manual and inefficient. Compliance and regulatory reporting were time-consuming, and the company's ability to detect, investigate and respond to threats was hampered by a lack of automation and integration. The 2014 breach, which compromised the personal information of 76 million households and 7 million small businesses,[10] served as a wake-up call for JPMorgan Chase. The company recognized that its approach to security had to change, and that this change would require a significant investment of resources and a fundamental shift in mindset. Rather than viewing security as a necessary evil, JPMorgan Chase made the strategic decision to embrace it as a driver of innovation and growth. The company allocated billions of dollars to enhance its security infrastructure, implement advanced threat detection and response capabilities, and train its employees on best practices. This investment was not just about shoring up defences; it was about transforming the way the organization approached security as a whole.

One of the most immediate and tangible benefits of JPMorgan Chase's security-driven innovation was the restoration of customer trust and loyalty. The 2014 breach had shaken the confidence of the company's clients, many of whom were understandably concerned about the safety of their personal and financial information. However, by demonstrating a strong and sustained commitment to security, JPMorgan Chase was able to rebuild trust and regain the confidence of its customer base. Within just two years of the breach, the company's customer retention rate had climbed back to pre-breach levels,[11] and by 2018, it had surpassed them, reaching an impressive 94 per cent.[12] This renewed trust has had a ripple effect across the organization. Customers have become more willing to engage with the company's expanded suite of secure financial services, leading to a significant increase in cross-selling and upselling opportunities. The company's new customer acquisition rate has also grown by approximately 15 per cent since 2014,[13] as clients are drawn to the enhanced security features and innovative products.

In addition to strengthening customer relationships, JPMorgan Chase's security-driven innovation has also led to significant improvements in operational efficiency. Investments into automated security tools and streamlining security processes allowed the company to reduce the time and resources required to detect, investigate and respond to security threats by 30 per cent. This increased efficiency has had a direct impact on the company's bottom line: JPMorgan Chase has reported a 15 per cent reduction in its overall cybersecurity-related operational costs since 2014, as it has been able to optimize its security spending and reduce the impact of security incidents. The benefits of this efficiency extend beyond cost savings. By freeing up its security team from manual tasks, JPMorgan Chase has been able to allocate more resources towards strategic initiatives and innovation. The company has seen a 25 per cent reduction in security-related manual tasks, allowing its security professionals to focus on more proactive and forward-thinking projects.[14]

In the highly regulated financial services industry, compliance is a critical aspect of business operations. JPMorgan Chase's security-driven innovation has enabled the company to streamline its compliance and regulatory reporting processes, leading to a 20 per cent reduction in the time and resources required to generate regulatory reports. This improvement in compliance efficiency has had a direct impact on the company's regulatory standing. JPMorgan Chase has reported better audit scores and a lower risk of costly fines or penalties related to non-compliance. Compared to its peers in the industry, the company has faced fewer major compliance violations, with an average of 3.5 significant breaches per year, which is lower than the industry average of 4.8. Moreover, JPMorgan Chase has been subject to a relatively lower number of regulatory enforcement actions, such as consent orders and cease-and-desist orders, compared to other major financial institutions. The company has faced an average of 2.2 enforcement actions per year since 2014, while the industry average for large banks is around 3.1 actions per year. These metrics demonstrate that JPMorgan Chase's proactive approach to security and compliance has enabled the company to navigate the regulatory landscape more effectively. By prioritizing security as a strategic priority, the company has been able to minimize the financial and reputational impact of regulatory penalties and fines, positioning it for long-term sustainable growth.

The security-driven transformation at JPMorgan Chase has also had a profound impact on the company's product innovation efforts. Embracing the principle of 'secure by design', the organization has been able to develop new products and services that prioritize security from the ground up, giving them a competitive edge in the market. One prime example of this is JPMorgan Chase's foray into the cryptocurrency and digital asset space. In 2020, the company became the first major US bank to offer a Bitcoin fund to its wealth management clients. Its entry into the cryptocurrency and digital asset space has positioned it to capitalize on the rapidly evolving fintech landscape, while its expansion into small business banking has allowed it to diversify its customer base and tap into new sources of revenue. This move was enabled by the company's robust security infrastructure, which allowed it to navigate the unique risks and regulatory requirements of this emerging market. Similarly, JPMorgan Chase has forged strategic partnerships with fintech companies, such as Plaid and Marqeta, to offer innovative financial services to its customers. These partnerships have been facilitated by the company's ability to securely integrate its systems with those of its fintech partners, ensuring the protection of customer data and the overall integrity of the financial ecosystem.

Beyond the digital realm, JPMorgan Chase has also leveraged its security expertise to expand its small business banking services. The company's secure digital banking platforms and advanced fraud detection capabilities have been instrumental in attracting and retaining small business clients, who are particularly vulnerable to cyber threats.

The security-driven innovation at JPMorgan Chase has not only fuelled product development but has also enabled the company to confidently expand into new geographic markets and business lines. Since the 2014 breach, JPMorgan Chase has made a concerted effort to expand its global footprint, entering new markets in Asia, Europe and Latin America. The company's enhanced security capabilities have allowed it to navigate the unique regulatory and cybersecurity challenges of these new markets, establishing a strong presence and capturing market share.

These new market entries demonstrate how JPMorgan Chase's security-driven innovation has enabled the company to diversify its business, explore new revenue streams and strengthen its competitive position in the financial services industry. The company has been able to confidently expand into emerging and high-growth markets by prioritizing security as a strategic imperative, positioning itself for long-term success.

The story of JPMorgan Chase's security-driven transformation is not just a tale of one company's success; it is a testament to the transformative power of security in the financial services industry as a whole. In an era where cyber threats are becoming increasingly sophisticated and customer expectations are constantly evolving, the importance of security as a strategic priority should not require much explanation. The lessons learned from JPMorgan Chase's experience can be applied across the financial services sector and beyond. Companies that are willing to invest in robust security infrastructure, streamline their security processes and integrate security into their product development and market expansion strategies will be better positioned to navigate the challenges of the digital age and thrive in the long run.

A significant impact of JPMorgan Chase's transformation has been the shift in industry-wide perceptions of security. Rather than being viewed as a necessary cost or a hindrance to growth, security is now being recognized as a strategic enabler that can fuel innovation and drive sustainable success. This shift in mindset is crucial, as it has the potential to inspire other financial institutions to follow in their footsteps. From enhanced customer trust and loyalty to improved operational efficiency and regulatory compliance – other organizations may be more inclined to invest in their own security-driven transformation efforts after seeing the concrete results of this achievement. The success of JPMorgan Chase's security-driven innovation has the power to influence the broader technology and innovation landscape within the financial services industry. As more companies recognize the value of security as a strategic priority, they may be more likely to collaborate with security-focused start-ups and technology providers, further accelerating the pace of innovation in the sector.

This collaborative approach to security and innovation could also have a ripple effect on the regulatory environment. As financial institutions demonstrate their commitment to security and their ability to navigate the complex regulatory landscape, policymakers may be more inclined to adopt a more flexible and supportive regulatory framework that encourages innovation while still maintaining robust security standards. In this way, the story of JPMorgan Chase's security-driven transformation is not just about one company's success; it is about the potential to reshape the entire financial services industry and, ultimately, the way that businesses approach security and innovation in the digital age.

KEY TAKEAWAYS

- Traditionally, security is often viewed as a cost centre which puts it at a disadvantage for significant investment beyond minimum operational status quo.

- Security will manifest itself as a driver for innovation in different ways, depending on the industry.

- Regulated industries are particularly rich targets for opportunities to innovate, as they are subject to outside influence (regulators).

- Companies – even non-technical ones – will continue to invest in security as a driver for innovation and growth.

Notes

1 Alex Wilhelm. Apple CEO Tim Cook: Apple Pay activated 1m cards in 72 hours, TechCrunch, 27 October 2014. https://techcrunch.com/2014/10/27/ apple-ceo-tim-cook-apple-pay-activated-1m-cards-in-72-hours/ (archived at https://perma.cc/HNC5-TH9Y)

2 Tom Warren. Apple Pay available on October 20th with 500 more banks on board, The Verge, 16 October 2014. www.theverge.com/2014/10/16/6981117/ apple-pay-release-date-available-october-20th (archived at https://perma.cc/ N2MP-8WWK)

3 Ben Lovejoy. Apple Pay now supports 90% of US credit cards by transaction volume, 9to5Mac, 16 December 2014. https://9to5mac.com/2014/12/16/ apple-pay-cards/ (archived at https://perma.cc/DFE9-VKPE)

4 Mikey Campbell. Apple Pay transactions totaled $10.9B in 2015, suffers growing pains, report says. https://appleinsider.com/articles/16/06/02/apple-pay-transactions-totaled-109b-in-2015-suffers-growing-pains-report-says (archived at https://perma.cc/X3MC-G2J8)

5 From Bloomberg News. Apple Pay supported by 2,500 banks as fraud concerns linger, Silicon Valley, 9 March 2015. siliconvalley.com/2015/03/09/ apple-pay-supported-by-2500-banks-as-fraud-concerns-linger/ (archived at https://perma.cc/3ZAE-MDYX)

6 Dumindu Buddhika. How Apple Pay works under the hood, freeCodeCamp. www.freecodecamp.org/news/how-apple-pay-works-under-the-hood-8c3978238324/ (archived at https://perma.cc/P9HA-S5KR)

7 How is Apple Pay secure? GB Times, 5 December 2024. https://gbtimes.com/ how-is-apple-pay-secure/ (archived at https://perma.cc/2JK9-STWS)

8 Apple Support. Payment authorisation with Apple Pay. https://support.apple.com/ en-gb/guide/security/secc1f57e189/web (archived at https://perma.cc/763X-7VZP)

9 Martin Armstrong. Infographic: Netflix is Responsible for 15% of Global Internet Traffic, Statista Infographics, 1 March 2023. www.statista.com/ chart/15692/distribution-of-global-downstream-traffic/ (archived at https:// perma.cc/TN6H-H2RP)

10 Jessica Silver-Greenberg, Matthew Goldstein and Nicole Perlroth. JPMorgan Chase hacking affects 76 million households. DealB%k, New York Times, 2 October 2014. https://archive.nytimes.com/dealbook.nytimes.com/2014/10/02/jpmorgan-discovers-further-cyber-security-issues/ (archived at https://perma.cc/D5AL-RA75)

11 https://www.jpmorganchase.com/content/dam/jpmc/jpmorgan-chase-and-co/ investor-relations/documents/2016-annualreport.pdf (archived at https://perma.cc/DQZ9-7R6W)

12 https://www.jpmorganchase.com/content/dam/jpmc/jpmorgan-chase-and-co/
investor-relations/documents/annualreport-2018.pdf (archived at
https://perma.cc/8NW7-MYC6)

13 https://www.jpmorganchase.com/content/dam/jpmc/jpmorgan-chase-and-co/
investor-relations/documents/annualreport-2023.pdf (archived at
https://perma.cc/U9AP-B7TV)

14 We continue to execute against our technology strategy. https://www.
jpmorganchase.com/content/dam/jpmc/jpmorgan-chase-and-co/investor-
relations/documents/events/2023/jpmc-investor-day-2023/global-technology.
pdf (archived at https://perma.cc/S233-9FKZ)

4

Embracing risk for strategic growth

In the previous chapter, I discussed the correlation between growth and risk: as you increase growth, you will inherently take on more risk. It is incredibly common – and sensible – that risk is first avoided (if possible), then mitigated where available. In larger, regulated organizations, taking on risk is no easy task even with the best of intentions. In those types of organizations, risk is typically managed centrally as the stakes are ever increasing to protect the reputation and safety of the market in which they operate. Consider healthcare and life sciences, where large companies are developing products and services which can directly impact the health of a human being (hopefully in a positive way), or the financial services industry whose users rely on for their personal and family's financial stability and security. Even in non-regulated industries, taking on new risk is costly and is often a barrier to rapid growth. Companies like these tend to incubate new projects by turning to the services or even startup world where they can transfer their own risks to a third party in exchange for a product that adds value to their own product offering without having to build it themselves. Even then, taking on a third party involves risk, as the data will now have to be sent outside of the comfort of their own data halls.

So far, what I have described is 'typical' or 'traditional' and possibly even necessary, but it is not the only way to overcome risk in favour of progress. A traditional lifecycle of a project often is as follows:

1 **Ideation.** This is the initial stage where new ideas are formed by customer feedback, internal feedback, product brainstorming,

industry trends, etc. The idea is often pitched to the necessary stakeholders and considered for what additional value it might add to their customer base.

2 **Feasibility assessment.** This is a cursory look at what it would take to implement the idea. Engineering costs, infrastructure, time, resources, systems, technology and so on. This is all weighed up against the values and benefits raised in the first stage to determine the return on investment (ROI) – how long until the costs are recovered and the idea becomes profitable.

3 **Business case.** This is where things start to firm up. A deeper consideration for the resources and costs are quantified and timelines for milestones are proposed (often to leadership) and aligned with strategic goals of the organization.

4 **Proof of concept.** This is a minimal implementation of the solution created to validate the technical integration as well as draw out any challenges that perhaps had not yet been considered during the previous stages. The intended outcome is often a pass/fail and possibly the gateway to full implementation.

5 **Risk assessment.** With the concept proven and loosely built out, this is an assessment of what risks the solution may have to the business, what controls apply to the solution and the data it uses.

6 **Project planning.** The project plan should contain details of the full implementation including scope, timeline, resource requirements and communications.

7 **Development.** This is where an actual engineering and implementation effort commences according to the established plan. Software development, integration with existing systems, resource provisioning, anything related to implementing the solution is executed.

8 **Validation.** Comprehensive regression, integration and user acceptance testing is performed and documented. Any inconsistencies with desired output (bugs) are raised and ideally fixed during this process.

9 **Integration.** The developed (and accepted solution) is integrated into the live systems.

10 **Go-live.** The new feature or solution is made available to beneficiaries. This may include user training, customer or technical support and performance monitoring.

11 **Continuous improvement.** A post-implementation review is conducted to compare project expectations compared to reality and how to better align, determine areas of improvement and track ongoing metrics to optimize performance and desired outcomes.

Risk assessment comes in at step 5 which many stakeholders would argue is the highest mountain to climb. That is typically the 'no' phase, where the risks appear to be too much for the business to handle at face value. This is probably the first time that anyone from the team responsible for security has seen or heard of this solution, so the risks are evaluated without much context – although risk is risk, no matter how much context you put around it, and it is up to the responsible team to enforce it.

However, the term 'risk versus reward' comes to mind, and risk can be mitigated. If you evaluate the cost of mitigation and the resulting risk delta (one of four risk sensitivity metrics utilized by options traders), and then compare that to the reward, you have something of a formula to test the feasibility of the full solution.

That said, security people are not business-illiterate. They are all marching toward the collective goals set forth by leadership. They do care about the outcomes of the business and want to grow and achieve, but they just aren't always given the chance to show it. Security minded people are creative problem solvers and if brought into the fold of a project in the ideation or feasibility assessment stages, they can help you build the business case. Instead of 'no', they will ask themselves 'how'.

A common mistake that the 'uninitiated' make is that compliance and security are the same thing. Spoiler: they aren't. Compliance focuses on aligning with laws, regulations and relevant industry standards which are both applicable to, and driven by, the need to meet external requirements. Compliance tends to be reactive and process-driven with periodic checkpoints over time to measure the adherence to those requirements. Security is a focus protecting the assets and systems of an organization from threats and vulnerabilities, and comes from the need to safeguard the confidentiality, integrity and availability of information. Security tends to be proactive and preventative to eliminate danger before it even arises. It is ongoing and ever evolving as it should be continuously measured for its effectiveness.

A classic example of the difference between the two is a house and its occupants: security is the homeowner's individual efforts to protect the contents and other inhabitants. A homeowner might install a deadbolt and an alarm system to prevent and deter break ins. Motion lights, wall-safe, fire extinguishers are also relative to securing the home. Compliance, in this example, is akin to building codes and zoning which the house must adhere to. Think electrical wiring standards, avoiding the use of prohibited building materials, permits for renovations, taxes and fees, etc.

The primary responsibility of a security team is to minimize risk. This is typically done by avoiding risk, transferring risk and mitigating risk, in that order. As a result, security teams naturally emphasize threat minimization and compliance. When evaluating new opportunities, security teams often take a compliance-driven approach, especially when the opportunities are considered out of context. This prevention-led approach is a direct headwind to grow an innovation, and the business will behave accordingly; it is a great way to not get invited to parties. When observed through the lens of prevention at all costs, security teams may lose sight of the 'greater good' when it comes to business objectives. In that way, they will be perceived as a roadblock to progress instead of part of the solution.

It is understandable that a security team would want to prioritize prevention. However, this approach has two potential extremes. On one end, the team could try to stop every single bad thing from happening. This would effectively stifle any potential for good outcomes as well. On the other end, the team could allow anything and everything to happen, removing any barriers to progress but also risking significant harm. The challenge is finding the right balance – preventing the most serious threats while still enabling positive opportunities to move forward. These are the two ends of the spectrum, and neither approach is the right one. Of course, every company and every business will have its own approach to what is appropriate for them, and it must also be considered that in some industries, a free-for-all approach is simply not an option.

If those two extremes represent the spectrum, then what lies in between is a sliding scale from less risk to more risk. As mentioned earlier, in terms of regulated companies, the risk level or risk appetite tends to be lower. These companies are more risk-averse, not only for the good of their own business but also because they are required to by their regulators. Regulators tend to look after the health of the entire industry rather than individual organizations, which is where the guidelines from these regulators come into play. These guidelines specify the minimum requirements or the maximum allowable risk.

It makes sense, then, that if you bring a problem or a new opportunity to any security team, with or without context, their natural reaction is to say 'no, too risky'. When I worked within the cloud, I was working with financial services customers who were looking to adopt cloud, which was immediately struck down by many of the security teams because it was inherently too risky. What I've seen in 10 out of 10 cases was that the immediate knee-jerk reaction was 'no, too risky'. This really came from a binary point of view. My default position was that a move to the cloud would benefit the company from a business perspective, and also from a security perspective (not without some effort), and their default position would be 'no, too risky'. Neither of us are correct, at least at face value, but that's where the spectrum comes into play. If we stop at face value, nothing will ever move, and nothing will ever change, because the security team is always going to have the last say in terms of risk management. Although they may not have a say in what is decided overall, they will measure the risk, and someone has to sign off on it. Nobody wants to be the one signing off on the risk and then having the threats come true on their watch, effectively losing their job and possibly experiencing some jail time, which makes objective risk evaluation a tricky situation for businesses.

What I found is that you have to dive deeper into what the needs of the business are from a risk point of view and find creative ways to mitigate those risks and navigate them. Onboarding new technology, vendors or services may require non-standard approaches which depend on the use case, the data involved, the jurisdiction and so on. Working with the technical personnel who understand the intended integration can help delve deeper into the actual, measurable risks facing the business. One of the key capabilities of a security team is their ability to qualify or quantify risk. Whether the risk assessment is qualitative or quantitative depends on the nature of the subject matter; not all risks can be quantified, so a relative scoring system may be employed. Alternatively, estimating the financial impact should the risk materialize, or the data that could be lost and subsequent knock-on effects, provides a quantitative assessment.

Ultimately, associating numerical values with risks is essential to determining if the level of risk is acceptable.

Drawing on some of my own experiences, I worked with a potential customer who was interested in moving to cloud. From a business point of view, the security team immediately rejected the idea, raising concerns over sharing infrastructure and hardware, how the neighbours of the cloud are unknown to them, and how they don't know if they are launching next to someone who's intentionally trying to come across tenant boundaries set by the hypervisor to do something with their data. At face value that is a sensible reason not to move forward. However, when we really understood what sort of workload they would be putting on there and what exactly they were afraid of, we could contact the cloud provider with their concerns.

We dived much more deeply into the technical architecture of the cloud infrastructure and compared it with the existing hardware and infrastructure of the particular customer. We looked at one of the risks they were mitigating in relation to shared hardware or shared resources. We know that the other virtual machines or containers running on the same physical server or in the same private data centre as our workloads are also under our control. This means we don't have to worry about our sensitive workloads being placed next to a potentially malicious actor, which could be a concern in a shared public cloud environment. Since the 'next-door neighbours' in our own data centre are part of our own infrastructure, we can be confident there is no such risk.

We have to take the risk out of isolation and into context and ask how you know that all the resource that is sitting next to that resource isn't still malicious. Just because it's internal to your data centre doesn't mean that malice is unavoidable – this comes down to who your employees are, who has access to certain systems and where you are co-locating your data.

So, for as many reasons not to move to the cloud in this example there were just as many reasons where I could argue in favour of it. What we did in the end was come up with a way to move to cloud, looking at the available protections and configurations that we might be able to leverage and utilize in order to make it OK to move to the cloud. There was an option to launch the workload with certain parameters which involved encrypting things before they hit the cloud. It was about making sure that the resources being used for the workload had the security properties required to help them mitigate risk.

Therefore, the exercise was to evaluate in context the risks that the company were potentially facing with this move. Now, if we take that same approach to more or less any vendor, solution or new technology, there is at least a better, more informed way of making those decisions. This also provides an opportunity to have more visibility while monitoring those risks which may cause stress or cost the business if these bad things were to happen.

Security professionals are obviously capable of understanding these business problems and needs, and can understand the benefits of launching into a new technology, vendor or whatever the project is. However, traditionally they are not brought to the table at the last minute, so they rarely have that context which makes it difficult for them to come up with those creative workarounds and ways to launch this new project as they haven't been involved in the process the whole way.

So, what is the antidote to stifled innovation and agility due to culture of risk avoidance and prevention? It is to bring security professionals in early on and invest in security. Security isn't a cost if brought in at the right time, with the right people in the right context. They become the 'how?' people rather than the 'no' people so they will be able to help cultivate opportunities for competitive advantage and an organizational growth if they are simply brought into the fold earlier in the stack.

Qualitative vs quantitative risk assessment

When it comes to security risk assessment, there are almost always two methods: a qualitative approach, which is a more subjective assessment based on risks and their potential impact, and a quantitative approach, which involves assigning numerical values to the likelihood and impact of security threats. A qualitative approach helps prioritize risks and draw more attention to which elements of the thing being assessed are important to the business. A quantitative approach would result in understanding the cost of a particular risk materializing, so that it can be decided whether the cost of mitigating that risk is more than what the risk might cost the business.

When we look at a qualitative approach, it is judgement-based and subjective. It involves understanding the needs of the business, the technology or service being added, as well as the security posture of the business itself. This requires some expertise on the security and technology side to evaluate the likelihood and severity of threats to the business. This is typically manifested using a scale or a rating system to categorize the subjective risk level in an easy to understand way such as 'low', 'medium' and 'high'. This is more practical and easier to implement, especially when dealing with complex or unknown situations where exact numerical data is not available. As a bonus, 'low', 'medium' and 'high' are not security 'jargon' and can be easily consumed outside of the security organization. Qualitative assessments can provide a more complete understanding of the security landscape and help prioritize risks based on their importance to the business.

In a qualitative risk assessment, the scale or rating system is a useful tool, if not the most necessary. Typically, the risk likelihood is qualified. This is the probability of a particular threat or event occurring on a qualitative scale. For example, if you adopt a third-party email service, the likelihood of being phished might be low or medium, as phishing is not entirely preventable, but an enterprise email solution can help mitigate it. Low, medium and high are a popular scale, with critical sometimes included as well. Alternatively, a numerical scale of 1 to 5 could be used, with 1–2 representing low, 3–4 representing medium and 5 representing high. In addition to likelihood, impact is also an important dimension of qualitative risk assessment. The impact is the potential consequence of a security threat or event, which is also assessed on a qualitative scale, such as 'insignificant', 'minor', 'moderate', 'major' and 'catastrophic'. As with likelihood, a numeric scale from 1 to 5 can also be used here for continuity.

These two dimensions – likelihood and impact – are commonly evaluated together through a risk matrix as shown in Figure 4.1. Risk likelihood is placed on one axis and risk impact on the other, with the scales overlapping in a matrix form. The intersection of each likelihood and impact are coded to create a gradient scale (commonly red, amber, and green, with red being high, amber being medium, and green being low) which can be used to make decisions about individual risks perceived to face the business, and priority can be assigned in order of most severe to least severe for mitigation.

FIGURE 4.1 An example risk matrix

Probability			Impact			
Very High 5	5	10	15	20	25
High 4	4	8	12	16	20
Normal 3	3	6	9	12	15
Low 2	2	4	6	8	10
Very Low 1	1	2	3	4	5
	Very Low 1	Low 2	Normal 3	High 4	Very High 5

With such a scale available, risks from a risk register can be scored for likelihood and impact and subsequently measured against the risk matrix to assess the severity of each.

The qualitative scale allows professional security professionals to prioritize and assess risk based on their subjective judgement and experience, as opposed to hard numbers. It's important to conduct a qualitative risk assessment with someone who understands the industry and has experience with your business, so that their judgement of the impacts is based on their knowledge. This approach is typically useful when dealing with solutions with high complexity or high degrees of uncertainty, where more quantitative data is not available to measure the risks numerically. The specific scales and thresholds used in this type of risk assessment can vary, depending on the security maturity of the organization. Some companies use greater than five gradients, while others use as few as three.

On the other hand, quantitative risk assessment is a more numerical and objective approach to evaluating risks. It means assigning relatively precise numerical values to the same dimensions which are potential impact and probability. The numerical values associated with probability or likelihood would be a percentage, a decimal or a number of occurrences of a successful attack per a given time period, usually a year.

These numbers are not always readily available to an organization, especially in its infancy. Instead, these numbers come from historical data, industry benchmarks, expert judgement, probability modelling and threat intelligence. Organizations can analyse their own records of past incidents, failures and breaches to determine the frequency or rate of occurrence relative to the risk being faced. This is a good way to provide a foundation for estimating the likelihood of similar events that could occur in the future. When looking at industry benchmarks, there are reports and research available that typically provide statistics on the prevalence of certain types of risk events that may map well to the assessment being done. This would help understand an organization's context in terms of the risk profile of experiencing similar events in a similar industry, maybe even in a similar region. Subject matter experts, such as security professionals, risk analysts or other industry specialists, can provide their informed estimates of the likelihood of a particular event based on their own knowledge, experience and understanding of the threat landscape. This is particularly valuable when historical data or industry benchmarks are not readily available.

Statistical modelling is also a useful way to come up with these metrics and is a more scientific approach to evaluating historical data. Probability distributions and Monte Carlo simulations are common ways of estimating the likelihood of a given risk event and are typically found within organizations with a mature security program (which is often the case in a regulated industry). These analyses can incorporate various factors, such as the frequency of past incidents, the effectiveness of existing controls and the potential for new threats to emerge. Intelligence data provides insights into the current and emerging threat landscape and can also help assess the likelihood of risk events. This information typically comes from sources such as security vendors, government agencies, industry-specific threat intelligence platforms or even product-based threat intelligence for some of the larger services available to enterprises today. While each figure on its own may have its own margin of error, which will vary from organization to organization, combining two or more of these sources can help develop more accurate and reliable estimates of the likelihood of a risk event occurring.

Impact is almost always measured in financial terms, such as: 'What is the estimated financial impact to the business if this risk event were to occur?' This focuses on quantifying the potential monetary consequences of the risk event. The obvious answer would be to consider the immediate, tangible costs associated with the risk, such as remediation, recovery and any regulatory fines. However, the actual financial impact is usually more complex. It also involves peripheral costs like productivity losses, reputational damage and loss of customer trust and business. Beyond that, the analysis must account for the costs of any disruption to normal business operations. This includes lost revenue, increased expenses and resources needed for business continuity measures. Importantly, the financial impact assessment should also factor in the potential business opportunities that may be missed or foregone as a result of the risk event.

This refers to revenue, new initiatives or other growth prospects that the organization may be unable to pursue if resources and attention have to be diverted to address the risk and its aftermath.

With those additional considerations in mind, the numerical value is often much higher than face-value.

Let's take a look at a simple quantitative risk assessment. Suppose over the past 5 years there have been 10 data breaches in an organization. The average cost of each data breach was $500,000, and the organization's network has 1,000 devices. To perform a quantitative risk assessment, the organization can use statistical analysis to estimate the probability and potential impact of a data breach. The organization can calculate the annual probability of a data breach using the historical data:

- Annual probability of a data breach = Number of data breaches (10) / Number of years (5)
- Annual probability of a data breach = 10 / 5 = 2%

The organization can use the average cost of past data breaches to estimate the potential financial impact by calculating the Annualized Loss Expectancy (ALE) – a common metric used in quantitative risk assessment which combines the probability and impact of a risk event:

- Average cost of a data breach = $500,000
- ALE = Annual probability of a data breach × Average cost of a data breach
- ALE = 2% × $500,000 = $10,000

This means that the organization can expect an average annual loss of $10,000 due to data breaches. The organization can then use this quantitative risk assessment to make informed decisions to determine the appropriate budget for security measures to mitigate the risk, evaluate the cost-effectiveness of the current control environment, and prioritize investments into further security measures based on the potential impact of the risk. Depending on the output, it may even be that the cost of impact is acceptable to the business to simply absorb without mitigating at all. Or it may be that just covering the costs with a suitable insurance product to transfer the risk is acceptable. The business may also deem it too expensive and avoid it entirely by not pursuing the opportunity.

Pushing through the barrier

When a business is faced with any risk whether it is low, medium, high or even critical they now have a choice on how to handle it: it could either be rejected or avoided, which means the project dies in its tracks, or it could be accepted which effectively means that the level of risk is acknowledged and that a responsible party is prepared to deal with the consequences of it. This is not something that is easily done, as in most cases where someone must be accountable for that risk as well as the consequences should they come to pass. This is an unfortunate outcome of some of these risk assessments. There is some rating, score or number at the end of the exercise that, if it is above a certain threshold, it gets implemented. If it's below a certain threshold then it gets rejected or avoided entirely. This is a 'the computer says no' scenario which has a definitive end point which can be a frustration for a hopeful business unit looking to expand capabilities and drive innovation.

If we take a step back, the reason a single numerical or qualitative output would yield a binary answer is because we're only looking at one side of the full equation. This equation consists of the organization's existing risk posture and the current risk assessment being conducted. The first component – the risk posture of the business – represents the left side of the equation. This risk posture has already been predetermined based on the organization's existing security controls, processes and overall risk tolerance. The second component – the risk assessment – represents the right side of the equation. This risk assessment is being calculated at a specific point in time, and is evaluated against the initial, predetermined risk posture of the organization.

In a better, healthier approach to risk management, I would argue that it's fair to continuously evaluate both sides of the equation.

That would involve a frequent assessment of the risk mitigation capabilities of the business to keep the number on the left side (the risk posture) as up-to-date as possible. What happens more often than not is that number stays static for much longer than the risk assessment gets evaluated. So, if we're talking about assessing risk every year for a particular vendor or a cyclical release schedule for new products, that output is being measured all the time. But perhaps the control environment hasn't been evaluated in a few years or rather, it has been evaluated, but it hasn't been updated in a few years. Therefore, that number will stay relatively the same.

To create a new paradigm for onboarding new risk and allowing for a more dynamic risk tolerance, it's important to implement more robust risk mitigation strategies and doing so more frequently. Try to treat your security program like any other application which has updates, release schedules, quality assurance and all sorts of ceremonies in pursuit of relevance. Also look at options for risk transfer, accepting risks with contingencies, diversifying risks by spreading them out, and an overall adjustment and appetite to mitigate additional risks. Evolving your control framework is essential as new risks emerge, but don't ignore the modernization and continuous improvement of the controls already in place to keep them relevant. For example, if your business has been operational for a long time, you might find that the commonly used control frameworks are very much out of date. As a consequence of evaluating new concepts to old controls, it would be no surprise to find that the concepts are out of tolerance, or just plain incompatible. By continuously evaluating and improving those controls, environments will help constantly update the mathematics of one side of the equation to be more fitting for taking on new risks.

Another option to change the 'right side' of the equation (the risk assessment) is to completely transfer the risk to a third party. Insurance is a great way to do that – more and more insurance companies are now offering things like cyber protection, phishing protection and other specialized coverage products for this world of emerging and evolving risks. You can also outsource specific risk-prone activities or add contractual clauses to your third-party vendors to cover off or effectively transfer some of these risks that you're facing to make it more palatable to your control environment.

Risk is a limit forever approaching zero, so at some point, some level of net-new risk must be taken on in the name of progress. Accepting risk is not just to accept it and move on, but it's accepting it and planning for contingencies. Acknowledging the high-risk nature of a particular opportunity and developing contingency plans to manage any potential consequences should any of those come to pass involves establishing clear incident response procedures, having an alternative supplier, as well as having a very defined and tested business continuity strategy.

Risk diversification is about spreading the risk across multiple initiatives instead of concentrating it into a single project. So, for example, if you look after a portfolio of opportunities, each with its own risk, you can balance the overall exposure so that the organization can reduce the potential impact of a single high-risk event and make the overall risk more manageable. For instance, imagine a company is considering three new product initiatives, each with their own risk profile:

1 Launching a new software application – this has a high-risk profile, as it's a completely new product in a competitive market.

2 Expanding an existing product line into a new geographic region – this has a medium-risk profile, as the product is established but entering a new market brings some uncertainty.

3 Upgrading the company's internal IT infrastructure – this has a lower-risk profile, as it's an internal project to improve efficiency and security.

Instead of putting all the company's resources into just the high-risk software application, the company could diversify its risk by investing in all three initiatives. This way, if the software application launch runs into unexpected challenges, the company has the other two lower-risk projects to help balance out the overall risk exposure, thus allowing the business to take on new initiatives. By having a portfolio of initiatives with varying risk levels, the company can reduce the potential impact of any single high-risk event. This makes the overall risk more manageable for the organization. The key is to spread out the risk across multiple projects rather than concentrating it in one area.

All these measures are ways to adjust the risk appetite of the business on the left side of the equation, and my proposal is to do this on a more frequent basis. Adjusting the appetite and tolerance levels and increasing or decreasing the sensitivity can help reframe what would normally be a high-risk opportunity into a lower risk classification by effectively changing the very definition of high risk. This isn't always easy to do, and it generally involves a strategic shift in an organization's risk management approach with a greater emphasis on innovation and growth and calculated risk-taking. Also, it may involve increasing the size of your security team, which is often seen as a cost centre as opposed to a profit centre. Therefore, this is not always easy to pitch at the board level, but by adjusting the risk of appetite, evolving it with the times, you can reframe the organization's look at risk to allow for new and exciting opportunities to grow the business.

Strategies for embracing and managing risk

Now that we have some idea of how risk is evaluated and how internal risk tolerances are assessed, we should have decent visibility of the decision-making process. The goal is now building an organization that fosters innovation by continuously improving their own risk posture and how it is actually evaluated to empower people within the business to identify and address risks, and implement robust risk management frameworks and strategies.

Security is often a cost centre for most organizations (unless the product is security) and it's hard to convince any accountant to add security staff under the banner of being able to innovate faster. Instead, a cultural shift to diversify and democratize risk management across everyone involved, especially the 'non-security' people, plays a big part in the organizational change required to keep up with the pace of innovation. For example, stakeholders involved in a particular project can be trained or should at least understand the process of risk assessment and qualification, as described previously, so that they be ahead of any potential objections when presenting to the risk board or going through the risk mitigation exercise required by the organization. Having some understanding of emerging threats and the risk landscape as it applies to modern technology will play a huge role in being able to predict and anticipate the challenges that are going to be faced for a particular business case as it moves through the process. Believe it or not, this approach is actually easier to achieve from within when comparing it to asking for an increase in security budget.

Risk-informed decision-making, now that we can qualify and quantify risk, is very helpful in incorporating considerations into the strategic decision-making process. Discussion of frameworks and methodologies for evaluating the trade-off between mitigation and business objectives is an important one to have. Frameworks are always evolving, and new bodies of practice are always emerging and seeking community input for the next set of control objectives with a clever acronym (e.g. NIST, COBIT, OWASP, MITRE ATT&CK). Making this information accessible and easy to consume is paramount in the encouragement of a self-service introduction to risk management. A first port of call could be to compare your internal control program to that of something more common in your industry, and you may find that your internal framework is out of touch with reality. This reveals the need for a holistic, risk-based approach to decision-making, as opposed to a silo compliance-driven approach, to change a conversation ender to a conversation starter.

Those industry frameworks that apply to your line of business or industry are very important because these frameworks are generally created in cooperation with players in the industry, which have agreed that these are good, if not best, practices in order to evaluate and mitigate common risks faced. To sweeten the deal, they are typically either known or even preferred by relevant regulatory bodies, should your industry be subject to regulation.

The way to change the culture to continuously update the risk equation involves measurement, just like assessing risk. To do this quantitatively where possible is probably the most mature way of doing this, because it yields a direct numerical comparison when measuring risk against risk appetite. Qualitative measurement is arguably less precise, but needs must. In order to give weight to a qualitative assessment, looking at key performance indicators (KPIs) around the success or effectiveness of your security program, like continuous monitoring, vulnerability management, ticket metrics such as mean time to resolution, and incident protocols will help justify the subjective nature of a qualitative assessment. These are all metrics that can help change that left side when looking at the risk equation. Always being aware of the current state of your control framework and your security program will help facilitate this conversation, and you don't have to be a security professional to understand it.

The security industry tends to be shrouded in a certain degree of specialized, tribal knowledge. Regardless of where I go, I still run into the same group of people that I've been working with in some capacity for years. The positive impact of such knowledge is that collaboration is crucial for the industry. When you get two security people in a room who haven't met each other, they tend to 'size each other up', at least metaphorically. However, security has such a broad catchment, that two specialists actually have very little in common beyond being able to solve maths equations directly in binary. A non-technical trait that most have in common is the willingness to share and to teach. Security is a never-ending race for superiority; an arms-race and the good guys need each other to succeed.

Discussing the importance of breaking down silos within organizations and fostering a collaborative environment amongst security, business and IT teams is paramount. Highlighting the value of industry benchmarking, peer learning and the adoption of best practices is crucial, as these often come from other organizations of similar size, jurisdictional requirements or even the same technology stack. People from organizations that have faced similar risks can provide valuable perspectives and different approaches to the same problem, which can be great ways to introduce a fresh look at your security and risk posture.

The best way to embrace something as sensitive as risk is to understand it completely, not just on the surface, but also how a particular risk could apply to the organization you work for. In most cases, whatever project you're working on has a finite number of risks, and those would be more or less the same across any business. However, it's how a particular business is prepared to manage that risk that makes the difference. For example, the risk of personal identifiable information being leaked is more or less universal across the world, but certain types of information being transferred across the network may be incredibly risky for some industries, yet completely innocuous in others. Understanding the risks you are about to undertake is relatively easy, but understanding how those risks apply to your business is the slightly more challenging part. This can be overcome by having those conversations upfront and gaining that knowledge from within, to say, 'I understand what we're facing, and here's how I propose that we face it.'

Balancing risk and security investments

It is a simple fact that evaluating security risks costs resources. Those resources might be time, it might be money, it might be both, but in most cases, it is a non-revenue-generating function which is typically minimized as much as possible from a financial point of view. You want to maximize your profits and minimize your costs; it is simple business economics. However, it doesn't preclude the need to actually create some sort of balance between security investment and enabling strategic growth. As we have covered before, growth without security investment is typically going to be too risky. Conversely, too much security investment will likely stifle growth because over-indexing on preventative measures will fundamentally disallow anything new and interesting to come across the business. As with anything else, understanding the factors at play are paramount to making informed trade-offs between risk mitigation and business.

The first step is to align security investments with the organization's overall business priorities, rather than just security priorities in isolation. This involves closely linking security spending initiatives to the organization's broader strategic objectives. For example, if the business is trying to expand into a new geographical market, they may face different environmental risks that they haven't had to deal with in their existing operations. In their current 'footprint' or area of operations, the organization likely has experience and familiarity managing the security challenges. However, venturing into this new market brings the potential for encountering unfamiliar risks and threats. Therefore, it would be worth that business's while to seek security specialists in that particular region to advise on the environmental risks that they may face. The long tail of deep security assessments is best left to the professionals to provide guidance by a strategic discussion about organizational priorities and on how to conduct a thorough risk assessment of an organization's risk profile and threat landscape.

Understanding the needs of the business is a great way to organically surface net-new security requirements before they become showstoppers and fuel a progressive conversation about security investment in context of strategic growth. For example, it's very easy for a security leader to make demands for adding new tools and personnel in pursuit of the greater good, but if some of those pursuits are much farther ahead than the roadmap of the business then those investments are probably not appropriate at that time. Having that conversation early on is a great way to gain the trust of senior leadership and further the position of security as a strategic function.

Just like with evaluating security controls, measurement is all but necessary to bring to the table during a discussion on security investment. Even though security is often a cost centre, there is a discussion to be had around a return on investment on security expenditure. Exploring methodologies and frameworks for qualifying the return on those investments helps rise above a cost-centric mindset. Just as quantified or qualified risk rises above the tolerance of business, it's easy to say no. The same is true for cost additional cost requirements. If the budget is X and the cost requirements for investment for security is X+Y, it's easy to say no. However, quantifying the return on those investments is an evolved version of that conversation which changes the discussion from a cost-centric mindset to a goal-oriented mindset. Navigating this conversation can be tricky, but it's important to include both the tangible and the intangible benefits, such as risk reduction, operational efficiency and even things way beyond the security landscape, such as brand reputation. Understanding the needs of the business in this frame of mind will help level the playing field and make you less intimidating as a security professional and more of a team player, as the organization will be moving towards a common goal. Highlighting the importance of establishing key performance indicators and metrics to track the effectiveness of these investments is a great way to continue building that trust. It signals to the investor that this is a well-thought-out plan, and the benefits from such an investment are already going to be communicated back to be measured for their efficiency and their effectiveness.

Having gathered information from both the business and the security side, it should enable an organization to make informed trade-offs between risk and business agility. We do have to acknowledge that there's an inherent tension between risk mitigation and the need for business agility and innovation. The business understands strategy and growth, and the security team understands security and risk. Providing guidance on how to strike a balance between security controls and flexibility is required to be able to seize those new opportunities. A security professional who talks about business agility has a clearly vetted interest in helping the business achieve their common goal and ends up being an ally to the stakeholders instead of a roadblock. Enabling stakeholders conduct their risk-benefit analysis in a self-serving way helps to make informed decisions that optimize the balance between risk and business objectives. In its final form, it will be part of the business case. It's very easy for a shiny new tool or a new opportunity to be run wild in the business side, not considering the risk impact. It's just as easy to look at the risk impact and immediately say no because the perceived risk exceeds the current risk threshold, but it's about meeting in the middle and understanding the needs from both sides of the table.

It can be argued that it is much easier for a security professional to get more involved in the business side than it is for a business side to get more involved in the security. Security professionals hone their skills over many years to develop and own their skills to be able to be a trusted partner and protector of that organization's risk profile. But it takes a lot less effort for a security professional to understand fundamentals of business strategy. Topics such as prioritizing investments based on risk exposure, business impact and a cost-benefit analysis indicate a material investment into the health and direction of a business, but does not really have a return path into the security world, thus the burden to 'reach across the aisle' is placed upon the security team.

Suggestions to explore approaches to optimize that security spending, such as leveraging cloud-based solutions, specialty tools, automation and even managed security services are best handled by the security organization but put into business terms like any other project. Highlighting the importance of continuous monitoring, review and adjustment of those security investments not only helps adapt to evolving threats and business requirements but also continues to underpin that business acumen which is needed to have these conversations in the first place, transforming the organization from a risk organization to an organization which makes informed risk decisions.

The security team providing tools, resources and easy-to-understand procedures for the business side – to help frontload some of that low-level security work or risk assessment – will pay dividends in the future for democratizing the conversation. It will help emphasize the need to cultivate a culture where security is viewed as an enabler of innovation rather than a constraint. This involves also discussing the role of security professionals in collaborating with business units to identify and address security challenges in a way that supports strategic goals as those strategic goals emerge.

KEY TAKEAWAYS

- Talking about risk without magnitude will always lead to negativity; be sure to put some kind of measurement – relative or otherwise – in front of your risk conversations.

- Risk is necessary for growth. Get comfortable with meeting risk and having difficult conversations head-on.

- Security on its own is obtuse, confusing and even scary for non-security professionals, so demystify it by putting it in context of day-to-day operations.

- Use the data in creative (but truthful) ways to secure a budget which bolsters security proportionally to the strategic initiatives of the entire business.

5

Cultivating a security-driven organization

A security-driven organization is one where security is in the very fabric of everyday life for every employee, relative to their job role. This is not achieved through a top-down, heavy-handed approach, but rather through a collaborative and inclusive culture that empowers all members of the workforce to be active participants in safeguarding the organization. In such an environment, security becomes an integral component that enables and accelerates the achievement of business objectives.

The foundation of a security-driven organization lies in cultivating a deep understanding and appreciation for security among employees at all levels. This is accomplished through comprehensive training programmes that go beyond mere compliance and instead focus on making security relatable, engaging and directly relevant to each individual's day-to-day responsibilities. By leveraging gamification, storytelling and real-world scenarios, security professionals can transform the learning experience, fostering a sense of ownership and personal investment in maintaining strong security practices. The key to this transformation lies in empowering the broader workforce to become active participants in the organization's security initiatives. Security professionals can no longer operate in isolation, dictating a set of rules and restrictions. Instead, they must adopt a more inclusive and user-centric approach, making security education and awareness accessible and engaging for all employees. For security to truly permeate the depths of an organization, it must be easy to understand, accessible to all, and complementary to the work of other disciplines.

Current state of organizational security

Security awareness training, which in most compliance frameworks requires employees to be educated on at least annually, is a type of security education that you may already be familiar with. Security awareness training is a fundamental component in cultivating a security-driven organization, with the intention of embedding security deeply into the everyday lives of employees. However, in many (possibly most) cases, these training programmes are viewed as a necessary evil by employees; an annoyance, a box to be checked off rather than an opportunity to meaningfully engage with the security principles of the organization.

It can easily be argued that a 30-minute training once per year is hardly enough exposure to make any material impact on how security is treated. Compounding that, many of these trainings lack relevance or any sort of personalization. They take a one-size-fits-all approach with generic content that fails to address the specific roles, responsibilities and pain points of different employee groups. When the training feels disconnected from an individual's day-to-day work, it becomes very easy to dismiss as irrelevant.

Also, much of the time the content is dry and delivered in a lecture-style presentation focusing heavily on compliance and reciting policy language. This is a dry, box-ticking approach which can demotivate and fail to engage employees on a practical or emotional level. The training then becomes an inconvenience for an employee, as they are required to complete these exercises, which are an unwelcome distraction, in addition to their day-to-day responsibilities. When training is not integrated into the workflow, it is often viewed as an obstacle rather than an investment of time.

Training is also usually passive and lacks opportunity for the trainee to engage interactively or provide feedback. A lack of interaction can make the training feel like a one-way communication rather than a collaborative learning experience. Ideally, security awareness should be an ongoing process rather than a point-in-time assessment which tests the ability of the taker to recall some language they read several slides before. Many organizations fail to provide regular refreshers, updates and opportunities for employees to apply and reinforce what they have learned and anything that was learned during the training quickly fades. Culturally speaking, when security is siloed within an organization, an employee who is forced to take a security training will perceive it as a 'security thing', or a security-specific initiative rather than being integrated into the broader organizational culture.

In a security-driven organization, security awareness training is transformed into a dynamic, interactive experience that fosters a deep understanding and appreciation for security among employees at all levels. Moving beyond the traditional, lecture-style format can enable an organization to leverage a variety of engaging techniques to make security relatable, relevant and even enjoyable for participants.

One such technique is gamification, which taps into the natural human desire for competition and recognition. Instead of passive learning, organizations can introduce interactive elements such as quizzes, challenges and leaderboards that make the training process fun and rewarding. Employees may be tasked with identifying phishing attempts, responding to simulated security incidents or even earning 'security points' for demonstrating exemplary security behaviours. This gamified approach not only enhances knowledge retention but also motivates employees to actively engage with security protocols, fostering a sense of ownership and personal investment in maintaining a robust security posture.

Storytelling is another powerful tool in security awareness training. Presenting security concepts through the lens of real-world case studies and personal narratives, security professionals can help employees understand the tangible consequences of security breaches and the importance of their individual roles in prevention. These stories can highlight the impact on customers, the financial implications or the reputational damage that can result from security incidents, resonating with employees on an emotional level and inspiring them to be more vigilant.

This transformative approach to security awareness training helps to break down the traditional perception of security as a hindrance, instead positioning it as an integral component that enables and accelerates the achievement of business objectives. Organizations can cultivate a security-conscious workforce that is actively invested in protecting the organization, rather than simply complying with mandated requirements, by making security training engaging and relevant.

This approach to security awareness training can also have a significant impact on the organization's overall security posture. When employees are equipped with a deep understanding of security best practices and the ability to identify and respond to threats, they become a powerful line of defence against cyber-attacks and data breaches. The resulting reduction in security incidents not only mitigates financial and reputational risks but also frees up security teams to focus on more strategic initiatives that drive business growth and innovation.

Perhaps most importantly, security awareness training that is both engaging and impactful can foster a culture of security-consciousness that reaches the entire organization. Empowering employees to be active participants in the security process can transform security from a siloed function into a shared responsibility, where everyone in the organization plays a role in safeguarding the business. This collaborative and inclusive approach is the foundation of a security-driven organization, where security is not just a necessity, but a strategic enabler for success.

Building a security-aware workforce

Security champions

The identification and empowerment of 'security champions' within the organization play a crucial role in driving this cultural transformation. Security champions are employees who, while not necessarily security experts themselves, have a deep understanding and appreciation for the importance of security within the organization. They may be respected leaders, influential figures or simply individuals who have a natural affinity for security and a desire to contribute to the organization's overall resilience. These champions serve as a critical bridge between the security function and the broader workforce, translating complex security concepts into practical, relatable terms that resonate with their colleagues. They are the security evangelists, the trusted advisors and the role models who inspire others to adopt and champion security initiatives. This grassroots approach to security evangelism helps to break down the traditional barriers between the security function and the broader workforce, creating a cohesive and security-conscious team. Identifying and empowering security champions within the workforce leverages the power and scalability of peer-to-peer influence to accelerate the dissemination of security best practices and cultivate a security-driven culture.

Security champion responsibilities

A security champion is not a job title. Instead, it is a loosely defined set of characteristics of an individual pursuant to the common goals of a security organization. Each champion will have a different style, level of seniority, even different domains of security (e.g. network security, application security, encryption and so on), but each of them contributes to the overall security posture of the organization by working alongside their peers.

Security champions can enhance any part of an organizational security programme. They play a crucial role in making security training and awareness programmes more engaging and impactful by providing valuable insights into the needs and pain points of their respective teams, helping to tailor the content and delivery to ensure maximum relevance and impact. In this way, they serve as an ambassador both to *and* from the security team with the ability to represent both sides accurately.

Champions can also serve as role models, demonstrating exemplary security behaviours and encouraging their peers to follow suit. They can share success stories, provide practical tips and offer hands-on support to help others integrate security into their daily workflows. As trusted members of their teams, security champions are often the first to become aware of security-related issues or concerns. For instance, a security champion might be diligent about using strong, unique passwords for all their accounts, and they might enthusiastically enable two-factor authentication on every platform they use. When their colleagues see the champion consistently practising these fundamental security hygiene habits, it normalizes these behaviours and encourages others to do the same.

Beyond just personal security practices, security champions can also model proactive risk awareness and incident response. If the champion spots a suspicious email or identifies a potential vulnerability, they might promptly report it to the security team and share their thought process with their peers. This not only helps to address the immediate concern but also educates others on how to recognize and respond to similar threats. Security champions can also showcase their security expertise by providing hands-on support and guidance to their colleagues. If a team member is struggling to set up a security tool or implement a new policy, the champion might offer to walk them through the process, sharing practical tips and troubleshooting advice. This personalized assistance helps to demystify security and empowers others to take ownership of their role in maintaining the organization's defences. Through these various role-modelling behaviours, security champions can have a profound impact on the organization's security culture. As their colleagues witness the champion's dedication and the tangible benefits it brings, they become more inclined to emulate those practices, creating a ripple effect that transforms security from a siloed function into a shared responsibility, thus turning the security programme into a force-multiplier.

Security champions can then serve as the conduit between the workforce and the security team, facilitating the timely identification and resolution of potential vulnerabilities or threats. Just as trained first aid responders are equipped with the knowledge and skills to assess and respond to medical emergencies, the security champions would be trained to identify, report and even mitigate potential security incidents. For example, when an employee encounters a suspicious email, a malfunctioning security tool or any other security-related concern, they would have a designated champion to turn to for guidance and support. The champion could then relay these issues to the central security team, providing valuable context and insights that help the professionals quickly diagnose and resolve the problem. This direct communication channel would enable a more timely and effective response, reducing the risk of escalating incidents and minimizing the impact on the organization.

The security champions could also play a proactive role in educating and empowering their colleagues, much like the first aid responders do in promoting health and safety awareness. The champions would help to build a more resilient and vigilant workforce by sharing security best practices, conducting training sessions and fostering a culture of security-consciousness. Just as the first aid responders are recognized and celebrated for their critical role in safeguarding the well-being of their colleagues, the security champions could be similarly acknowledged and rewarded for their contributions to the organization's cybersecurity posture. This formal recognition would not only motivate the champions themselves but also inspire others to follow in their footsteps, further strengthening the security-driven culture.

They can be also powerful advocates for security-related projects and investments, leveraging their influence and credibility to garner support from leadership and secure the necessary resources to drive security transformation. For example, a security champion within the software development team may recognize the need for implementing robust access controls and encryption protocols to protect sensitive customer data. As the champion effectively communicates the business value and risk mitigation benefits to the executive team, they possibly can secure the funding and resources required to implement these critical security measures. This not only strengthens the organization's overall security posture but also enables the development of innovative customer-facing applications, as the security champion is able to align security requirements with the organization's strategic objectives. The security champion's ability to bridge the gap between security and other business functions, such as product development, allows them to advocate for security investments that support the organization's growth and innovation initiatives.

Identifying security champions

The process of identifying and empowering security champions within an organization requires a strategic and inclusive approach. It is not enough to simply designate a few individuals and expect them to single-handedly drive security transformation. Instead, organizations must create a structured programme that supports and nurtures these champions, providing them with the necessary resources, training and recognition to be effective in their roles.

When looking to identify security champions within an organization, it is important to focus on employees who have demonstrated a keen interest in security, either through their actions, questions or participation in security-related initiatives. These individuals have already shown a natural inclination towards safeguarding the organization and are more likely to be receptive to taking on a more active role as a security champion.

Organizations should also seek out individuals who are respected and influential within their respective teams or departments. These respected figures are more likely to have the credibility and reach to effectively drive security adoption across the organization. Leveraging the influence of these security champions is a great way for an organization to ensure that security-related messages and initiatives resonate with their intended audience, fostering a collaborative and security-conscious mindset throughout the business. Implementing a nomination process can also be an effective way to identify security champions. Allowing managers and peers to recommend individuals they believe would make effective security champions can tap into the collective knowledge and insights of the broader workforce. This approach not only helps to identify the most suitable candidates, but also encourages a sense of ownership and investment in the security champion programme.

Regardless of the methodology, it is crucial to ensure diversity in the selection of security champions, representing a cross-section of the organization's departments and job functions. This diversity helps to create a well-rounded team of champions, each with their own unique perspectives, experiences and areas of expertise. Embedding champions across the organization can seamlessly integrate security into the day-to-day operations of the business, fostering a holistic and collaborative approach to risk management and innovation.

When it comes to empowering security champions within an organization, they need to be provided with the necessary resources and support to be effective in their roles. This begins with offering comprehensive security training and education, equipping the champions with the knowledge and skills they need to navigate the complex landscape of cybersecurity. Organizations must also allocate dedicated time and resources for the champions to focus on their security-related responsibilities, ensuring that the champions have the bandwidth to dedicate themselves to their roles which can empower them to make a meaningful impact on the organization's security posture. This may involve adjusting workloads, providing access to relevant tools and technologies or even designating specific security-focused projects for the champions to lead.

Depending on the size of the organization, establishing a security champions network can also be a powerful tool for fostering collaboration and knowledge-sharing. Bringing these influential individuals together can create a platform for the champions to collaborate, share best practices and support one another in their efforts to drive security transformation. This network can serve as a valuable resource, allowing the champions to learn from each other's experiences and develop innovative solutions to address emerging threats.

Offering recognition and rewards programmes can be an effective way to acknowledge the champions' contributions and inspire others to follow in their footsteps. By highlighting the successes and achievements of the security champions, organizations can create a culture of security-driven innovation, where individuals are motivated to take on active roles in safeguarding the business. This recognition can take many forms, such as awards, promotions or even financial incentives, depending on the organization's specific needs and culture.

To integrate security champions into the security function, a company should:

- Encourage close collaboration between the security champions and the security team, fostering a spirit of partnership and shared responsibility.

- Empower the champions to serve as a conduit between the security function and the broader organization, helping to bridge the gap and improve communication.

- Leverage the champions' unique perspectives and understanding of the organization's culture and workflows to inform the development of more effective security strategies and initiatives.

- Consider formalizing the security champion role, with clear responsibilities, KPIs and career development opportunities to further incentivize and retain these valuable assets.

The power of peer-to-peer influence

The success of a security champion programme lies in its ability to harness the power of peer-to-peer influence. Employees are often more receptive to security advice and guidance when it comes from a trusted colleague or respected leader, rather than from the security team alone.

Security champions, by virtue of their credibility and influence within their respective teams, can effectively break down the traditional barriers between security and the broader workforce. They can translate complex security concepts into practical, relatable terms, and they can inspire their peers to adopt security best practices as a natural extension of their daily responsibilities.

Moreover, the grassroots approach of a security champion programme can foster a sense of ownership and personal investment in security among the workforce. When employees see their colleagues actively championing security initiatives, they are more likely to feel empowered to do the same, creating a ripple effect that can transform the organization's security culture.

Ongoing support

Ongoing support and development are crucial for ensuring the long-term success and effectiveness of security champions within an organization. This means at least regularly checking in with the champions to understand their challenges, successes and evolving needs; it is important to maintain open lines of communication to gain valuable insights into the champions' experiences and tailor their support accordingly. As the security organization learns more about the needs of other parts of the business, they must also provide continuous learning opportunities for the champions to keep their knowledge current. This may include advanced security training, industry events and mentorship programmes that help the champions deepen their expertise and stay ahead of emerging threats. Investing in the champions' professional development help organizations ensure that they remain at the forefront of the ever-evolving cyber-security landscape, enabling them to identify and address new risks with confidence.

Establishing feedback loops and communication channels is also essential for fostering a collaborative and responsive security culture. Providing the champions with a platform to share their insights, concerns and recommendations directly with the security team and leadership can leverage the champions' unique perspectives to inform strategic decision-making and drive continuous improvement. This two-way dialogue not only strengthens the champions' sense of ownership and investment in the organization's security initiatives, but also helps to ensure that the security programme remains aligned with the evolving needs of the business.

Finally, it is important to celebrate the champions' achievements and share their stories of success to inspire and motivate the broader workforce. By highlighting the positive impact that the champions have had on the organization's security posture and overall perfor-mance, organizations can create a culture of security-driven innovation, where individuals are encouraged to take on active roles in safeguarding the business. This recognition can take many forms, such as public acknowledgements, awards or even the opportunity to share their experiences with their peers, further reinforcing the value and importance of the security champion programme.

Implementing a comprehensive approach to ongoing support and development of their security champions, organizations can ensure that they remain engaged, empowered and equipped to drive meaningful change. This holistic approach not only strengthens the organization's security posture, but also fosters a culture of collaboration, innovation and continuous improvement, positioning the business for long-term success in the face of evolving digital risks.

Security champions

The benefits of a well-executed security champion programme can be far-reaching and measurable, both in terms of security outcomes and broader organizational impact.

One of the most tangible outcomes is improved security awareness and adoption across the organization. Security champions can drive higher participation and engagement in security training and awareness programmes, leading to better knowledge retention and more consistent security-conscious behaviours among employees. These influential individuals can help to normalize security best practices, making them an integral part of the organization's daily operations by serving as role models and providing hands-on support. This heightened security awareness and adoption can translate directly into reduced risk exposure. Security champions are often able to identify and address vulnerabilities more quickly, as they have a deep understanding of the organization's security posture and the ability to effectively communicate security requirements to their peers. Additionally, by fostering a culture where security is viewed as an enabler rather than a hindrance, security champions can encourage the proactive reporting of security incidents and near-misses, allowing the security team to respond more effectively and mitigate potential threats before they can cause significant damage.

Beyond the security realm, security champions can also have a measurable impact on the organization's overall performance and competitiveness. By aligning security initiatives with the organization's strategic objectives, these individuals can help to unlock new opportunities for innovation and growth. For instance, a security champion within the product development team may advocate for the implementation of robust data protection measures, enabling the organization to develop and market customer-centric applications that prioritize privacy and security – a key differentiator in today's digital landscape. The presence of security champions can also contribute to improved employee morale and retention. When employees feel that their organization values their safety and the security of their work, they are more likely to feel engaged, empowered and committed to the company's success. This positive sentiment can translate into higher productivity, better collaboration and reduced turnover, all of which can have a direct impact on the organization's bottom line.

One of the most impactful benefits of a robust security champion programme is the ability to identify and resolve security issues more quickly and effectively. Security champions, with their deep understanding of their teams' workflows and pain points, can often spot potential vulnerabilities or threats more readily than the security team alone. These individuals are embedded within the various business units, giving them a unique vantage point to observe and understand the day-to-day operations and challenges faced by their colleagues. Security champions can facilitate the timely reporting and resolution of security concerns by serving as the bridge between the workforce and the security function. Employees may feel more comfortable raising issues or seeking guidance from a trusted peer, rather than going directly to the security team. This open line of communication allows security champions to quickly escalate critical issues, ensuring that the security team can respond swiftly and mitigate potential threats before they can cause significant damage.

Security champions can also play a crucial role in translating complex security requirements into practical, user-friendly solutions. They possess the ability to fill the gap between technical jargon and the language of the business, helping to ensure that security measures are not only effective, but also intuitive and aligned with the organization's workflows. The presence of security champions not only enhances the overall security posture, but also fosters a culture of security ownership, where employees feel empowered to participate in the organization's risk management efforts. The ability to identify and resolve security issues more rapidly can have a tangible impact on the organization's bottom line, as minimizing the time between the detection of a vulnerability and its remediation can help to reduce the potential for costly data breaches, system downtime and regulatory fines.

Proactively approaching security management can also free up the security team to focus on more strategic initiatives, further strengthening the organization's resilience and preparedness in the face of evolving threats. Overall, the security champions' unique position within the organization and their deep understanding of both security best practices and business operations make them invaluable assets in the quest for faster identification and resolution of security issues. By leveraging the power of these influential individuals, organizations can enhance their security posture, drive operational efficiency and ultimately, position themselves for long-term success in the digital age.

Security champions play a crucial role in reframing the security narrative within the organization. When security is positioned as a strategic asset, these individuals can help to shift the mindset of their colleagues which fosters a culture where security is seen as a key driver of competitive differentiation and business success. For instance, a security champion within the product development team may advocate for the implementation of advanced data protection measures, enabling the organization to develop and market customer-centric applications that prioritize privacy and security. These features can become a unique selling point, setting the organization apart from its competitors and attracting a growing customer base that values the security and integrity of their personal information.

Similarly, security champions can help to identify opportunities for security-enabled innovation in other areas of the business, such as supply chain management, remote work infrastructure or even employee wellness programmes. When security initiatives are aligned with the organization's strategic objectives, these champions can demonstrate how a proactive, security-driven approach can unlock new avenues for growth, efficiency and customer engagement.

Culturally, the presence of security champions can inspire a sense of shared responsibility and collaboration across the organization. When employees feel that their safety and the security of their work are valued, they are more likely to engage in the organization's risk management efforts, contributing their unique insights and ideas. This collaborative approach can lead to the development of innovative security solutions that not only protect the business, but also enhance the overall user experience and operational effectiveness. Through fostering a culture of security-driven innovation, an organization can position themselves as industry leaders, attracting top talent, securing lucrative partnerships and ultimately, achieving sustainable growth and success in the face of evolving digital risks.

At the heart of a successful security champion programme lies the potential to significantly enhance the organization's overall resilience to cyber threats and other disruptive events. Underpinned by a network of engaged and empowered security champions, organizations can embed security into the very fabric of their operations, better equipping themselves to withstand and recover from potential crises by fostering a security-driven culture. Security champions play a crucial role in this process, serving as force multipliers for the security team and catalysts for a more proactive, collaborative approach to risk management. With these individuals embedded across various business units, they can help to identify and address vulnerabilities more quickly, leveraging their deep understanding of their teams' workflows and pain points. Facilitating the timely reporting and resolution of security concerns will minimize the potential impact of security incidents, reducing the risk of costly data breaches, system downtime and reputational damage.

The security champions' ability to translate complex security requirements into practical, user-friendly solutions can help to ensure that security measures are not only effective, but also seamlessly integrated into the organization's day-to-day operations. This level of security ownership and collaboration across the workforce can significantly enhance the organization's overall resilience, as employees are better equipped to recognize and respond to potential threats, and the security team can focus on more strategic, proactive initiatives. In the event of a disruptive incident, such as a natural disaster or a cyber-attack, the security-driven culture fostered by the champion programme can also play a crucial role in the organization's ability to bounce back quickly. With security deeply embedded into the organization's processes and mindset, the impact of such events can be more effectively mitigated, and the organization can leverage its collective resilience to restore normal operations and minimize downtime.

Security champions can help to position the organization for long-term success, not only by safeguarding against immediate threats by strengthening organizational resilience, but also by enabling the organization to adapt and thrive in the face of evolving challenges. This holistic approach to security management can be a true competitive advantage, setting the organization apart in an increasingly volatile and unpredictable business landscape.

Quantifying the measurable impact of security champions can help organizations build a compelling business case for investing in these influential individuals and the broader security champion programme. A data-driven approach not only helps to secure the necessary resources and support from leadership, but also reinforces the strategic value of security as a key driver of innovation, growth and competitive advantage.

Seeding long-term success

Establishing a successful security champion programme is not a one-time event, but rather an ongoing process that requires sustained commitment and investment. To ensure the long-term viability and impact of the programme, organizations must adopt a holistic and strategic approach that addresses the continuous recruitment and succession planning of security champions.

Regularly assessing the evolving needs of the organization and identifying new opportunities to expand the security champion network is crucial for maintaining the programme's relevance and effectiveness. As the business landscape and security threats continue to evolve, the required skills, expertise and areas of focus for security champions may shift over time. Proactively evaluating the organization's changing requirements can help leaders ensure that the security champion programme remains aligned with the organization's strategic priorities and emerging risk profile.

This continuous recruitment process should be underpinned by a structured onboarding and training regimen for new champions. Ensuring a smooth transition and the preservation of institutional knowledge is key to maintaining the programme's momentum and avoiding disruptions to the security-driven initiatives. Comprehensive training programmes, mentorship opportunities and knowledge-sharing sessions can equip new champions with the necessary skills and support to hit the ground running and seamlessly integrate into the existing network. Encouraging current security champions to identify and mentor potential successors can also be a powerful strategy for fostering a sense of ownership and continuity within the programme. Empowering the champions to play an active role in shaping the next generation of leaders will cultivate a self-sustaining ecosystem where security expertise and best practices are continuously passed down and refined. This approach not only strengthens the overall resilience of the programme but also reinforces the champions' commitment to the organization's long-term security and success.

In addition to the continuous recruitment and succession planning, organizations must also invest in the ongoing training and professional development of their security champions. As the cybersecurity landscape continues to evolve at a rapid pace, it is essential that the champions remain at the forefront of emerging threats, technologies and best practices. Providing security champions with access to advanced training, industry events and mentorship opportunities can help them to deepen their expertise and expand their sphere of influence within the organization. Equipping the champions with the latest knowledge and skills has a scaling effect, and organizations can ensure that their security-driven initiatives remain relevant, effective and responsive to the changing needs of the business.

Encouraging the champions to share their knowledge and insights with the broader workforce can further strengthen the organization's security culture. Leveraging the champions' credibility and communication skills can more effectively disseminate security-related information, foster cross-functional collaboration and inspire employees to take a more active role in safeguarding the business. Moreover, the security champions' deep understanding of the organization's unique challenges and pain points can be invaluable in the development of tailored security awareness and education programmes. By tapping into the champions' expertise, organizations can create training materials and initiatives that resonate with the workforce, driving higher engagement and better retention of security best practices.

Lastly, a successful security champion programme must be underpinned by a culture of continuous feedback and iterative improvement through the establishment of regular communication channels and feedback loops, whereby organizations can ensure that the champions' insights, concerns and recommendations are heard and acted upon. This two-way dialogue not only strengthens the champions' sense of ownership and investment in the programme but also helps to inform strategic decision-making and drive continuous enhancements to the security initiatives. The security team and leadership can leverage the champions' unique perspectives to identify areas for improvement, address emerging challenges and align the programme more closely with the organization's evolving needs.

Analysing the programme's performance metrics, such as the rate of security incident reporting, the adoption of security best practices and the overall improvement in the organization's security posture, can also help to guide the iterative refinement of the programme. By regularly evaluating the programme's impact and adjusting the strategy and support structures accordingly, organizations can ensure that the security champions remain empowered and effective in their roles, continuously driving the organization towards greater resilience and security-driven innovation.

Celebrating the champions' achievements and sharing their success stories can also be a powerful tool for inspiring and motivating the broader organization. By highlighting the positive impact that the champions have had on the organization's security posture and overall performance, leaders can create a culture of security-driven excellence, where individuals are encouraged to take on active roles in safeguarding the business. This recognition can take many forms, such as public acknowledgements, awards or even the opportunity for the champions to share their experiences with their peers. Amplifying the champions' voices and showcasing their contribution will reinforce the value and importance of the security champion programme, further strengthening the organization's security culture and positioning it for long-term success.

Ultimately, the key to sustaining a successful security champion programme lies in the organization's ability to continuously evolve, adapt and invest in the development of these influential individuals. Adopting a holistic and strategic approach that addresses the programme's continuous recruitment, training and feedback mechanisms unlocks the true potential of security champions as catalysts for enhanced resilience, security-driven innovation and long-term competitive advantage.

For a security champion programme to truly thrive and deliver sustainable impact, it is essential that the programme is closely aligned with the organization's overall strategic objectives and security roadmap. By ensuring this alignment, organizations can unlock the full potential of their security champions, empowering them to drive initiatives that directly support the achievement of the company's key goals and priorities. This alignment should be an ongoing process, with regular reviews and adjustments to the programme's focus and initiatives. As the organization's needs and challenges evolve over time, the security champion programme must be agile enough to adapt and remain relevant. This may involve shifting the champions' areas of focus, introducing new training and development opportunities or even expanding the network of champions to address emerging threats or business imperatives.

Integrating the security champion programme into the organization's broader change management and transformation efforts can be a powerful strategy for driving cultural change. Organizations can more effectively embed security into the fabric of the business, ensuring that it is viewed as an enabler of innovation and growth, rather than a constraint by leveraging the champions as catalysts for this transformation. The security champions, with their deep understanding of the organization's operations and their credibility among their peers, are uniquely positioned to champion this cultural shift. Aligning the programme's initiatives with the organization's overarching vision and priorities, the workforce can be inspired by these influential individuals and be motivated to embrace security as a strategic advantage, ultimately strengthening the organization's resilience and competitive edge. Maintaining this strategic alignment requires ongoing communication, collaboration and feedback loops between the security champion programme, the security team and the organization's leadership.

Ensuring the long-term success and impact of a security champion programme requires a steadfast commitment to providing the necessary resources and securing strong executive sponsorship. Organizations must be willing to allocate sufficient budget, time and personnel to support the programme and enable the champions to be effective in their roles. This dedicated resourcing not only allows the champions to focus on their security-related responsibilities but also signals to the broader workforce the organization's commitment to the programme and its strategic importance. When employees see that the company is willing to invest in the security champions and empower them to drive meaningful change, it fosters a culture of trust, collaboration and security ownership.

Securing strong executive sponsorship is equally crucial, as it provides the security champion programme with the necessary visibility, authority and resources to drive impact across the organization. Champions having the backing of senior leadership can more effectively collaborate with decision-makers, ensuring that security initiatives are aligned with the organization's strategic objectives and receive the necessary funding and support. Empowering the security champions to engage directly with senior leadership, giving them a voice in the strategic decision-making process, further strengthens the programme's influence and impact. This open dialogue allows the champions to share their unique insights, advocate for security-driven initiatives and ensure that the organization's security posture remains responsive to evolving threats and business needs.

With dedicated resources and strong executive sponsorship, the security champion programme can become a powerful catalyst for cultural transformation, driving the organization towards a more resilient, innovative and security-conscious future. Sustaining the long-term impact and effectiveness of a security champion programme requires a steadfast commitment to the continuous learning and development of the champions themselves. Organizations must prioritize providing ongoing training and education opportunities, enabling these influential individuals to stay ahead of emerging threats, technologies and best practices in the rapidly evolving cybersecurity landscape. This investment in the champions' professional development not only strengthens their technical expertise but also empowers them to become more effective communicators and change agents within the organization. Equipping the champions with the latest knowledge and skills reinforces that their security-driven initiatives remain relevant, impactful and responsive to the organization's evolving needs.

Encouraging the champions to share their knowledge and experiences with one another can further enhance the learning and collaboration within the programme, by fostering a supportive network where the champions can exchange insights, troubleshoot challenges and identify innovative solutions. Offering career development pathways and recognition programmes can also be a powerful tool for incentivizing the champions and retaining their valuable expertise within the organization. When champions feel that their contributions are valued and that there are opportunities for professional advancement, they are more likely to remain engaged and committed to the programme's long-term success.

Ensuring the long-term success and sustainability of a security champion programme is best served by a system of measurement and evaluation. Establishing clear key performance indicators (KPIs) and metrics to track the impact and effectiveness of the programme, enables data-driven decision-making and continuous improvement. These KPIs should be aligned with the organization's overall security and business objectives, capturing metrics such as the rate of security incident reporting, the adoption of security best practices, and the improvement in the organization's overall security posture. Quantifying the programme's impact can build a compelling business case for ongoing investment and demonstrate the strategic value of the security champions to senior leadership. Regularly collecting feedback from the champions, the broader workforce and the security team can provide valuable insights for refining the programme's strategies and addressing emerging challenges. This feedback loop allows organizations to identify areas for improvement, address pain points and ensure that the programme remains responsive to the evolving needs of the business and its employees.

Communicating the programme's successes and achievements to the organization will reinforce the value of the security champions and inspire others to get involved. This transparent approach not only strengthens the security champion programme but also positions it as a strategic asset within the organization, securing the necessary resources, support and buy-in to drive meaningful, lasting change. Addressing these key considerations creates a sustainable and impactful security champion programme that serves as the foundation for a security-driven culture. These empowered and engaged employees, acting as force multipliers for the security function, can be the catalysts for transformative change, turning security constraints into competitive advantages and driving the organization forward in the face of evolving digital threats.

The security champion programme is not a silver bullet, but rather a critical component of a holistic security strategy that recognizes the power of the workforce in shaping the organization's security posture. Investing in the development and empowerment of these security ambassadors can unlock the true potential of their most valuable asset – their people – and position security as a strategic enabler for innovation, growth and long-term resilience.

Integration of security into development lifecycles

Beyond the workforce, the integration of security considerations into the organization's product development and delivery processes is a critical component of cultivating a security-driven culture. Adopting a 'shift-left' security approach – where security testing and risk assessments are incorporated early in the development lifecycle – organizations can proactively address vulnerabilities and design security into the core of their systems and applications. The 'shift-left' security approach is a fundamental concept that can significantly enhance an organization's ability to proactively address vulnerabilities and design security into the core of its systems and applications.

The traditional approach to security often involved testing and risk assessments being conducted towards the end of the development lifecycle, just before the product or system was deployed. This 'shift-right' mentality meant that security was treated as an afterthought, leading to costly rework, delayed releases and increased exposure to potential threats.

Incorporating security testing, threat modelling and risk assessments during the initial design and planning phases helps organizations identify and address vulnerabilities before they become embedded in the codebase or infrastructure. This proactive approach offers several key benefits. Firstly, it allows development teams to address security issues at a fraction of the cost compared to remediating them later in the lifecycle. Fixing a security flaw during the design phase is significantly less expensive than having to retrofit a solution or roll back a deployment due to a critical vulnerability. Secondly, the shift-left approach encourages a shared responsibility for security across the entire development team, rather than relegating it solely to the security specialists. Involving developers, architects and product managers in the security planning and implementation process fosters a security-conscious mindset and empowers cross-functional collaboration. This collaborative culture, underpinned by the principles of DevSecOps, further reinforces the shift-left security approach. Breaking down the traditional silos between development, operations and security, DevSecOps enables a continuous, iterative process of building, testing and deploying secure applications. Security becomes an integral part of the software development lifecycle, with automated security checks, vulnerability scanning and compliance monitoring integrated into the continuous integration and continuous deployment (CI/CD) pipeline. This seamless integration of security practices into the software development lifecycle helps to identify and address vulnerabilities more quickly, reducing the risk of costly breaches and ensuring that security remains a top priority throughout the product's evolution.

The shift-left approach also allows organizations to better align security requirements with the product's functionality and user needs. Development teams can design security controls that enhance the user experience rather than hindering it by involving security experts early on, creating a 'secure by design' mindset to ensure that security is not perceived as a constraint, but rather as an enabler of innovation and customer trust. This mindset empowers cross-functional teams to share the responsibility for security, fostering a collaborative environment where developers, security professionals and product managers work together to identify and mitigate risks.

Ultimately, the shift-left security approach is a fundamental pillar of building a security-driven organization because it proactively addresses vulnerabilities, fosters cross-functional collaboration and embeds security into the core of the development process, thus enhancing their overall security posture and reducing the risk of costly breaches, and delivers innovative, secure products that meet the evolving needs of their customers.

Automation plays a crucial role in this security integration, as tools and technologies that automate security checks, vulnerability scanning and compliance monitoring can streamline the development process and free up security professionals to focus on more strategic initiatives. Embedding these automated security controls into the development pipeline establishes that security is not an afterthought but an integral part of the product delivery lifecycle. For example, the integration of static application security testing (SAST) and dynamic application security testing (DAST) tools into the CI/CD pipeline can help to identify and remediate security flaws early in the development process. These automated scans can be triggered at various stages, such as during code commits, pull requests or before deployment, allowing the development team to address issues before they can be introduced into the production environment. Similarly, the use of infrastructure-as-code (IaC) tools, such as Terraform or CloudFormation, can enable the automated provisioning and configuration of cloud resources with built-in security controls. By defining the desired state of the infrastructure in code, organizations can ensure that security best practices are consistently applied, reducing the risk of human error and ensuring that the deployment process is both secure and scalable.

Conclusion

Developing a security-driven organization requires a multi-faceted approach that addresses both the human and technical aspects of security. Security awareness training, a security champions programme and incorporating security into the software development lifecycle work together to create a strong security culture and posture within the organization.

Security awareness training is the foundation for building a security-driven culture. Educating all employees on security best practices, common threats and their individual role in protecting the organization empowers the workforce to be the first line of defence. Regular, engaging training sessions that cover evolving risks help keep security top-of-mind and equip employees with the knowledge to identify and report suspicious activity. This baseline of security awareness is critical, as even the most robust technical controls can be undermined by careless or uninformed user behaviour.

Building on this foundation, the security champions programme taps into the power of peer influence and internal subject matter experts. Identifying and empowering security-minded individuals throughout the organization to serve as champions and advocates creates a network of security ambassadors. These champions can help reinforce training messages, provide localized support and guidance, and identify security improvement opportunities within their respective business units or functions. The champions programme harnesses the trust and credibility of internal role models to drive security culture change in a bottom-up, grassroots manner.

Lastly, incorporating security into the software development lifecycle (SDLC) ensures that security is a core design principle, not an afterthought. By embedding security practices, controls and testing throughout the SDLC, you can identify and remediate vulnerabilities early in the process when they are much less costly to fix. This proactive, 'shift-left' approach to security enables developers to build in security from the ground up, rather than bolting it on later. It also promotes a DevSecOps mindset where security is everyone's responsibility, not just the security team's. When developers, operations and security personnel collaborate closely, they can deliver secure, resilient applications and infrastructure.

Taken together, these three elements create a comprehensive security programme that addresses both human and technical risk factors. Security awareness training empowers the workforce, the security champions programme cultivates internal security leadership and advocacy, and SDLC integration bakes security into the organization's core business processes and technology. This holistic approach helps transform security from a compliance-driven, reactive function into a strategic, business-enabling capability.

Ultimately, the goal of a security-driven organization is to make security a natural, embedded part of the culture and day-to-day operations. Aligning people, processes and technology around security as a shared responsibility aim builds solid defences, reduces risk and unlocks new opportunities for innovation and growth. While the journey to becoming truly security-driven is an ongoing one, the strategies outlined in this chapter provide a strong foundation for getting started and sustaining security excellence over the long term.

KEY TAKEAWAYS

- Security awareness training is a great opportunity to lay the groundwork for a security culture.

- Security champions are very effective in the creation and promotion of a security culture.

- Technology is not the only place where security 'happens', but it is an excellent catalyst for it.

6

Leadership's role in security empowerment

In the modern business landscape, the role of leadership in shaping security-driven culture has become increasingly pivotal. As organizations adapt to escalating complexities of the digital arena, the need for a practical and empowered security approach is more important than it has ever been. That said, leadership's role is not without its nuances, and must be treated delicately, as organizations must embrace a transformative approach which sends a signal to the wider business that security is a strategic asset that safeguards against risks and also propels the organization forward in the face of evolving digital challenges.

At the heart of the cultural transformation to embed security lies the critical role of executives and senior managers who hold the power to shape the cultural narrative, allocate resources and drive the strategic direction of the organization. Their actions and decisions can either reinforce the status quo or catalyse a seismic shift in the way security is perceived and integrated within the broader business ecosystem. Without the commitment and active engagement of the executive suite, even the most well-conceived security strategies are destined for adversity. Leaders will need to recognize the evolving nature of the threat landscape, communicate the urgency and importance of security to the broader organization, and demonstrate a tangible commitment to security through resource allocation and leading by example.

Later in the chapter, we will build on the foundation of executive buy-in and examine the critical process of incorporating security into the organization's strategic planning. Effective security empowerment requires the seamless integration of security considerations into the organization's overall objectives and decision-making processes. This will explore strategies for aligning security goals with broader business priorities, creating cross-functional governance frameworks, and embedding security assessments into the innovation lifecycle, so that leaders can transform security from a reactive function to a strategic enabler.

One of the critical factors that can make or break the success of security empowerment initiatives is the ability of leaders to communicate security effectively. Translating technical security concepts into business-relevant terms and crafting compelling narratives that resonate with various stakeholders is a crucial skill for leaders to cultivate. Too often, security professionals have struggled to bridge the gap between the technical complexities of their work and the strategic priorities of the C-suite and broader business units. This disconnect can lead to a lack of understanding, buy-in and support for security initiatives, undermining the organization's ability to build a security-empowered culture. Leaders must take an active role in developing clear and compelling security communication strategies. This involves distilling complex security issues into easily digestible insights, aligning security messaging with the organization's overall brand and messaging, and ensuring that security communication is tailored to the specific needs and concerns of different stakeholder groups.

Executive buy-in: the cornerstone of security empowerment

Securing the commitment and active participation of an organization's executive leadership is a critical prerequisite for cultivating a robust culture of security. Executives must not only recognize the evolving threat landscape and the profound impact of security breaches, but also demonstrate a tangible commitment to strengthening the organization's security posture through the allocation of necessary resources and by leading by example. When executives embrace security as a strategic priority, they can inspire a cultural shift where security is viewed as an integral component of the organization's success.

The threat landscape is constantly shifting, with cybercriminals, nation-state actors and other malicious entities continuously devising new and increasingly sophisticated methods of attack. Ransomware, data breaches, phishing scams and other cyber threats pose a grave risk to organizations of all sizes and across all industries. I generally refer to it as an 'arms race', where criminals and defences are both constantly gaining advantage over the other as technology evolves so quickly. The consequences of a successful attack can be devastating, ranging from the immediate financial impact of stolen funds or extortion payments to the long-term reputational damage that can erode customer trust and undermine an organization's competitive position. Executives must therefore develop a comprehensive understanding of threats to their business and the potential consequences of security failures. This requires staying informed about the latest cyber threats, industry trends and emerging best practices in security management. Executives must also be able to effectively communicate the importance of security to the broader organization. This involves translating complex technical concepts into language that resonates with stakeholders at all levels, from the frontline employees to the board of directors.

Of course, effectively communicating the importance of security is only the first step. Executives must also be willing to allocate the necessary resources – both financial and human – to bolster the organization's security posture. This includes investing in cutting-edge technologies, recruiting and retaining top-tier security talent, and providing ongoing training and development opportunities for the security team. Through demonstrating a tangible commitment to security through resource allocation, executives send a powerful message to the entire organization. They signal that security is a strategic priority, not merely a cost centre, and that the organization is willing to make the necessary investments to protect its assets and safeguard its future. This commitment to security must also be reflected in the executive team's own decision-making processes and daily operations. By consistently prioritizing security considerations at this level, leaders can inspire a cultural shift where security is embedded into the fabric of the organization.

Consider the case of a large financial institution that suffered a devastating data breach due to a vulnerability in its legacy IT infrastructure. In the aftermath of the breach, the organization's executives realized that they had underinvested in security, relying on outdated technologies and a small, understaffed security team. To rectify this, the executives committed to a multi-year, multi-million-dollar initiative to overhaul the organization's security posture. This included investing in cutting-edge security technologies, such as advanced threat detection and response systems, secure cloud infrastructure and AI-powered analytics tools. Additionally, the executives allocated significant resources to recruiting and retaining a team of highly skilled security professionals, offering competitive salaries, comprehensive benefits and opportunities for professional development and career advancement. They recognized that the security team's effectiveness was not solely dependent on the tools and technologies at their disposal, but also on their ongoing training and development. As such, the organization committed significant resources to providing the security team with regular training opportunities, including industry conferences, certification programmes and in-house workshops, to ensure that they remained up-to-date on the latest security threats, best practices and emerging technologies. This investment in the security team's professional development not only enhanced their technical skills and knowledge, but also helped to boost morale and job satisfaction, reducing the risk of high turnover and ensuring the continuity of the organization's security efforts.

Embracing this security-minded leadership can better position organizations to withstand the complex and persistent threats that characterize their industry. However, securing executive buy-in is often easier said than done, as many leaders may be tempted to prioritize short-term financial gains or operational efficiency over long-term security considerations.

Quantifying ROI

One of the key challenges in garnering executive support for security initiatives is the inherent difficulty in quantifying the return on investment (ROI). Unlike investments in revenue-generating projects or operational improvements, security expenditures are often perceived as a cost of doing business rather than a strategic enabler. Executives may struggle to justify the allocation of scarce resources to security initiatives, particularly when the benefits are intangible, and the consequences of inaction are not immediately apparent. To overcome this hurdle, security leaders must become adept at translating the technical aspects of security into business-centric language that resonates with the executive team. This may involve developing detailed risk assessments that outline the potential financial, reputational and operational impacts of security breaches, as well as crafting compelling business cases that demonstrate how security investments can contribute to the organization's overall strategic objectives. For example, an executive may be more receptive to a security proposal that highlights the potential cost savings associated with preventing a data breach, such as the avoidance of regulatory fines, legal fees and customer churn, rather than one that focuses solely on the technical details of the security solution. By framing security as a strategic enabler, rather than a necessary evil, security leaders can help to shift the executive mindset and secure the necessary resources and support.

Conflicting priorities

Securing executive buy-in for security initiatives can be a significant challenge, as security often competes with other organizational priorities such as operational efficiency, customer experience and innovation. One of the key obstacles is the inherent tension between security and these other priorities. Executives may be hesitant to implement stringent security measures that could potentially slow down business processes, inconvenience customers or hinder the organization's ability to adapt to changing market conditions. This is a valid concern, as overly burdensome security measures can negatively impact an organization's competitiveness and agility. To navigate this delicate balance, security leaders must work closely with their executive counterparts to identify creative solutions that address security concerns without compromising other critical business objectives. This requires a deep understanding of the organization's unique needs, constraints and priorities.

One approach is to explore innovative technologies or security frameworks that enhance protection without unduly disrupting operations. For example, an executive may be more receptive to a security proposal that incorporates user-friendly authentication methods, such as biometric identification or single sign-on, rather than one that requires cumbersome password requirements or multi-factor authentication. By demonstrating how these solutions can improve security while minimizing the impact on the user experience, security leaders can make a stronger case for their initiatives. Another strategy is to develop security policies and procedures that are tailored to the specific needs and constraints of the organization. This may involve finding ways to streamline security processes, automate routine tasks or integrate security seamlessly into existing workflows. By aligning security with the organization's operational realities, security leaders can help to alleviate executive concerns and demonstrate the value of their proposals. Taking a holistic, collaborative approach that balances security with other organizational priorities can build the necessary trust and support from executive stakeholders. This may require a degree of flexibility and creativity, as well as a willingness to engage in ongoing dialogue and negotiation to find the right balance between security and other critical business objectives.

Ultimately, the key to garnering executive buy-in for security initiatives lies in demonstrating a nuanced understanding of the organization's unique needs and priorities, and proposing solutions that address security concerns without compromising the organization's ability to thrive in an evolving business landscape.

Cognitive biases and psychological barriers

In addition to the practical and strategic challenges of garnering executive buy-in for security initiatives, security leaders must also contend with the inherent cognitive biases and psychological barriers that can hinder the executive decision-making process. Executives, like all human beings, are susceptible to a range of cognitive biases that can significantly impact their perceptions and judgements when it comes to security-related decisions. Cognitive biases and psychological barriers will be discussed further in relation to employees in Chapter 8.

One of the most prevalent cognitive biases is the availability heuristic, which leads individuals to judge the likelihood of an event based on how easily they can recall similar occurrences. In the context of security, executives may underestimate the likelihood and severity of security threats simply because they have not personally experienced a major breach or incident. This can lead them to prioritize other business objectives over security investments, despite the growing prevalence and sophistication of cyber threats.

Another common bias is the optimism bias, which causes people to overestimate the likelihood of positive outcomes and underestimate the probability of negative events. Executives may be inclined to believe that their organization is less vulnerable to security threats than others, or that their current security measures are sufficient to protect against emerging risks. This overconfidence can lead to complacency and a reluctance to invest in more robust security solutions.

The sunk cost fallacy is another cognitive bias that can hinder executive decision-making. This bias leads individuals to continue investing resources in a course of action simply because they have already invested significant time, money or effort, even if the current situation suggests that a different approach would be more effective. In the security domain, executives may be reluctant to abandon outdated security technologies or practices, despite evidence of their ineffectiveness, because they have already invested heavily in them.

To overcome these cognitive biases and psychological barriers, security leaders must employ a range of persuasive techniques and psychological strategies. One effective approach is to frame security initiatives in terms of potential gains rather than losses. Instead of emphasizing the potential negative consequences of a security breach, security leaders can highlight the positive outcomes that can be achieved through proactive security measures, such as improved customer trust, reduced liability and enhanced regulatory compliance.

Leveraging social proof and peer influence can also be a powerful tool in persuading executives, by showcasing successful security initiatives implemented by industry peers or respected organizations that can help to normalize the need for strong security measures and overcome the perception that their organization is an outlier.

Additionally, appealing to the executive's sense of responsibility and risk aversion can be an effective strategy. This can be achieved by emphasizing the potential reputational and financial damage that a security breach can inflict on the organization to tap into the executive's innate desire to protect the company and its stakeholders.

Understanding and addressing the underlying psychological factors that shape executive decision-making can increase the likelihood of securing the necessary support and resources for security initiatives. This may involve providing targeted training or educational resources to help executives recognize and mitigate their own cognitive biases, or collaborating with organizational psychologists or behavioural economists to develop more effective communication and persuasion strategies. Ultimately, the ability to navigate the complex interplay of practical, strategic and psychological factors is essential for security leaders seeking to garner executive buy-in. Using a multifaceted approach that addresses both the rational and emotional aspects of decision-making can build the trust, support and commitment needed to implement effective security measures and protect their organizations from threats.

Fundamentally, the cultivation of a security-centric culture within an organization is a long-term, iterative process that requires sustained commitment and leadership from the executive team. Executives can inspire a cultural shift by leading by example and embedding security principles into their own decision-making processes and daily operations. Through this security-focused leadership, organizations can enhance their resilience, agility and long-term sustainability in the face of increasingly sophisticated security threat, prioritizing security as a strategic imperative where the protection of critical assets and the maintenance of stakeholder trust are essential to sustained competitive advantage.

Incorporating security into strategic planning

Effective security empowerment necessitates the seamless integration of security considerations into the organization's overarching strategic planning. This holistic approach embeds security considerations at the core of the planning framework which cultivates a resilient security posture that is closely aligned with their broader business goals and priorities. This, in turn, empowers employees at all levels to actively contribute to the organization's security efforts, fostering a culture of shared responsibility and proactive risk mitigation. When security is woven into the fabric of the strategic plan, it becomes a shared imperative, with each department and function recognizing their role in safeguarding the organization's assets, reputation and operational continuity. Additionally, the integration of security into the strategic planning cycle enables organizations to anticipate and adapt to emerging threats, rather than merely reacting to them. Considering security implications at the strategic level can help decision-makers make informed choices that balance risk, opportunity and resource allocation, ensuring that security investments and initiatives are strategically aligned and deliver maximum impact. Ultimately, this approach empowers organizations to navigate an increasingly complex and volatile threat landscape with confidence, agility and a heightened sense of security empowerment. It allows them to stay ahead of the curve, identify and mitigate risks proactively, and seize opportunities that enhance their overall security posture and competitive advantage. In doing so, organizations can foster a culture of security-minded innovation.

Governance framework

One of the key elements in this process is the establishment of a comprehensive governance framework that bridges the gap between security and business stakeholders. Creating cross-functional teams and collaborative decision-making processes can foster a shared understanding of security risks and their potential impact on the organization's strategic priorities. This collaborative approach not only enhances the effectiveness of security measures but also cultivates a sense of shared ownership and accountability across the organization. The development of a comprehensive framework is important to ensure that security considerations are seamlessly integrated into the organization's strategic planning. This framework should bring together key stakeholders from various departments, including IT, risk management, compliance and business operations, to create a cohesive and aligned approach to security.

Establishing cross-functional teams can leverage the diverse expertise and perspectives of their employees to identify and address security risks more effectively. These teams should be empowered to collaborate on risk assessments, threat analysis and the development of security strategies and policies. A collaborative approach helps to break down silos and fosters a shared understanding of the organization's security posture and its potential impact on strategic objectives. The framework should facilitate collaborative decision-making processes that enable security and business stakeholders to work together in a transparent and inclusive manner. This could involve the creation of steering committees or security councils, where representatives from different functions can discuss, debate and reach consensus on security-related decisions. Organizations can ensure that security measures are aligned with the organization's overall strategic priorities and operational needs by giving a voice to both security and business stakeholders.

The establishment of this collaborative governance framework also helps to cultivate a sense of shared ownership and accountability across the organization. When security is viewed as a shared responsibility, rather than solely the domain of the IT or security team, employees at all levels are more likely to engage with and contribute to the organization's security efforts. This, in turn, strengthens the overall security posture and resilience of the organization. To further enhance the effectiveness of the governance framework, organizations should consider implementing formal communication and reporting mechanisms. This could include regular security updates, risk assessments and performance metrics that are shared with all stakeholders, ensuring transparency and enabling informed decision-making. Providing visibility into the organization's security posture and the impact of security initiatives better align security investments with strategic priorities and demonstrate the value of security empowerment. The framework should also be designed to be agile and adaptable, allowing the organization to respond quickly to evolving threats, changing business requirements and emerging technologies. This may involve regular reviews and updates to security policies, the establishment of incident response and crisis management protocols, and the incorporation of lessons learned from security incidents or near-misses. Organizations can ensure that security considerations are not only integrated into the strategic planning process but also continuously monitored, evaluated and refined by cultivating a collaborative and adaptive governance framework. This approach empowers security and business stakeholders to work together in identifying and mitigating risks, seizing new opportunities, and ultimately strengthening the organization's overall resilience and competitive advantage.

Integrated into new products

It is up to leadership to insist that security is a central consideration in the development and implementation of new products, services and business initiatives. This requires the integration of security assessments and risk analyses into the early stages of the innovation lifecycle, enabling the proactive identification and mitigation of potential vulnerabilities. Integrating security considerations into the innovation process is a critical step in ensuring the long-term success and resilience of an organization. As businesses strive to stay competitive and meet evolving customer demands, the pace of product and service development has accelerated, often outpacing the implementation of robust security measures. This can leave organizations vulnerable to a range of threats, from data breaches and cyber-attacks to regulatory non-compliance and loss of trust.

To address this challenge, leaders must adopt a proactive and holistic approach to security, one that is deeply embedded within the organization's innovation and product development lifecycle. This begins with the establishment of a comprehensive security framework that is closely aligned with the organization's strategic objectives and risk appetite. This framework should outline clear security requirements, guidelines and processes that must be followed throughout the innovation process, from ideation and design to testing and deployment. The framework supplements the governance framework nicely.

Integrating security assessments and risk analyses into the early stages of product or service development can help identify and mitigate potential vulnerabilities before they become embedded within the final offering. This involves conducting threat modelling, vulnerability scanning and penetration testing to uncover and address security weaknesses, as well as incorporating secure-by-design principles into the product architecture and development practices.

A key aspect of collaborative security integration is the establishment of clear communication and decision-making processes. Forums and mechanisms which facilitate the exchange of information, the identification of security risks and the prioritization of mitigation strategies make for excellent platforms which encourage collaboration. The formation of security councils, the implementation of secure development lifecycles, and the adoption of agile security practices that enable rapid response to emerging threats are also good ways to establish security as a cooperative function of the business. The integration of security into the innovation lifecycle must be an ongoing and iterative process, with regular reviews and updates to address evolving threats, changing business requirements and the introduction of new technologies. This agile approach to security empowerment allows organizations to stay ahead of the curve, anticipate and mitigate risks, and seize new opportunities that enhance their overall security posture and competitive advantage.

One such opportunity lies in the potential for security to become a strategic differentiator. Organizations can enhance their reputation, build trust with customers and partners, and position themselves as industry leaders in security-conscious innovation by demonstrating a strong and proactive approach to security. This, in turn, can open up new market opportunities, strengthen customer loyalty and enable the organization to command a premium for its products and services. To realize this potential, development investments for robust data and analytics capabilities that support the organization's security integration efforts must be made by those who control the investments. By collecting, analysing and interpreting security-related data, an organization can gain deeper insights into their threat landscape, vulnerabilities and the effectiveness of their security measures. This data-driven approach enables more informed decision-making, resource allocation and the development of tailored security solutions that address the organization's unique needs and risk profile.

The integration of security considerations into the development and implementation of new products, services and business initiatives is a critical component of effective security empowerment. Adopting a proactive and collaborative approach to security can help leaders transform security from a reactive function to a strategic enabler, unlocking new avenues for growth, innovation and competitive advantage. This holistic integration of security into the organization's operations not only enhances the overall security posture but also fosters a culture of security-minded innovation that is better equipped to handle current threats and those that are not yet known.

Metrics

Developing a security metrics framework is a helpful way to transform security from a cost centre to a strategic enabler. Although traditional aspects such as compliance, risk mitigation and the prevention of security incidents remain important, leaders must now also shift their perspective to demonstrate how security can actively contribute to the organization's overall success and competitive advantage. To achieve this, security metrics must be closely tied to the organization's strategic objectives and key performance indicators (KPIs). This requires a deep understanding of the organization's critical assets, the potential impact of security breaches or disruptions, and the specific business outcomes that security initiatives are designed to support.

One example of a strategic security metric could be the impact of security measures on customer trust and loyalty. Data breaches and cyber-attacks can quickly erode customer confidence. Organizations that can demonstrate a strong security posture and a commitment to protecting customer information may enjoy a significant competitive edge. Tracking metrics such as customer churn rates, brand reputation or the financial impact of security-related incidents quantifies the value of security investments and makes a compelling case for continued support. Similarly, security metrics can be aligned with operational efficiency and productivity. Effective security measures that streamline access controls, automate threat detection and response, or minimize downtime during security incidents can contribute directly to improved operational performance, reduced costs and enhanced business resilience. Metrics such as the mean time to detect and respond to security incidents, the percentage of automated security processes, or the financial impact of security-related disruptions can help leaders demonstrate the tangible benefits of security investments.

In addition to these business-oriented metrics, organizations should also maintain a comprehensive set of technical security metrics that provide insights into the overall security posture and the effectiveness of specific security controls. These may include metrics related to vulnerability management, patch compliance, identity and access management, or the detection and mitigation of cyber threats. The organization's security infrastructure remains aligned with evolving threats and industry best practices through the monitoring of these technical metrics that identify areas for improvement, help allocate resources more effectively, and ensure that the organization's security infrastructure remains aligned with industry best practices.

An effective security metrics framework is often underpinned by thorough data collection and analysis capabilities that includes the implementation of security information and event management (SIEM) systems, the integration of security data with other business intelligence tools, and the development of advanced analytics and visualization capabilities. Leveraging data-driven insights can lead to more informed decisions and communicate the value of security investments to key stakeholders.

Going even further to reinforce the strategic importance of security, leaders should also consider integrating security-related performance metrics into the organization's overall compensation and incentive structures. Associating a portion of employee compensation to the achievement of security-related goals and objectives can foster a culture of security-minded behaviour and accountability, where employees at all levels are incentivized to actively contribute to the organization's security efforts. It can also help to attract and retain top talent in the security and risk management fields. As the demand for skilled security professionals continues to grow, organizations that can demonstrate a strong commitment to security and offer competitive compensation packages tied to security performance are more likely to attract and retain the best talent in the industry. This approach helps to align individual and team performance with the organization's security priorities and contributes to the overall success, allowing every employee to have a role to play in safeguarding the organization's assets and reputation. Security-related performance metrics should be carefully crafted to ensure that they are closely aligned with the organization's strategic objectives and risk profile. These metrics should be transparent, measurable and regularly reviewed to ensure that they continue to drive the desired behaviours and outcomes.

Communicating security effectively

With frameworks and metrics in place, effective communication becomes a critical component of successful security management. As organizations grapple with an increasingly complex and volatile threat environment, the ability to convey a wealth of security-related information in a clear, concise and compelling manner is essential for driving stakeholder engagement, securing buy-in for security initiatives, and positioning security as a strategic enabler.

However, the task of communicating security effectively is not without challenges. Security professionals, steeped in technical jargon and risk-focused mindsets, may struggle to translate their expertise into language that resonates with business leaders, end-users and other key stakeholders. Conversely, executives and decision-makers may lack the necessary understanding of security concepts to fully appreciate the importance and implications of security-related decisions. This disconnect can lead to a breakdown in communication, undermining the organization's ability to implement robust security measures, foster a security-conscious culture, and leverage security as a competitive advantage. To overcome these challenges, a comprehensive approach to security communication that bridges the gap between technical security requirements and the broader strategic and operational needs of the business is needed. At the heart of this approach is the ability to craft clear and compelling security narratives that resonate with the diverse stakeholder groups. It is imperative to understand the unique perspectives, priorities and pain points of each audience so that messaging can be tailored to effectively convey the value, impact and urgency of security initiatives. Framing security in terms of business outcomes, such as customer trust, operational resilience or regulatory compliance, rather than focusing solely on technical details or risk mitigation are important themes for effectiveness.

For instance, when communicating with the executive team, the security narrative may focus on the financial implications of security breaches, the reputational damage that can result from high-profile incidents, and the competitive advantages that a robust security posture can provide. This frames security in terms of business outcomes, such as customer trust, operational resilience and regulatory compliance that better demonstrate the strategic value of their initiatives and secure the necessary resources and support to implement them effectively. On the other hand, when engaging with end-users or operational teams, the security narrative may emphasize the practical benefits of security measures, such as streamlined access controls, reduced downtime or enhanced productivity. Highlighting how security can enable and empower employees to perform their roles more efficiently and effectively promotes a sense of shared ownership and responsibility for the organization's security efforts. Either way, crafting these tailored security narratives requires a delicate balance of technical expertise and storytelling prowess. Security leaders must possess a deep understanding of the organization's security landscape, the evolving threat environment, and the latest industry best practices. However, they must also be skilled communicators, capable of translating complex security concepts into language that resonates with their target audience.

Effective security communication requires a deep understanding of the organization's brand, culture and communication channels. Security messages should be aligned with the organization's overall messaging and visual identity, ensuring a consistent and cohesive experience for stakeholders. This, in turn, helps to build trust, credibility and a shared sense of ownership in the organization's security efforts. Equally important is the ability to translate technical security concepts into language that is accessible and meaningful to non-technical stakeholders. Breaking down complex security topics into clear, jargon-free explanations will empower decision-makers to make informed choices, encourage a security-conscious culture among employees, and engage with external partners and customers on security-related matters. Ultimately, the effective communication of security is not just a matter of conveying information; it is a strategic soft skill that can unlock new opportunities for growth, innovation and competitive advantage. A comprehensive approach to security communication will strengthen security posture, enhance stakeholder engagement and position security as a critical component of the organization's overall business strategy.

An effective technique for developing compelling security narratives is the use of real-world examples and case studies. Sharing stories of how other organizations have successfully navigated security challenges or leveraged security as a strategic advantage make the abstract more tangible and inspire their stakeholders to take action. These narratives can also incorporate data-driven insights, such as industry benchmarks or the financial impact of security incidents, to further strengthen the business case for security investments. It plays to the human nature of social proof bias, which is the tendency for someone to assume that the actions of others reflect the correct behaviour for a given situation – people are more likely to believe something if they see others doing or believing it.

The narrative should be aligned with the organization's overall brand and communication strategy which ensures that security messaging is consistent, coherent and reinforces the organization's core values, positioning and reputation. To achieve this level of alignment, security leaders may need to collaborate closely with the organization's marketing, communications and public relations teams.

Together, they can develop a comprehensive security communication plan that outlines key messages, target audiences, communication channels and metrics for success. This collaborative approach not only enhances the effectiveness of security communication but also helps to break down silos and foster a shared understanding of the organization's security priorities. Once released, continuous improvements to refine and adapt the security narrative in response to changing business requirements, emerging threats and stakeholder feedback is also required. The content should be regularly reviewed and updated according to their communication strategies, incorporating lessons learned, industry trends and the evolving needs of their target audiences. An agile approach to security communication ensures that the organization remains responsive, relevant and well-positioned.

KEY TAKEAWAYS

- Building a security culture needs buy-in from the top levels of the organization.

- Security at every organization is unique – however, a well-thought-out governance framework underpins many activities which support a security mindset.

- Putting security further up in the product lifecycle will keep products safe and build customer trust.

- Justify how much security 'improves' products by establishing a form of measurement.

- Share the measurements in a way that is meaningful to the business, not just self-fulfilling security's mission.

7

Strategies for effective risk management

Risk management is an overarching theme that can be applied to nearly any situation, even in the physical world. In fact, we are assessing risk all the time, but each of us have different tolerances for it. For example, there are plenty of people who enjoy the thrill of a roller coaster – so many that there are entire parks centred around rides that people travel to from all over the world for an adrenaline rush. However, there are possibly even more people who do not. You may choose not to walk a dangerous treacherous path on a wilderness hike for fear of being injured, but you can also be injured walking your dog just outside your own home. Do you hold the handrail when walking down the stairs? Why or why not? The answer to 'why or why not' is a rhetorical question, but the answer in reality is probably an assessment of data over time. It is a calculation of how many times you have gone down the stairs safely while holding (or not holding) the handrail versus how many times you have fallen down the stairs. People who always hold the handrail have either never fallen while doing so, or they have fallen at least once while not holding it, thus they decide that holding the handrail is in their best interest. All of that has been calculated at the moment you approach a set of stairs and your hand subconsciously extends to meet the rail as you take your first step, but it is a great example of a measurement of risk efficacy.

When discussing strategies for effective risk management, one should first understand how to define 'effective'. Just like some of us hold the handrail and some of us don't, that is a subjective calculation depending on the risk appetite of the organization – their willingness to accept a certain level of risk – and their obligations (e.g. regulations). Even still, an easy measurement of success (in the context of risk management at an organization) is comparing the number and severity of security incidents over time; it can be easily argued that risk management is effective if there are fewer security incidents during one period than there were in the one before it. Other dimensions of the same metric could be comparing the financial impacts of security incidents, recovery time and downtime sustained. It would be a good assumption that if these metrics were trending in the right direction, the risk management is effective. However, this simplistic view of 'fewer incidents equals better risk management' may not tell the whole story. After all, an organization could theoretically achieve this by taking an overly conservative approach, locking down every possible attack vector and grinding operations to a halt. Clearly, that would not be an effective long-term strategy. True effectiveness in risk management must balance the need to protect the organization with the imperative to enable the business to function and thrive.

One way to strike this balance is to take a more holistic view of risk management metrics. In addition to incident reduction, organizations can also track compliance and regulatory adherence. Successful completion of audits, reduction in compliance violations and avoidance of regulatory fines all speak to the organization's ability to manage risk within the bounds of their legal and industry obligations. This is a critical consideration, as failure to meet compliance standards can result in significant financial penalties and reputational damage – outcomes that no organization can afford.

Stakeholder confidence is another key indicator of effective risk management. If customers, partners and investors perceive the organization as a secure and reliable entity, it suggests that the risk management strategies in place are resonating and instilling a sense of trust. Conversely, a tarnished brand reputation or loss of business due to security incidents would indicate that the risk management approach is falling short.

Operational efficiency is yet another dimension to consider. Streamlined incident response and recovery processes, reduced security-related costs and improved business continuity all point to a risk management programme that is well-integrated into the organization's overall operations. When security measures enhance, rather than hinder, the organization's ability to function, it is a clear sign of effectiveness.

Threat intelligence and situational awareness are also crucial elements of effective risk management. The ability to detect and mitigate emerging threats in a timely manner, as well as the organization's capacity to share threat information and best practices, demonstrate a proactive and adaptive approach to risk management. In an ever-evolving threat landscape, organizations that can stay ahead of the curve are far more likely to maintain a robust security posture.

The overall maturity and continuous improvement of the risk management programme should be evaluated. This includes tracking the progression of security capabilities over time, successful implementation of industry frameworks and standards, and the incorporation of lessons learned. An organization that is consistently enhancing its risk management strategies is one that is well-positioned to navigate the challenges of the future.

Regardless of how it is measured, effective risk management is a critical component of any organization's security posture. Proactively identifying, assessing and mitigating potential risks will lead to better protection of company assets, maintain business continuity and safeguard their reputation.

Identifying potential digital risks

Now that we understand what it means for risk management to be effective, the first step towards that goal is to identify the potential digital risks facing the organization. This includes threats such as cyber-attacks, data breaches, system failures and regulatory non-compliance. Conducting a comprehensive risk assessment helps to gain a clear understanding of the likelihood and impact of these risks, giving way to prioritizing their mitigation efforts.

The process of identifying digital risks begins with a thorough inventory of the organization's assets, both tangible and intangible. This includes not only the obvious IT infrastructure and data repositories, but also the less visible elements such as intellectual property, brand reputation and employee knowledge. Understanding the full scope of what needs to be protected is crucial, as it provides the foundation for the risk assessment. Identifying *all* the risks can be tricky, and it helps to ask the question: 'What value does this have to an attacker?' The answer to this question can vary depending on the perspective of the person you ask. For example, if you ask someone in the finance department, the answer might be 'money' – an attacker could be interested in stealing funds or sensitive financial information. If you ask someone in the human resources department, the answer might be 'employee data' – an attacker could be interested in stealing personally identifiable information or using it for social engineering attacks. And if you ask someone in the marketing department, the answer might be 'reputation' – an attacker could be interested in damaging the organization's brand or public image through a cyber-attack.

It is important to collaborate across departments to gain a comprehensive understanding of the potential risks and their impact on the organization. This cross-functional approach helps to identify risks from multiple perspectives and ensures that the risk assessment covers all critical assets and potential attack vectors.

Next, the organization must delve into the threat landscape, analysing the various actors and vectors that could potentially compromise their assets. Cybercriminals, nation-states, hacktivists and even disgruntled insiders all pose unique threats, each with their own motivations and methods of attack. Cybercriminals are often financially motivated, seeking to steal sensitive data, disrupt operations or hold systems for ransom. They may use techniques like phishing, malware or exploiting vulnerabilities to gain unauthorized access. Nation-state actors, on the other hand, may have broader geopolitical goals, such as espionage, sabotage or disrupting critical infrastructure. Their attacks can be highly sophisticated, leveraging zero-day exploits and advanced persistent threats. Hacktivists, driven by ideological or political agendas, may target an organization to make a statement or draw attention to a cause. Their attacks can range from website defacement to distributed denial-of-service (DDoS) attacks. Disgruntled insiders, such as current or former employees, can pose a significant threat as they already have intimate knowledge of the organization's systems and processes.

Mapping these threats to the organization's assets will begin to provide an understanding of the likelihood and potential impact of different scenarios. This could involve assessing the value and sensitivity of the data, the criticality of the systems, and the potential consequences of a successful attack.

Regulatory compliance is another critical consideration in the risk assessment process. Organizations must ensure that they are adhering to industry standards, data privacy regulations and other legal requirements relevant to their operations. This includes complying with frameworks like HIPAA for healthcare organizations in the United States, PCI-DSS for those handling payment card data, or the GDPR for companies operating in the European Union. Failure to comply with these regulations can result in hefty fines, legal battles and irreparable damage to the organization's reputation. Regulatory bodies can impose significant monetary penalties for non-compliance, which can quickly add up and severely impact the organization's bottom line. Additionally, legal proceedings and lawsuits stemming from compliance failures can be time-consuming, costly and detrimental to the organization's public image. Beyond the financial and legal consequences, non-compliance can also lead to a loss of customer trust and brand reputation. Customers and stakeholders expect organizations to handle their data and operations responsibly and in accordance with established standards. A high-profile compliance breach can quickly erode that trust, making it difficult for the organization to recover and maintain its competitive edge in the market. Thoroughly understanding the relevant compliance requirements and proactively addressing any gaps or vulnerabilities will inevitably mitigate the risks associated with regulatory non-compliance. Implementing data protection measures, conducting regular audits and staying up-to-date with evolving regulations are great ways to address this, as integrating compliance considerations into the overall risk assessment process can help ensure the organization remains compliant, protected and trusted by its customers and stakeholders.

System failures and operational disruptions also fall under the purview of digital risk assessment. Whether caused by hardware malfunctions, software bugs or natural disasters, these events can have a crippling effect on an organization's ability to function. Hardware failures, such as server crashes, network outages or storage device failures, can lead to the loss of critical data and the inability to access essential systems. Software bugs and glitches can also cause applications to malfunction, leading to service interruptions and data integrity issues. Natural disasters, like floods, earthquakes or power outages, can physically damage infrastructure and disrupt the organization's operations. Identifying potential points of failure and understanding the cascading impacts of such incidents is essential for developing robust business continuity and disaster recovery plans. The likelihood and potential impact of various system failure scenarios must be assessed, considering factors such as the criticality of the affected systems, the availability of redundant infrastructure, and the time required to restore normal operations. Mapping out the interdependencies between different systems and processes will enable an organization to better anticipate the ripple effects of a disruption. For example, a server failure may not only impact the specific application running on that server but could also affect downstream services, customer-facing interfaces and even the organization's ability to generate revenue.

Comprehensive business continuity planning, including the implementation of backup systems, failover mechanisms and incident response protocols, can help mitigate the risks associated with system failures and operational disruptions. Regular testing and updating of these plans are crucial to ensure they remain effective in the face of evolving threats and changing business requirements. An organization can enhance their resilience, minimize downtime and maintain the trust of their customers and stakeholders, even in the face of unexpected challenges, by proactively addressing the risks posed by system failures and operational disruptions.

Assessing risk likelihood and potential impact

With the threats and assets now clearly defined, the organization can begin to assess the likelihood and potential impact of each risk scenario. This is where the risk assessment process becomes more quantitative, leveraging data-driven methodologies to assign numerical values to the various risk factors. Probability-impact matrices are a common tool used to visualize and prioritize risks, as described in Chapter 4.

A brief refresher: the probability-impact matrix plots the likelihood of a risk occurring (probability) against the potential consequences if it were to occur (impact). Risks with a high probability and high impact are typically considered the most critical, requiring immediate attention and mitigation efforts. Risk scoring models take this a step further by assigning numerical values to the probability and impact of each risk. These values can be based on historical data, industry benchmarks or expert assessments.

For more complex scenarios, Monte Carlo simulations can be employed to model the potential outcomes and their associated probabilities. This technique involves running multiple iterations of a risk scenario, each with slightly different inputs, to generate a distribution of possible outcomes. This can help security teams better understand the range of potential impacts and the likelihood of different risk levels occurring. Ultimately, leveraging these data-driven methodologies can objectively inform and prioritize the most critical risks facing the organization. This allows them to focus their limited resources on the areas of greatest concern, ensuring that the most valuable assets are adequately protected.

One of the key challenges in this phase is the inherent uncertainty and unpredictability of many digital threats. Cyber-attacks, for example, can evolve rapidly, with new vulnerabilities and attack vectors emerging on a near-constant basis. To address this, a more dynamic and adaptive approach to risk assessment must be considered, continuously monitoring the threat landscape and updating their evaluations accordingly. This is where threat intelligence and information sharing become invaluable. Security teams can gain a more comprehensive understanding of the risks facing their organization by tapping into industry-wide threat data, as well as the strategies and best practices employed by their peers to mitigate those risks. Collaboration with government agencies, security vendors and industry associations can further enhance threat awareness and risk assessment capabilities.

Another critical aspect of effective risk assessment is the involvement of cross-functional stakeholders. While the security team may be responsible for leading the process, input from IT, legal, compliance and business units is essential for ensuring a holistic view of the organization's risk profile. A collaborative approach strengthens the risk assessment and also fosters a shared understanding of the organization's security priorities and the potential impacts on day-to-day operations.

With the results of the risk assessment calculated, the organization can then proceed to prioritize its mitigation efforts based on the identified risks. This involves evaluating the various risk treatment options, each with its own advantages and drawbacks. One approach is to implement security controls to directly address and mitigate the identified risks. This could include deploying technical solutions like firewalls, intrusion detection systems and encryption, as well as implementing administrative controls such as access management policies, employee training programmes and incident response plans. Alternatively, an organization may choose to transfer certain risks to third-party providers or through insurance policies such as outsourcing specific functions or services to vendors with more robust security capabilities or purchasing cyber insurance to cover the financial consequences of a successful attack. While this approach does not eliminate the underlying risks, it can help an organization offload the responsibility and potential impact of certain threats.

In some cases, an organization may decide to accept certain risks as part of its overall strategy. This could be due to the low likelihood or impact of a particular threat, or because the cost of mitigating the risk outweighs the potential benefits. Consciously accepting these risks allows an organization to focus its resources on addressing the most critical threats while maintaining a balanced and cost-effective risk management plan.

The goal is to develop a comprehensive risk management strategy that aligns with the risk appetite and strategic objectives of the organization by using a combination of security controls, risk transfer mechanisms and risk acceptance, all tailored to the specific needs and constraints of the organization. Regularly reviewing and updating the risk management plan is equally important, as the threat landscape and the risk profile can evolve over time. Incorporating feedback from incident response activities, threat intelligence and industry benchmarking can help refine the risk management strategy and ensure it remains effective in the face of emerging threats. It's important to note that the risk assessment process is not a one-time exercise; it must be an ongoing, iterative endeavour. As an organization's assets, threat landscape and business requirements evolve, the risk assessment must be regularly reviewed and updated to ensure its continued relevance and effectiveness. This agile approach to risk management allows an organization to stay ahead of emerging threats and adapt its strategies accordingly.

Incident response planning

Even with hand-crafted risk management strategies in place, incidents can still occur, so effective incident response planning is critical to minimizing the impact of these events and ensure a swift and coordinated recovery. An organization must develop and regularly test their incident response plans, incorporating lessons learned to continuously improve their processes.

When an incident does occur, the incident response team will spring into action and follow a well-defined protocol to contain the damage, mitigate the immediate threat and begin the recovery process. This team, typically composed of security professionals, IT specialists and key stakeholders, must be trained and empowered to make critical decisions under pressure. The plan should outline clear procedures for identifying, classifying and prioritizing the incident. Is it a data breach, a system failure or a DDoS attack? Depending on the nature and severity of the incident, the response team must determine the appropriate course of action, whether it's isolating affected systems, activating backup and recovery mechanisms, or notifying relevant authorities and stakeholders.

Effective communication is key during an incident response. Clear lines of communication must be established by the team – both internally and externally – to ensure that all relevant parties are informed and aligned. Regular status updates to executive leadership, coordination with external partners or law enforcement, and the provision of timely and transparent updates to customers or the public, as appropriate, are found in all well-defined plans. Incident response plans should also incorporate detailed procedures for evidence collection and forensic analysis. In the event of a security breach or other malicious activity, it is important to preserve and analyse relevant data to understand the root cause, the extent of the damage and the potential impact on the organization. This information can then be used to strengthen defences and prevent similar incidents from occurring in the future. Once the immediate crisis has been addressed, the organization must shift its focus to recovery and restoration. Restoring data from backups, rebuilding affected systems and gradually returning to normal operations are common avenues following such an incident. Throughout this process, the incident response team must continuously monitor the situation, identify any lingering issues and ensure that critical business functions are restored in a timely and secure manner.

If data was lost or corrupted, restoring the 'last known good' from backups is a critical first step in the recovery process. Data may reside in offsite storage, cloud-based backup solutions or redundant on-premises systems and must be retrieved safely and securely. The integrity of the backed-up data must be carefully validated for completeness to ensure that no corruption or gaps exist when it is restored. This may require running checksum verifications, testing sample data and comparing the backup data to any remaining live data sources.

Rebuilding affected systems is the next crucial step. Activities such as reinstalling operating systems, redeploying applications and reconfiguring network settings to restore the technology infrastructure are common. Depending on the scope and severity of the incident, this process may require the provisioning of new hardware, the restoration of virtual machine images or the redeployment of containerized applications. Throughout this process, the incident response team must carefully monitor the status of the recovery efforts, identify any lingering issues or unexpected complications, and address them in a timely manner by troubleshooting connectivity problems, resolving software conflicts or addressing data integrity concerns.

The gradual return to normal operations is a delicate and deliberate process, as the organization must ensure that its critical business functions are fully restored and operating securely before resuming regular activities. Depending on company size and incident blast radius, a phased approach – where certain mission-critical systems or services are brought back online first, followed by less essential components – would be appropriate. 'Normal operations' in this context refer to the pre-incident state, where all essential business processes, customer-facing services and internal workflows are functioning as intended: the 'last known good', including seamless transaction processing, uninterrupted delivery of products or services, and the reliable exchange of information both within the organization and with external stakeholders.

These activities are the perfect opportunity to inform key performance indicators related to programme effectiveness, such as:

- Time to restore critical data from backups: the duration from the initiation of the data restoration process to the point where all mission-critical data is successfully recovered and validated.

- Time to rebuild and redeploy affected systems: time required to reinstall, reconfigure and bring back online the various technology components that were impacted by the incident.

- Time to resume normal operations: the total time measured from the initial incident to the point where the organization has fully returned to its pre-incident state, with all critical business functions operating as expected.

Closely monitoring these KPIs can assess the efficiency of its recovery efforts and also use the data to inform future incident response planning and continuous improvement initiatives. For example, if the time to restore critical data from backups is consistently longer than the recovery time objective, it may indicate a need to invest in more robust backup and recovery infrastructure.

Ultimately, the recovery and restoration process is a delicate balance of speed, security and thoroughness. The incident response team must work diligently to bring the organization back to normal operations as quickly as possible, while ensuring that the underlying issues have been addressed and that systems and data have been fully restored and secured.

Post-incident review

Equally important is the post-incident review and continuous improvement process. A thorough analysis of the incident should be conducted to evaluate the effectiveness of the response plan, identify areas for improvement and document the lessons learned. This information can then be used to update the incident response plan, enhance security controls and improve overall resilience. For example, if the incident response team identified delays in communication or decision-making during the crisis, more streamlined reporting structures or empowering the team with greater autonomy to make time-sensitive decisions may be used. If the analysis reveals vulnerabilities in the backup and recovery systems, investments may be made to enhance data redundancy, improve recovery times and ensure the availability of critical systems. Continuous improvement also involves staying up-to-date with the latest threat intelligence, industry best practices and emerging technologies. Actively monitoring for new threats and adapting security strategies accordingly help stay one step ahead of potential attackers and minimize the risk of future incidents.

Regular testing and simulation exercises are another component of the continuous improvement process, and are sometimes required by certain compliance frameworks. Conducting tabletop exercises (like the ones mentioned in the previous chapter), penetration tests and incident response drills will help identify gaps in the plans, assess the readiness of the teams and refine the procedures to ensure they are prepared to respond effectively to a wide range of potential incidents. Also consider establishing formal feedback loops and knowledge-sharing mechanisms to learn from peers and industry counterparts. Participating in security forums, industry associations and information-sharing initiatives can provide valuable insights into emerging threats, successful mitigation strategies and best practices for incident response and recovery.

Embracing a culture of continuous improvement can transform an organization's incident response capabilities from a reactive, firefighting approach to a proactive, resilience-focused mindset. This not only enhances the ability to withstand and recover from incidents but also strengthens its overall security posture, making it a less attractive target for potential attackers.

Adaptive risk management

It should be obvious by now that static risk management strategies are no longer sufficient to properly mitigate against a technical world where change is the only constant. Effective risk management means implementing flexible security controls, ongoing review and updating of risk assessments, and ultimately a cultural shift to continuous learning and improvement. The pace of technological change, the proliferation of new attack vectors, and the increasing sophistication of cyber threats have made it challenging to maintain a comprehensive and up-to-date understanding of an organization's risk profiles. Traditional risk management frameworks, which often rely on point-in-time assessments and predefined mitigation strategies, quickly become outdated and ineffective in the face of these dynamic challenges.

To address this, embrace an adaptive risk management approach that is designed to be agile, responsive and resilient. This starts with cultivating a deep understanding of the risk landscape, which requires continuous monitoring, analysis and adaptation.

At the heart of an adaptive risk strategy is the ability to continuously monitor and assess the risk landscape by leveraging a range of data sources, including threat intelligence feeds, security event logs, vulnerability scans and industry benchmarks, to maintain a real-time understanding of the threats and vulnerabilities faced. Aggregating and analysing this data leads to the identification of emerging trends, detecting anomalies, and gaining early warning of potential threats. This information can then be used to update the risk assessments, refine security controls and prioritize mitigation efforts.

For example, if an organization's threat monitoring system detects a surge in phishing attacks targeting the industry, the risk assessment team may need to reevaluate the likelihood and potential impact of a successful phishing incident. This could lead to the implementation of enhanced employee training programmes, the deployment of more stringent email security controls, and the allocation of additional security analysts to address this evolving threat.

Adaptive risk strategies also require the implementation of flexible security controls that can be easily adjusted and scaled in response to changing conditions. Using modular, cloud-based security solutions that can be rapidly deployed, configured and updated, as opposed to relying on monolithic, on-premises systems that are more difficult to maintain and adapt are worth investigating for feasibility, in this situation. Additionally, consider adopting a 'defence-in-depth' approach, which involves layering multiple security controls to create a more resilient and adaptable security posture. This is achieved using a combination of preventive measures (e.g. firewalls, intrusion prevention systems), detective controls (e.g. security information and event management tools, user behaviour analytics), and responsive mechanisms (e.g. incident response plans, automated remediation workflows). Implementing this layered approach prepares an organization to better withstand the failure or compromise of individual security controls, as the remaining layers can continue to provide protection and enable a swift response to emerging threats. Furthermore, the flexibility of these controls allows an organization to quickly scale up or down its security measures based on the evolving risk landscape, ensuring that resources are allocated efficiently and effectively.

Alongside the implementation of flexible security controls, adaptive risk strategies require the regular review and updating of the organization's risk assessments. This is an important step in ensuring that risk management efforts remain aligned with evolving business objectives, threat landscape and resource constraints. Rather than relying on a single, comprehensive risk assessment conducted at the beginning of the year, an organization can adopt a more iterative and continuous approach on a quarterly or semi-annual basis, where the risk assessment team re-evaluates the likelihood and potential impact of various risk scenarios, adjusts the prioritization of mitigation efforts, and reallocates resources as needed. This continuous risk assessment process should also incorporate feedback from incident response activities, threat intelligence and industry benchmarking. Learning from past incidents, monitoring emerging threats and comparing their performance to industry means peers can refine an organization's risk models, identify new areas of concern and ensure that risk management strategies remain relevant and effective. For example, if an organization experiences a successful ransomware attack, the risk assessment team may need to reevaluate the likelihood and potential impact of similar attacks, as well as the effectiveness of the organization's existing controls and recovery mechanisms. This could lead to the implementation of more robust backup and recovery systems, the enhancement of employee security awareness training, and the allocation of additional resources to address the ransomware threat.

Developing an adaptive risk strategy also requires the cultivation of a culture of continuous improvement within the organization. Employees at all levels would be empowered to actively participate in the risk management process, share their insights and experiences, and contribute to the ongoing refinement of the organization's security posture. One key aspect of this is promoting a 'no-blame' approach to incident reporting and analysis. Employees should feel comfortable and encouraged to report security incidents, near-misses and potential vulnerabilities without fear of repercussion. An open and transparent reporting culture allows an organization to quickly identify and address emerging threats, while also gathering valuable data to inform future risk assessments and mitigation strategies. Additionally, formal feedback loops and knowledge-sharing mechanisms to facilitate the exchange of information and best practices are a great way to normalize participation in the risk process. Regular security awareness training sessions, cross-functional risk management workshops, and internal communities of practice where employees can collaborate, share insights and learn from one another are excellent avenues for collaborative opportunities.

By fostering this culture of continuous improvement, an organization can tap into the collective intelligence and diverse perspectives of its workforce, leveraging their unique experiences and domain expertise to enhance overall resilience. This, in turn, can lead to the identification of innovative security solutions, the development of more effective risk mitigation strategies, and the cultivation of a more security-conscious and engaged workforce.

Embracing emerging technologies and methodologies

Adaptive risk strategies must also keep pace with the rapid advancements in security technologies and methodologies by actively exploring and evaluating the potential benefits of emerging tools and techniques.

AI and ML

Artificial intelligence (AI) and machine learning (ML) are powerful tools that can significantly enhance adaptive risk strategies as they can be leveraged to automate the analysis of security data, detect anomalies and predict potential threats, enabling a faster material response to evolving risks. Applying AI and ML algorithms to the vast amounts of security data generated by the various systems and tools will help security teams uncover patterns, identify anomalies and detect potential threats that may have gone unnoticed using traditional, rule-based approaches. For example, AI-powered security analytics can analyse user behaviour, network traffic and system logs to identify unusual activity that could indicate a security breach or an emerging threat. Predictive models based on ML can also help anticipate and prepare for future threats. When these models are trained on historical security data, threat intelligence and industry benchmarks, they offer valuable insights into the likelihood and potential impact of various risk scenarios. The speed and accuracy of AI and ML-driven threat detection and prediction can significantly enhance the ability to respond to evolving risks. Automating the analysis of security data and providing real-time alerts will enable security teams to identify and address threats much faster, reducing the potential for damage and minimizing the disruption to business operations.

Threat hunting and proactive monitoring

Threat hunting and proactive monitoring is another great addition to an adaptive risk strategy, as they allow for taking a more proactive approach to security. It allows an organization to actively search for and identify threats that may have evaded traditional detection mechanisms, allowing them to address vulnerabilities before they can be exploited. Unlike traditional, reactive security approaches that rely on waiting for alerts and responding to incidents, threat hunting involves the systematic and continuous search for signs of malicious activity within the network and systems. Security teams employ advanced analytical techniques, threat intelligence and contextual knowledge to uncover hidden threats, identify anomalies and detect indicators of compromise that may have gone unnoticed by conventional security controls. The insights gained through threat hunting activities can be used to refine and enhance security controls, threat detection capabilities and incident response procedures. Integrating threat hunting and proactive monitoring into an adaptive risk strategy empowers security teams to take a more proactive and agile approach to security, enabling them to identify and address threats in a timely manner and minimize the potential impact on operations and assets.

Cyber threat intelligence

Cyber threat intelligence (CTI) can also provide a deeper understanding of the threat landscape, enabling an organization to anticipate and prepare for emerging threats. Integrating and analysing threat intelligence from a variety of sources, including government agencies, security vendors, industry forums and open-source intelligence, help to gain rich insights into the tactics, techniques and motivations of potential adversaries, such as new vulnerabilities, emerging attack vectors and the activities of specific threat actors which allow security teams to stay informed and responsive to the evolving threat landscape. Leveraging CTI enables the proactive identification and assessment of the risks posed by these threats and inform the prioritization of their mitigation efforts based on the likelihood and potential impact of each scenario. These insights, too, can be used to enhance an overall security posture, informing the development of more robust security policies, employee training programmes and threat detection mechanisms. As new threat intelligence becomes available, security teams can quickly adapt their controls, update their risk assessments and adjust their mitigation strategies accordingly, ensuring that the organization remains resilient and responsive to new threats.

DevSecOps and secure software development

DevSecOps and secure software development as part of an adaptive risk strategy are great ways to build more secure and resilient applications, reducing the risk of vulnerabilities and ensuring that security is a core consideration throughout the entire product lifecycle. These methodologies integrate security practices seamlessly into the software development lifecycle, promoting security as a fundamental part of the development process from the very beginning. Security-focused activities, such as threat modelling, secure coding practices and automated security testing, are integrated into the various stages of the development pipeline so that applications are inherently more secure and resilient, reducing the risk of vulnerabilities that could be exploited by threat actors. This strengthens overall security posture as the applications themselves become a more reliable component of the infrastructure. The continuous integration of security practices throughout the software development lifecycle enables security to identify and address vulnerabilities much earlier in the process when they are typically less costly and disruptive to remediate. This proactive approach to security helps stay ahead of potential threats, rather than reacting to incidents after the fact.

XDR

Extended detection and response (XDR) is a powerful approach that can significantly enhance an adaptive risk strategy by providing a more comprehensive and coordinated response to security incidents. Traditional security tools and technologies often operate in silos, with each solution focusing on a specific aspect of the security landscape, such as endpoint protection, network monitoring or threat detection. This fragmented approach can lead to gaps in visibility, making it challenging for security teams to detect, investigate and remediate threats in a timely and effective manner. XDR addresses this challenge by combining data from multiple security tools and sources, including endpoints, networks, cloud environments, and security information and event management systems, to provide a unified and holistic view of an organization's security posture. This cross-correlation of data enables security teams to identify patterns, detect anomalies and uncover hidden threats that may have gone unnoticed using individual security solutions. XDR solutions can provide security teams with a more comprehensive understanding of the threat landscape by integrating and analysing data from these diverse sources, allowing them to respond more effectively to security incidents. The enhanced visibility and coordinated response capabilities of XDR can significantly improve the ability to detect, investigate and remediate threats, reducing the potential for damage and minimizing the disruption to business operations, thus strengthening the overall security posture and resilience.

Embracing the challenges of adaptive risk strategies

Developing and implementing an adaptive risk strategy is not without its challenges. Organizations may face a range of obstacles ranging from cultural to technical and all the way to institutional. Understanding these challenges is important to be able to overcome them, by applying the known benefits of an adaptive risk strategy.

Overcoming organizational inertia

One of the most significant challenges in implementing an adaptive risk strategy is overcoming the natural resistance to change within an organization. Organizational inertia, the tendency for an organization to maintain its current state and resist transformative change, can be a formidable obstacle to the successful adoption of more agile and responsive risk management practices. Employees, accustomed to established risk management protocols and comfortable with familiar processes and technologies, may be hesitant to embrace new approaches, even in the face of an evolving threat landscape. Employees may be apprehensive about the potential disruptions and uncertainties associated with adopting new technologies and processes. The prospect of learning new skills and adapting to different ways of working can be daunting, leading to resistance and a desire to maintain the familiar. If employees do not have confidence in the leadership or believe that the proposed changes are not well-conceived or communicated, they may be less inclined to support the transition to an adaptive risk strategy. Employees may also worry that the implementation of new technologies and automated processes could threaten their job security, leading to a defensive posture and resistance to change. In some cases, the prevailing culture may not be conducive to adaptability and continuous improvement. A risk-averse, hierarchical or siloed culture can hinder the cross-functional collaboration and information sharing that are essential for effective adaptive risk management.

Overcoming these challenges and fostering a culture of adaptability and continuous improvement requires strong leadership and effective change management strategies. Employees need to understand how the proposed changes will enhance the security posture, improve business resilience and create new opportunities for growth and innovation. Encouraging employee participation in the design and implementation of the adaptive risk strategy can help build buy-in and ownership, reducing resistance to change. Investing in employee training and development to equip them with the necessary skills and knowledge to navigate the new risk management processes and technologies can help ease the transition. Fostering an environment where employees are encouraged to experiment, learn from failures and continuously refine their risk management practices can help sustain the momentum of the adaptive risk strategy over the long term. Ensuring that the reward and recognition systems reinforce the desired behaviours and outcomes associated with the adaptive risk strategy can help drive sustained engagement and commitment from employees.

Overcoming technical hurdles

In addition to the cultural and organizational challenges of implementing an adaptive risk strategy, organizations also face significant technical hurdles in aggregating and analysing the vast amounts of data required to maintain a real-time understanding of their risk landscape. Developing the necessary data integration and analytics capabilities is a complex and resource-intensive undertaking. The goal is to be able to effectively collect, integrate and interpret data from a wide range of sources, including internal systems, external threat intelligence feeds and industry benchmarks, in order to identify emerging risks and inform their adaptive response strategies. This data-driven approach to risk management requires significant investments in advanced analytics and data management technologies. Organizations may need to invest in sophisticated data integration platforms, deploy machine learning algorithms to detect anomalies and patterns, and establish robust data governance frameworks to ensure the accuracy, reliability and security of the information being used to drive decision-making.

The technical complexity of this task should not be underestimated. Integrating data from disparate systems, normalizing and enriching the data to enable meaningful analysis, and translating the insights into actionable risk mitigation strategies can be a significant challenge, particularly for organizations with legacy IT infrastructures or siloed data environments. Leveraging cloud-based data lakes, data warehouses and advanced analytics tools can help centralize and analyse data more effectively, enabling them to identify and respond to emerging threats in near real-time. Implementing strong data governance policies, data quality controls and data security measures can help ensure the integrity and confidentiality of the information being used to inform the adaptive risk strategy. Bringing together teams from across the organization, including IT, security, risk management and business operations, can help break down data silos and facilitate the sharing of critical information and insights. Integrating data from external threat intelligence sources, such as industry-specific information sharing initiatives or commercial threat intelligence services, can provide organizations with a more comprehensive and up-to-date understanding of the threat landscape.

Implementing an effective adaptive risk strategy often requires significant investments in new technologies, processes and personnel – resources that may be in short supply for many, particularly those operating with limited budgets and staffing. Deploying flexible security controls that can respond to changing conditions can be a resource-intensive undertaking. Organizations may need to invest in advanced analytics platforms, automation tools and specialized cybersecurity expertise. At the same time, they are often faced with a myriad of competing priorities, from maintaining core business operations and driving innovation to complying with regulatory requirements and meeting customer expectations. Balancing the need for adaptive risk strategies with these other pressing demands can be a delicate and challenging exercise. For many, the strategic allocation of scarce resources is easier said than done. Prioritizing investments in adaptive risk management over other critical initiatives can be a difficult decision, especially when the tangible benefits may not be immediately apparent or quantifiable.

Aligning with regulation and law

Organizations must also grapple with the complexities of aligning these practices with the requirements of industry regulations and data privacy laws. Adaptive risk management, with its emphasis on real-time monitoring, data-driven decision-making and flexible security controls, can introduce potential conflicts with established compliance frameworks. Organizations must ensure that their adaptive risk management practices not only enhance their security posture, but also maintain compliance with relevant regulations, such as data protection laws, industry-specific standards and cybersecurity guidelines. This balancing act can be particularly challenging, as the rapid pace of technological change and threats may outpace the ability of regulatory bodies to keep up. As a result, organizations may find themselves in a situation where the most effective adaptive risk strategies are not necessarily aligned with the letter of the law, creating a delicate and potentially risky situation.

Despite these challenges, the benefits of embracing an adaptive risk strategy far outweigh the potential drawbacks. Cultivating a culture of continuous improvement, leveraging emerging technologies and methodologies, and fostering collaborative relationships will enhance the ability to anticipate, detect and respond to threats, thus strengthening their overall security posture and resilience.

Information is power

Adopting a data-driven approach that leverages advanced analytics and threat intelligence is one of the most impactful forms of establishing an effective risk management strategy. At the core of this data-driven approach is the recognition that information is power when it comes to risk management. Continuously collecting, analysing and acting on relevant data will yield a deeper understanding of the risks they face and develop more effective strategies for mitigating those risks.

Identifying patterns and detecting anomalies

A key benefit of this approach to risk management is the ability to identify patterns and detect anomalies that may signal emerging threats. Through the use of advanced analytics and machine learning algorithms, vast amounts of data, from internal systems and external sources, can be quickly correlated to identify trends and patterns that may not be immediately apparent to the human eye. For example, a global supply chain organization may use data analytics to monitor a range of factors, such as supplier performance, transportation delays and geopolitical events, in order to identify potential disruptions before they occur. Should anything look out of place, it can quickly adapt its supply chain strategies to mitigate the impact of these disruptions and ensure the continued flow of goods and services to its customers. Similarly, in the realm of cybersecurity, organizations can leverage data analytics and threat intelligence to detect and respond to cyber threats more effectively by analysing network traffic, user behaviour and other security-related data. Suspicious activity detected early on can result in taking proactive measures to prevent data breaches and other cyber-attacks which is why advanced statistical models and machine learning algorithms are such powerful tools for risk management.

Enabling pattern and anomaly detection is the ability to integrate and synthesize data from a variety of sources. Modern datasets are vast and ever-expanding, from internal systems and processes to external sources such as social media, news reports and industry databases. To effectively leverage this data for risk management, comprehensive data integration and data management strategies are needed. Components such as data lakes, data warehouses and other data management technologies to consolidate and organize data from disparate sources, as well as the implementation of data governance policies to ensure the quality, security and accessibility of this data, are needed. Integrating and synthesizing data from multiple sources will result in a comprehensive understanding of the risks, and inform the development of more effective strategies for mitigating risks.

Continuous monitoring

Hand in hand with predictive analytics is the ability to continuously monitor changing conditions to quickly adjust risk management strategies. This requires a flexible and agile approach to data collection and analysis, as well as a willingness to experiment with new tools and techniques. One way to achieve this level of agility is through the use of real-time data dashboards and visualization tools. These tools allow quick and easy access to interpret the data needed to make informed decisions and respond to changing conditions in a timely manner. However, these types of tools and skills may not be feasible in-house. External experts and service providers provide specialized expertise and tools to support data-driven risk management efforts, which may be more appropriate for an organization just starting this pursuit. These experts may be from cybersecurity firms that enhance an organization's threat detection and response capabilities, or data analytics consultants that develop sophisticated predictive models and forecasting tools.

Continuous improvement and adaptation

The effective use of data and analytics for risk management is not a one-time event, but rather an ongoing process that requires continuous improvement and adaptation. New sources of data, more sophisticated models, new tools and technology are always emerging and need to be assessed in context of supporting the risk management process. As always, regularly review and assess effectiveness of these strategies and make needful adjustments to remain relevant and effective. The effective use of data and analytics is essential for organizations that are looking to develop and implement effective risk management strategies. The successful implementation of a data-driven approach requires a holistic and cross-functional effort, involving the participation and collaboration of stakeholders from across the organization. It also requires a willingness to continuously adapt and evolve, as the business environment becomes increasingly complex and unpredictable. A data-driven approach to risk management will position an organization for long-term success and resilience, and can better navigate the challenges and uncertainties that lie ahead.

KEY TAKEAWAYS

- Effective risk management can only be realized after risks have been assessed.
- Even when risk management is 'effective', it will never replace a strong incident response function.
- The most well-intentioned risk strategies are worthless if they do not account for the unknown.
- Risk must be quantified in order to be considered 'effective' as it must be measured against something.

8

Human factors in security

When building a strong cybersecurity culture, it is important to remember that technology alone is not enough. The human element plays a pivotal role in the overall security posture of any enterprise, and understanding the human-centric security challenges is the first step towards cultivating a security-conscious workforce.

An organization can invest heavily in state-of-the-art cybersecurity solutions, including advanced firewalls, intrusion detection systems and encryption protocols, however despite these technological safeguards, they may still experience security breaches and data leaks. The root cause is often traced back to employee behaviour and decision-making. Employees, regardless of their technical expertise, are often the weakest link in the security chain. They may inadvertently fall victim to social engineering tactics, click on malicious links or fail to follow established security protocols. This is particularly problematic in an era where cyber threats are becoming increasingly sophisticated and targeted. Others may neglect to follow established security protocols, such as using strong passwords or reporting suspicious activities. Human tendency towards complacency and resistance to change can also hinder the implementation of effective security measures – employees may become complacent about security practices over time, or they may resist the adoption of new security technologies and processes, perceiving them as inconvenient or disruptive to their daily workflows.

Additionally, the diverse nature of the modern workforce, with remote and hybrid work arrangements, can introduce additional security challenges. Employees working from home or on the go may be more susceptible to security risks, such as unsecured Wi-Fi networks or the use of personal devices for work-related tasks. Driven by a complex interplay of cognitive biases, heuristics and competing priorities, they can inadvertently expose their employers to a wide range of cyber threats, undermining even the most robust technological defences, leaving the organization exposed to significant risks.

However, while humans are 'often the weakest link in the security chain', they are also any organization's strongest asset given the right education and opportunity. A holistic approach to security awareness and up-skilling which combines technical solutions with a strong focus on employee engagement helps the tools and the people who use the tools work together to safeguard the assets of the organization.

Consider this all-too-familiar scenario involving a mid-sized company's production manager. They were going about their day when an urgent email from the CEO landed in their inbox. The message requested an immediate wire transfer of a significant sum of money to a foreign bank account, citing a time-sensitive business opportunity that required prompt action. Recognizing the CEO's email signature and the tone of the message, they felt a sense of pressure to comply quickly. Eager to demonstrate their responsiveness and support for the company's leadership, they hastily reviewed the details and proceeded to authorize the wire transfer without taking the time to independently verify the legitimacy of the request.

What they didn't know was that the email was the product of a sophisticated phishing attack orchestrated by a group of cybercriminals. These attackers had meticulously studied the company's organizational structure, the CEO's communication style and the typical procedures for approving financial transactions. Armed with this contextual information, the attackers were able to craft an email that appeared to be authentic, complete with the appropriate branding, language and sense of urgency. By the time the manager realized the transfer was part of a scam, the funds had already been siphoned out of the company's accounts and were likely beyond recovery.

In another case, the organization's IT administrator was working remotely and decided to connect to the corporate network using a public Wi-Fi hotspot at a local coffee shop. Despite the company's strict policies prohibiting the use of unsecured public Wi-Fi networks, they prioritized the convenience of being able to access the corporate resources they needed to get their work done. As the IT administrator logged into the coffee shop's public Wi-Fi network and connected to the company's virtual private network (VPN), they were unaware that they had just exposed their login credentials and sensitive corporate data to a hacker lurking on the same network.

Cybercriminals are well-aware of the risks posed by public Wi-Fi hotspots, which often lack the security measures found in private, enterprise-grade networks. An attacker can position themselves on the same network and employ a variety of techniques to intercept and steal the data transmitted by unsuspecting users. One common tactic is known as a 'man-in-the-middle' attack, where the hacker inserts themselves between the user and the intended destination, intercepting all communication. They may also set up a rogue access point that mimics the legitimate public Wi-Fi, tricking users into connecting to the attacker's network instead. Once connected, the hacker can use specialized tools to monitor and capture the user's login credentials, email messages, documents and other sensitive information as it flows through the network. This stolen data can then be used for further malicious activities, such as gaining unauthorized access to the company's systems, initiating fraudulent transactions or launching targeted phishing campaigns against other employees.

Even outside the confines of a well-defined corporate security policy, both of the dangers illustrated above are relatively common knowledge these days, as these types of attacks are among the most frequent, so we end up hearing about them in our daily lives. If you've ever checked your email's spam folder, you will likely find plenty of phishing attempts, albeit very *un*sophisticated. Most of us will laugh them off considering how lazy the messaging is, but it begs the question: why are criminals still sending these low-effort phishing attempts? The answer is simple: they work.

To address and understand the human factor in cybersecurity, we must investigate the psychological and cognitive processes that influence employee decision-making. Behavioural science research has identified several key factors that contribute to security-related mistakes, such as cognitive biases, mental shortcuts, lack of awareness and conflicting priorities. Employees, like all human beings, are susceptible to various cognitive biases that can lead to poor security decisions. For example, the 'authority bias' may cause them to blindly trust requests from individuals perceived as being in a position of power, such as the CEO in the first example. Also at play is the 'optimism bias' that can lead employees to underestimate the likelihood of a security breach, making them less vigilant about following security protocols. Employees also often rely on mental shortcuts, or heuristics, to make quick decisions in the face of time pressure or information overload. While these heuristics can be useful in certain situations, they can also lead to security-related errors, such as failing to verify the legitimacy of a request or overlooking potential red flags.

Many employees simply lack a comprehensive understanding of cybersecurity threats and best practices. Without proper training and education, they may not recognize the signs of a phishing attack, the importance of using strong passwords, or the risks associated with using unsecured public Wi-Fi networks. This is why it is so important to have a comprehensive security awareness training. Also, employees are often juggling multiple tasks and responsibilities, and security may not always be their top priority. In the heat of the moment, they may prioritize productivity or convenience over security, leading to risky behaviours that expose the organization to potential threats, just like the IT administrator did in the second example above.

Cognitive biases

Central to the human factor in cybersecurity lies a complex web of cognitive biases – unconscious mental shortcuts and tendencies that can lead employees to make poor security decisions. These biases, deeply ingrained in the human psyche, can undermine even the most robust technological defences, exposing organizations to a wide range of cyber threats.

Authority bias

One of the most prevalent cognitive biases in the context of cyber-security is the 'authority bias'. This bias causes individuals to place a disproportionate amount of trust in the directives and requests of those perceived to be in positions of power or authority, such as executives or IT administrators.

Authority bias is a well-documented cognitive bias that has significant implications for decision-making, problem-solving and the acceptance of new ideas or information. At its core, authority bias refers to the tendency of individuals to place a higher value on the opinions, judgements and directives of those in positions of authority or perceived expertise, even when those opinions may be flawed or biased. This bias is rooted in our innate human tendency to defer to those we perceive as knowledgeable, experienced or holding a position of power. From a young age, we are socialized to respect and obey the instructions of authority figures, such as parents, teachers and other respected professionals. This conditioning will inevitably carry over into adulthood, where we continue to place a disproportionate amount of trust in the opinions and decisions of those we view as authoritative.

One of the key characteristics of authority bias is the lack of critical thinking that often accompanies it. When faced with information or recommendations from an individual or institution that is perceived as authoritative, people may be less inclined to scrutinize the validity or accuracy of the information. Instead, they may simply accept it at face value, assuming that the authority figure's expertise and position of power are sufficient justification for the information's credibility. This overconfidence in the competence and infallibility of authority figures can lead to a number of problematic outcomes. In the earlier example of the phishing attack, the production manager's tendency to blindly trust the email from the CEO, without verifying its legitimacy, was a direct result of the authority bias.

Optimism bias

Another significant cognitive bias is the 'optimism bias', which leads employees to underestimate the likelihood and severity of security breaches. Driven by a false sense of confidence, they may become complacent about following security protocols, believing that 'it won't happen to me'. This bias can be particularly dangerous in the context of cybersecurity, as it can lull employees into a false sense of security and make them less vigilant about potential threats.

Optimism bias has significant implications for decision-making, risk assessment and overall personal and professional well-being. Fundamentally, optimism bias refers to the tendency of individuals to overestimate the likelihood of positive events occurring and underestimate the likelihood of negative events. This bias is particularly evident in the case of the IT administrator who prioritized convenience over security protocols. Like many individuals, they were susceptible to the allure of optimism bias. As they worked remotely, they were faced with the decision of how to connect to the corporate network. Despite their organization's strict policies prohibiting the use of unsecured public Wi-Fi networks, they chose to prioritize the convenience of being able to access the necessary corporate resources. In their mind, the likelihood of something going wrong was low, and the benefits of being able to work efficiently outweighed the potential risks.

This overconfidence in their ability to avoid negative outcomes is a hallmark of optimism bias. They likely believed that they were more capable than the average person of avoiding the pitfalls of using a public Wi-Fi network given their knowledge, or that the chances of a hacker being present and intercepting their login credentials were slim. Unfortunately, this optimistic outlook led them to make a decision that exposed their company's sensitive data to potential compromise. The implications of these actions can be far-reaching. As an IT administrator, they were entrusted with the responsibility of safeguarding the organization's digital assets and ensuring the security of its network. Disregarding established security protocols can jeopardize a user's access to the corporate resources but also potentially put the entire organization at risk.

From a broader perspective, individuals may underestimate the constant evolution of cybersecurity threats, making it more difficult to implement effective mitigation strategies.

To address the negative effects of optimism bias, it is essential to cultivate a more balanced and realistic perspective on the world around us. In the IT administrator's case, this could have involved actively seeking out information about the risks associated with using public Wi-Fi networks, engaging in critical self-reflection, and seeking the input of their colleagues or cybersecurity experts. It is important to note that optimism bias is not inherently negative; in fact, a certain degree of optimism can be beneficial for mental health, motivation and overall well-being. The key is to strike a balance between maintaining a positive outlook and acknowledging the realities of the world around us.

Confirmation bias

Confirmation bias is yet another cognitive bias at play that can have significant implications for effective cybersecurity practices. This bias causes individuals to seek out and interpret information in a way that confirms their existing beliefs or preconceptions, while ignoring or dismissing evidence that contradicts them. In a security context, this bias can lead employees to overlook or rationalize potential red flags, ultimately jeopardizing digital assets and overall security posture. Confirmation bias is related to our natural tendency as humans to seek information that aligns with our existing beliefs and to avoid or discount information that challenges those beliefs. This cognitive shortcut can be a useful heuristic in many situations, as it allows us to quickly process and make sense of the vast amount of information we encounter daily. However, in the context of cybersecurity, this bias can have serious consequences.

Consider the case of an employee who has been tasked with reviewing incoming emails for potential phishing attempts. They have been trained to identify suspicious characteristics, such as unusual sender email addresses, generic greetings or requests for sensitive information. However, due to confirmation bias, they may be inclined to focus on the aspects of an email that align with their preconceptions of what a legitimate message should look like, while overlooking or rationalizing the red flags. For example, if they receive an email that appears to be from a trusted colleague, they may be more likely to assume the message is legitimate, even if it contains subtle indicators of a phishing attempt, such as a slightly altered email address or an unusual request for login credentials. Their confirmation bias leads them to seek out and interpret the information in a way that confirms their belief that the email is from a trusted source, rather than objectively evaluating the potential risks.

This selective attention and biased interpretation of information can have severe consequences for an organization's cybersecurity posture. Failing to identify and report potential phishing attempts could result in the employee, and other employees like them, inadvertently enabling cybercriminals to gain access to sensitive data, compromise the organization's systems or even launch more sophisticated attacks.

That said, the impact of confirmation bias is not limited to individual employees; it can also manifest at the organizational level, influencing the way cybersecurity policies and procedures are developed and implemented. For instance, a security team may be inclined to focus on threats that align with their existing perceptions of risk, while overlooking emerging or evolving cyber threats that do not fit their preconceived notions.

Confirmation bias can also lead to a reluctance to adopt new security technologies or strategies, as decision-makers may be more inclined to stick with familiar approaches, even if they are less effective or efficient. The desire to confirm the validity of their existing security measures can blind them to the potential benefits of innovative solutions. The impact of confirmation bias can also be seen in the way cybersecurity policies and strategies are developed and implemented. Imagine a scenario where a security team is tasked with evaluating the effectiveness of the organization's existing access control measures. Due to confirmation bias, the team may be inclined to focus on the aspects of the current system that appear to be working well, while dismissing or downplaying the potential weaknesses or vulnerabilities. This bias can lead the security team to resist or delay the adoption of new access control technologies or approaches, even if they may be more effective in addressing the organization's security needs. The desire to confirm the validity of the existing system can blind the team to the potential benefits of innovative solutions, ultimately leaving the organization vulnerable to emerging threats.

Framing effect

In cybersecurity, decision-makers are constantly faced with a myriad of challenges that require careful consideration and sound judgement. A cognitive bias that can significantly influence these decisions is the 'framing effect'. This bias occurs when the way information is presented, or 'framed', affects an individual's perception and response to that information.

The framing effect is the human tendency to make decisions based on the way a problem or choice is presented, rather than solely on the objective merits of the options. On a positive note, this cognitive shortcut allows us to quickly process and respond to the vast amount of information we encounter daily. However, in the context of cybersecurity, the framing effect can have serious implications for the effectiveness of security practices and the overall resilience of an organization.

Consider the example of a security training programme designed to educate employees on the importance of strong password practices. If the programme emphasizes the negative consequences of a security breach, such as the potential loss of sensitive data or the reputational damage to the organization, employees may be more likely to adopt more cautious behaviours, such as using longer and more complex passwords. Conversely, if the training focuses on the benefits of secure practices, such as the peace of mind that comes with knowing their accounts are well-protected or the potential cost savings associated with avoiding a data breach, employees may be more motivated to comply with the organization's password policies.

The framing effect – as with authority, optimism and confirmation biases – can also influence how cybersecurity policies and strategies are developed and communicated. If a security team that is tasked with implementing a new access control system frames the initiative as a necessary measure to mitigate the growing threat of unauthorized access, employees may be more likely to view the new system as a burdensome security requirement. However, if the team frames the initiative as an opportunity to streamline and enhance the organization's access management capabilities, employees may be more receptive to the changes and more willing to adapt to the new system. The way the information is presented can significantly impact the employees' perceptions and their subsequent buy-in and compliance with the new security measures.

The cybersecurity community as a whole can play a crucial role in addressing the impact of the framing effect. Industry associations, research institutions and policymakers can collaborate to develop and disseminate best practices, case studies and educational resources that highlight the importance of cognitive bias awareness and mitigation in the context of cybersecurity. For example, industry associations could organize workshops or conferences that bring together security professionals, behavioural scientists and communication experts to explore the intersection of cognitive biases and effective security practices. These collaborative efforts can help foster a deeper understanding of the framing effect and its implications, ultimately leading to more informed and effective cybersecurity decision-making across the industry.

Heuristics

In the realm of cybersecurity, the human factor plays a crucial role in determining the overall security posture of an organization. Beyond the cognitive biases that can influence decision-making, the use of heuristics by employees can significantly impact the effectiveness of security measures. Some of these heuristics were discussed previously in relation to executives in Chapter 6.

Heuristics are cognitive strategies that individuals employ to simplify complex decision-making processes. These mental shortcuts allow people to make quick judgements and solve problems efficiently, often without the need for extensive analysis or deliberation. While heuristics can be beneficial in many situations, they can also lead to security-related errors and vulnerabilities when applied in the context of cybersecurity.

One of the primary ways in which heuristics can undermine cybersecurity is through the tendency to rely on past experiences or intuitions rather than carefully evaluating the current situation. Employees may, for instance, assume that a particular email or website is safe based on their previous interactions, without thoroughly verifying the authenticity of the source. This can lead to the inadvertent exposure of sensitive information or the installation of malware on corporate systems. The desire for convenience and efficiency can also influence the way employees approach security-related tasks. Individuals may choose to bypass security protocols or use unsecured communication channels to save time, prioritizing productivity over the potential security risks. This can create vulnerabilities that cybercriminals can exploit, compromising the organization's overall security posture.

Another challenge posed by heuristics in cybersecurity is the tendency to underestimate the likelihood of rare or unexpected events. Employees may dismiss the possibility of a sophisticated cyber-attack or a novel threat, relying on their past experiences or intuitions rather than considering the evolving nature of the threat landscape. This can result in a false sense of security and a failure to implement appropriate preventive measures.

Availability heuristic

The 'availability heuristic' causes individuals to judge the likelihood of an event based on the ease with which they can recall similar occurrences, which can lead to a distorted perception of risk and a false sense of security within an organization. The availability heuristic can manifest in various ways. Employees may, for instance, underestimate the risk of a security breach if they have not personally experienced one or if they do not have a clear understanding of the frequency and severity of such incidents within their organization. This can be particularly problematic in industries or organizations that have not yet been the target of a major cyber-attack, as the lack of salient examples can lead to a complacent attitude towards security measures.

The availability heuristic can also influence the way employees perceive the effectiveness of existing security protocols. If an employee has not encountered any significant security breaches or incidents in the past, they may be inclined to believe that the current security measures are sufficient, even if they are not keeping pace with the evolving threat landscape. This can result in a reluctance to invest in new security technologies or to implement more robust security practices, ultimately leaving the organization vulnerable to emerging threats. The availability heuristic can also shape the way employees respond to security-related warnings or alerts. If an employee has not experienced a specific type of cyber threat, they may be less likely to take the necessary precautions or to report suspicious activity, assuming that the risk is low or that the warning is not relevant to their particular situation. This can create blind spots within the organization, allowing potential threats to go undetected and increasing the likelihood of a successful cyber-attack.

The availability heuristic can also influence the way employees prioritize security-related tasks and responsibilities. If an employee has not been directly impacted by a security breach, they may be more inclined to focus on other, more immediate priorities, relegating cybersecurity to a lower position on their list of concerns. This can lead to a lack of attention and resources being dedicated to the implementation and maintenance of effective security measures, ultimately compromising overall security posture.

The impact of the availability heuristic on cybersecurity can be particularly pronounced in organizations with a high turnover rate or a decentralized workforce. In such environments, the lack of institutional memory and the constant influx of new employees can make it challenging to maintain a consistent understanding of the organization's security history and threat landscape. This can lead to a fragmented approach to cybersecurity, with individual employees making decisions based on their own limited experiences rather than a comprehensive understanding of the organization's security needs and vulnerabilities. It can also influence the way organizations respond to security incidents. If a particular type of cyber-attack has not occurred in the recent past, the response may be less coordinated and effective, as employees may not have a clear mental model of the necessary steps to mitigate the threat. This can result in delayed or ineffective responses, allowing the attack to cause more significant damage and disruption to operations.

Representativeness heuristic

Another heuristic with implications for organizational cybersecurity is the 'representativeness heuristic'. The representativeness heuristic leads individuals to make judgements based on how closely an event or object resembles their mental prototypes or stereotypes, and may result in a distorted perception of risk and a failure to recognize emerging threats. It can cause employees to overlook potential threats that do not fit their preconceived notions of what a 'typical' cyber-attack looks like. This can lead to missed opportunities for detection and prevention, as security measures may be focused on addressing threats that are perceived as more representative or familiar, while neglecting less conventional or novel attack vectors.

For example, an employee may be more likely to recognize and respond to a phishing email that closely resembles the classic 'Nigerian prince' scam, as it aligns with their mental prototype of a fraudulent message. However, they may be less likely to identify a more sophisticated phishing attempt that uses a legitimate-looking email address or mimics the branding of a trusted organization, as it does not fit their mental model of a typical phishing attack. Similarly, employees may be more inclined to prioritize the protection of assets or systems that they perceive as being at a higher risk of cyber-attacks, based on their mental representations of what a 'high value' target looks like. This can result in a disproportionate allocation of security resources, leaving other areas of the organization vulnerable to threats that do not align with the employees' preconceived notions.

The representativeness heuristic can also influence the way employees respond to security alerts or warnings. If an employee does not perceive a particular threat as being representative of the types of attacks they have encountered or been trained to address, they may be less likely to take the necessary action to mitigate the risk. This can lead to a delayed or ineffective response, allowing the threat to potentially escalate and cause more significant damage. Cybersecurity training and awareness programmes may also fall victim to the representativeness heuristic, especially if the training materials or simulations focus primarily on threats that are perceived as being more representative or familiar. Employees may develop a limited understanding of the broader threat landscape, leaving them ill-equipped to recognize and respond to less conventional or emerging cyber-attacks.

The impact of the representativeness heuristic can be particularly pronounced in organizations that have experienced specific types of cyber-attacks in the past. In such cases, employees may be more attuned to the detection and prevention of threats that resemble the previous incidents, while overlooking the potential for new and different types of attacks. This can create a false sense of security and a failure to adapt to the evolving threat landscape. Going further, it can also influence the way security investments are prioritized and the way that new strategies are developed. If decision-makers within the organization have a limited understanding of the broader threat landscape or a biased perception of the most pressing security risks, they may allocate resources and focus their efforts on addressing threats that are perceived as more representative, rather than taking a more comprehensive and proactive approach to cybersecurity.

Therefore, the representativeness heuristic can have significant implications for the cybersecurity of an organization. By causing employees to overlook potential threats that do not fit their mental prototypes or stereotypes, this bias can lead to missed opportunities for detection and prevention, ultimately leaving the organization vulnerable to a wide range of cyber-attacks.

Anchoring heuristic

The 'anchoring heuristic' causes individuals to rely heavily on the first piece of information they receive, even if that information is incomplete or inaccurate, and can lead to poor decision-making in the context of security-related threats.

Considering cybersecurity, the anchoring heuristic can manifest in various ways. For instance, during a phishing attack, employees may be more likely to trust the initial email request, without thoroughly verifying its legitimacy. The first piece of information they receive, which may be a seemingly legitimate email from a trusted source, can become the anchor that shapes their subsequent judgements and actions, even if further investigation reveals the message to be fraudulent. This shortcut can be particularly problematic in situations where employees are presented with time-sensitive or high-stakes security-related information. Under pressure, they may be more inclined to rely on the initial details they receive, rather than taking the time to gather additional information and critically evaluate the situation. This can lead to hasty decisions that expose the organization to unnecessary risks, such as the inadvertent disclosure of sensitive data or the installation of malware on corporate systems.

Employees' ability to perceive and respond to security alerts or warnings are influenced by the anchoring heuristic. If the first notification they receive about a potential threat downplays the severity or likelihood of the risk, employees may be less inclined to take the necessary precautions, even if subsequent information suggests a more serious situation. This can result in a delayed or ineffective response, allowing the threat to escalate and potentially cause significant damage.

Just like other heuristics, training and awareness are impacted also. If the initial information or guidance provided to employees focuses on a specific type of threat or security practice, it can become the anchor that shapes their understanding and expectations, even if the threat landscape evolves or more effective security measures become available. This can lead to a lack of adaptability and a failure to keep pace with the changing cybersecurity landscape.

Policies and decisions are also subject to anchoring: if the initial risk assessment or security strategy is based on incomplete or inaccurate information, it can become the anchor that guides subsequent decisions, even if new evidence or insights emerge that suggest a different course of action. This can result in the perpetuation of suboptimal security practices and the misallocation of resources, ultimately compromising the organization's overall security posture.

The interplay of cognitive biases and heuristics

The human factor in cybersecurity is a complex and multifaceted challenge that must be navigated with great care. The interplay between cognitive biases and heuristics further exacerbates the programme, which can lead to a profound impact on the effectiveness of an organization's security measures. While technological advancements have undoubtedly enhanced our ability to protect against cyber threats, the inherent cognitive biases and heuristics that govern human decision-making can often undermine even the most robust security protocols. When these biases and heuristics are experienced in combination, the challenge of maintaining effective cybersecurity becomes even more daunting.

One of the most prominent examples of this interplay is the authority bias and the optimism bias. The authority bias can lead individuals to blindly trust the directives of those in positions of power, even if those directives are flawed or ill-advised. This can result in the adoption of security measures that are not optimized for the organization's specific needs, or the failure to question the validity of security protocols that may be outdated or ineffective.

Consider the case of a large financial institution that has recently experienced a series of successful phishing attacks targeting its employees. In response, the executive team, led by the Chief Information Security Officer (CISO), mandates the implementation of a new security protocol that requires all employees to undergo extensive cybersecurity training and to use a complex password system that must be changed every 30 days. At the same time, the optimism bias may lead these same employees to believe that the new security measures will be highly effective in preventing future phishing attacks, despite the fact that research has shown that frequent password changes and extensive training can actually decrease employee compliance and increase the risk of security breaches.[1] For example, frequent password changes can lead to employees reusing or slightly modifying their previous passwords, making them easier to guess. Additionally, the cognitive burden of remembering multiple complex passwords that must be changed regularly can cause employees to engage in insecure password management practices, such as writing down passwords or storing them in easily accessible locations. This increases the risk of passwords being compromised and exploited by attackers through phishing or other social engineering tactics. Additionally, the inconvenience of constantly changing passwords may reduce employee compliance with the security protocol, undermining its overall effectiveness. However, due to the authority bias, many employees within the organization are inclined to trust the directives of the CISO and the executive team. Employees may feel that questioning the CISO's decisions would be a sign of insubordination or a lack of trust in leadership.

The combination of the authority bias and the optimism bias can create a dangerous situation where employees blindly accept the CISO's directives, even if those directives are not grounded in evidence-based best practices. This can result in the adoption of security protocols that are not appropriate for the needs of the organization, leaving the institution vulnerable to cyber threats.

For example, the complex password system may be so burdensome that employees resort to writing down their passwords or using easily guessable ones, undermining the very security measures that the CISO has implemented. Similarly, the extensive cybersecurity training may be perceived as a waste of time by employees who already believe that the organization's security measures are sufficient, leading to a lack of engagement and a failure to adopt the recommended security practices. In this way, the interplay between the authority bias and the optimism bias can create a false sense of security within the organization, ultimately compromising the effectiveness of its cybersecurity efforts.

Compounding the issue is the optimism bias, which can cause individuals to underestimate the likelihood of a cyber-attack occurring, or to believe that their organization is somehow immune to such threats; 'it won't happen to *me*'. This false sense of security can lead to a lax approach to cybersecurity, with employees failing to adhere to best practices or to report suspicious activities. An employee who is influenced by the authority bias may be reluctant to question the security measures implemented by their superiors, even if those measures are undermined by the optimism bias.

Another example of the interplay between cognitive biases and heuristics in cybersecurity is the confirmation bias and the framing effect. The confirmation bias can cause individuals to seek out and interpret information in a way that aligns with their preexisting beliefs, rather than objectively evaluating the available evidence. This bias can result in the dismissal of warning signs or the failure to consider alternative security solutions that may be more effective. The framing effect, on the other hand, can influence the way in which individuals perceive and respond to cybersecurity risks. If a security breach is framed as a technical failure rather than a human error, employees may be less inclined to take personal responsibility for their actions and to adopt more vigilant security practices. When these two biases work in tandem, the impact on cybersecurity can be significant. An employee who is influenced by the confirmation bias may be unwilling to consider alternative perspectives or to acknowledge the limitations of the organization's current security protocols. At the same time, the framing effect may reinforce the belief that cybersecurity is primarily a technical challenge, rather than one that requires a holistic approach that addresses both technological and human factors.

The availability heuristic and the representativeness heuristic can also contribute to the complexity of the human factor in cybersecurity. The availability heuristic can lead individuals to judge the likelihood of an event based on how easily it comes to mind, while the representativeness heuristic can cause them to judge the likelihood of an event based on how closely it resembles a typical or stereotypical scenario. These heuristics can result in the misidentification of cyber threats. For example, an employee may fail to recognize a phishing attempt because it does not match their preconceived notion of what a cyber-attack should look like, or they may overestimate the likelihood of a particular type of attack because it has received significant media attention.

When these heuristics are combined with other cognitive biases, the impact on cybersecurity can be even more pronounced. An employee who is influenced by the availability heuristic may be more likely to focus on high-profile cyber-attacks, while overlooking less publicized threats that may be just as dangerous. At the same time, the representativeness heuristic may lead them to dismiss certain types of cyber threats as being 'unlikely' or 'not relevant' to their organization, even if the evidence suggests otherwise.

Finally, the anchoring heuristic can also contribute to the complexity of the human factor in cybersecurity. This heuristic refers to the tendency to rely heavily on the first piece of information encountered when making decisions. In the context of cybersecurity, this can lead to a situation where an organization's security protocols are based on outdated or incomplete information, with employees becoming anchored to those protocols even as the threat landscape evolves.

As an example, consider an organization that has historically focused its cybersecurity efforts on protecting against traditional malware and phishing attacks. When they first implemented their security measures, these threats may have been the most prevalent and well-known. However, as the cybersecurity landscape has shifted, new and more sophisticated threats have emerged, such as ransomware, advanced persistent threats and supply chain attacks. Due to the anchoring heuristic, employees may be reluctant to deviate from the security protocols that they have become accustomed to, even if those protocols are no longer adequate for addressing the current threat landscape. They may continue to focus their efforts on defending against the types of attacks that were prevalent in the past, rather than adapting their security measures to address the evolving threats. This can be particularly problematic when the security protocols are based on outdated or incomplete information, such as outdated threat intelligence or security best practices that have since been superseded. Employees who are anchored to these protocols may be resistant to adopting new security measures, even if they are more effective at mitigating the current threats.

New challenges in the modern workplace

The Covid-19 pandemic ushered in a seismic shift in the modern workplace, accelerating the transition towards remote and hybrid work arrangements. While this shift has brought about a host of quality-of-life benefits for employees, it has also introduced a new set of cybersecurity challenges that organizations must grapple with. Positively, the distributed workforce model has provided employees with unprecedented flexibility and autonomy. No longer tethered to a physical office, workers can now enjoy greater work–life balance, with the ability to integrate their professional and personal responsibilities more seamlessly. This enhanced flexibility has been a boon for employee morale and well-being, with studies showing that remote workers often report higher levels of job satisfaction and productivity.[2] The distributed nature of the workforce has also enabled organizations to tap into a wider talent pool, unencumbered by geographic constraints. Employees can now work from the comfort of their own homes, or even from remote locations around the world, allowing companies to access a more diverse and skilled labour force. This has been particularly beneficial for organizations operating in niche or specialized industries, where the available talent may be scarce in any one particular region.

However, the very factors that make the distributed workforce model so appealing from an employee and organizational perspective also introduce significant cybersecurity risks. The expansion of the attack surface is perhaps the most pressing concern, as employees now access sensitive data and systems from a variety of locations and devices, many of which may lack the robust security controls found in a traditional office environment. Without the physical security of an on-site network, remote workers become prime targets for cyber-criminals seeking to exploit vulnerabilities in home Wi-Fi networks, personal devices and cloud-based applications. This increased risk of data breaches is particularly problematic for industries that handle highly sensitive information, such as healthcare, finance and government, where the consequences of a successful attack can be devastating. The distributed nature of the workforce also makes it more challenging for IT teams to maintain visibility and control over the digital ecosystem. With employees scattered across different locations, it becomes increasingly difficult to monitor and secure all the endpoints, applications and cloud services in use. This lack of centralized oversight can lead to the proliferation of shadow IT, where employees use unauthorized software and services to perform their work, further complicating the security risks.

The shift towards a distributed workforce has also heightened the vulnerability to social engineering attacks, and the advancements in AI technology have only exacerbated this threat. Cybercriminals can now leverage AI-powered tools to craft highly personalized phishing emails and vishing (voice phishing) scripts that mimic the tone and writing style of legitimate communications. Furthermore, the development of voice synthesis and deepfake technologies has enabled attackers to create remarkably realistic-sounding impersonations of trusted figures, such as company executives or customer support representatives. This makes it increasingly difficult for remote workers, who are often isolated from their colleagues and IT support, to distinguish these malicious attempts from authentic correspondence. The scalability and adaptive learning capabilities of AI-powered phishing and vishing tools have also allowed cybercriminals to target a larger number of victims more efficiently, further compounding the security challenges faced by organizations with a distributed workforce.

IT and security teams are also feeling the additional strain as they must now manage a more complex and dispersed digital infrastructure. Maintaining the security and availability of critical systems and data across multiple locations and devices requires a significant investment of time, resources and expertise, which can be particularly challenging for small and medium-sized businesses. The proliferation of shadow IT, where employees use unauthorized software and services to perform their work, further aggravates the security risks. Without the visibility and control afforded by a centralized IT infrastructure, organizations may be unaware of the various applications and cloud services being used, leaving them vulnerable to data breaches, compliance violations and other security incidents.

As organizations continue to navigate the complexities of the distributed workforce, they must strike a delicate balance between embracing the non-security benefits such as employee well-being and addressing the cybersecurity risks. This will require a comprehensive and proactive approach to security, one that leverages advanced technologies, robust policies and ongoing employee training to mitigate the evolving threats posed by the distributed work environment.

Impacts of security incidents on employees

Security incidents can have far-reaching consequences that extend well beyond the immediate technical vulnerabilities or breaches. When a security incident occurs due to employee negligence or mistakes, it can set off a chain reaction that undermines the credibility of the organization's security efforts and erodes the trust of the very people who should be the first line of defence against cyber threats. The impact of a security breach on employee trust and morale can be devastating. Employees may feel a deep sense of guilt and shame, knowing that their actions or inactions have directly contributed to the vulnerability. This can lead to a reluctance to report future security incidents, as they fear being blamed or facing repercussions. The erosion of trust can also make employees less inclined to follow security protocols, share information or collaborate with the security team, further adding to the organization's existing security obligations.

The cascading effect of a security breach can be particularly damaging where security is a critical component of the business. In these environments, employees are expected to be vigilant, proactive and responsive to potential threats. When a breach occurs, it can shatter the confidence that employees have in the organization's ability to protect itself and its assets. This can lead to a general sense of unease and a loss of faith in the leadership's ability to effectively manage security risks. The impact on employee morale and productivity can be equally severe. The stress and anxiety associated with a security incident, coupled with the potential disruptions to business operations, can lead to decreased job satisfaction, increased absentee-ism and a general sense of disengagement among the workforce. In some cases, the fallout from a security breach can even result in legal and regulatory consequences, such as fines, lawsuits and reputational damage that can threaten the very survival of the company.

The ripple effect of a security incident can be particularly pronounced in organizations with a strong security culture, where employees are expected to be actively engaged in the security process. When a breach occurs in these environments, it can feel like a personal betrayal, as employees may have invested significant time and effort into building and maintaining the security posture. The loss of trust and the sense of failure can be deeply demoralizing, leading to a breakdown in communication, collaboration and overall morale. The impact of a security breach can extend beyond the organization itself, affecting the broader ecosystem of partners, suppliers and customers. When a breach occurs, it can erode the trust and confidence that these stakeholders have in the organization's ability to protect sensi-tive information and maintain the integrity of its operations. This can lead to a loss of business, strained relationships and long-term repu-tational damage that can be difficult to recover from. One of the key factors that can make the ripple effect of a security incident worse is the way in which the organization responds to the breach. If the organization fails to communicate effectively with its employees, or if it appears to be more concerned with damage control than with addressing the underlying issues, it can further undermine trust and morale. Employees may feel that the organization is more interested in protecting its own reputation than in addressing their concerns or providing them with the support they need to recover from the inci-dent. In addition, the way in which the organization handles the aftermath of a security breach can have a significant impact on its ability to retain and attract talent. Employees who feel that their organization has failed to protect them or to address their concerns may be more likely to seek employment elsewhere, leading to a loss of valuable expertise and institutional knowledge. This can further weaken the security posture and make the company more vulnerable to future attacks.

Another factor that can contribute to the ripple effect of a security incident is the overall approach to security. If the organization has a reactive, rather than proactive, approach to security, it may be more vulnerable to the cascading effects of a breach. Organizations that prioritize security as a strategic priority, and that invest in ongoing training and education for their employees, may be better equipped to mitigate the impact of a security incident and to maintain the trust and confidence of their workforce.

Finally, the nature of the security incident itself can also play a role in the ripple effect. Incidents that involve the theft or compromise of sensitive personal or financial information, for example, may have a more significant impact on employee trust and morale than incidents that are more technical in nature. Employees may feel that their personal information has been put at risk, and may be less willing to trust the organization's ability to protect them in the future.

Understanding the human factors that contribute to the impact of security breaches can help an organization to better prepare for and mitigate the potential consequences, ensuring that their security efforts remain effective and resilient in the face of evolving threats. Ultimately, the success of any security strategy will depend not only on its technical capabilities, but also on its ability to engage and empower its employees as active participants in the security process.

Accounting for human factors

Despite our awareness of the psychology that impacts decisions and the risks associated with a distributed workforce, the human factor remains a persistent challenge that continues to vex organizations of all sizes. Even with the advancements in technological solutions and the growing recognition of the importance of human behaviour in security, addressing this challenge remains a formidable task due to the inherent unpredictability and variability of human behaviour. Employees, who are often the first line of defence against cyber threats, can inadvertently undermine even the most sophisticated security systems and protocols. Whether it's falling victim to phishing scams, using weak passwords or simply failing to adhere to established security practices, the human factor introduces a level of uncertainty that cannot be easily eliminated.

The constant evolution of cyber threats further complicates the problem. As cybercriminals develop new and increasingly sophisticated attack vectors, employees must remain vigilant and adaptable, constantly updating their knowledge and skills to keep pace. This dynamic nature of the threat landscape makes it challenging to develop a one-size-fits-all approach to security training and awareness. The human factor in cybersecurity extends beyond individual employees; it also encompasses the broader organizational culture and leadership. If an organization's leadership fails to prioritize security, communicate its importance effectively and foster a security-conscious mindset among the workforce, the human factor will continue to undermine the overall security posture. A lack of a cohesive and consistent security culture can lead to a fragmented approach, where employees may view security measures as burdensome or unnecessary, rather than as a critical component of their daily responsibilities. This disconnect between the organization's security objectives and the employees' perceptions can create a breeding ground for security breaches and incidents. Between leadership and individual employees, the human factor also includes the decision-making processes and risk management strategies employed by security professionals and IT teams. Even the most knowledgeable and experienced security personnel can make misjudgements or overlook potential vulnerabilities, leading to costly security incidents.

The complexity of the human factor in cybersecurity is further compounded by the diverse range of employee backgrounds, skill levels and personal motivations. Individuals may have varying levels of security awareness, technological proficiency and risk tolerance, making it challenging to develop a one-size-fits-all approach to security training and awareness. In addition, the increasing prevalence of remote work and the blurring of personal and professional boundaries have introduced new layers of complexity to the human factor in cybersecurity. Employees working from home may be more susceptible to distractions, personal device usage and the potential for unauthorized access to sensitive information, further complicating the security landscape.

The rapid pace of technological change and increasing complexity of modern information systems contribute to the persistent challenge of the human factor. As new technologies and digital tools are introduced, employees must quickly adapt and learn to use them securely, often with limited training or guidance. This dynamic environment can lead to a sense of information overload, where employees struggle to keep up with the security protocols and best practices. The temptation to take shortcuts or bypass security measures in the name of efficiency can be strong, further undermining the organization's overall security posture.

By recognizing the inherent unpredictability and variability of human behaviour, organizations can begin to develop more effective and adaptive security strategies that account for the human factor. This may involve leveraging behavioural science insights, implementing gamification techniques, and fostering a security-centric mindset throughout the organization. However, the challenge of the human factor in cybersecurity is not one that can be easily solved. It requires a continuous and collaborative effort, with organizations, security professionals and employees working together to address the evolving threats and adapt to the changing landscape of human behaviour.

KEY TAKEAWAYS

- Humans will always be both the strongest and the weakest part of any security programme.

- Despite the best intentions and the most advanced prevention and defence techniques, humans still have biases that impact their decision-making which must be accounted for.

- Since Covid-19, working from home is more prevalent which makes user-security more complicated as the work environment is no longer homogenous.

- Biases, and human nature in general, are reasons enough to continuously bring security into as many conversations as possible around the workplace to normalize good practices.

Notes

1 Lorrie Cranor. Time to rethink mandatory password changes, Federal Trade Commission, 2 March 2016. www.ftc.gov/policy/advocacy-research/tech-at-ftc/2016/03/time-rethink-mandatory-password-changes (archived at https://perma.cc/S8GX-P8R5).

2 Mubashira Fathima and B. N. Suresh Kumar. The impact of remote work on employee productivity and satisfaction: analyze how remote work trends have affected various aspects of employee performance and well-being, *Educational Administration: Theory and Practice*, 2024, 30 (5), 1323–9.

9

Practical implementation: from theory to action

Much of the material that has been covered so far in this book has been anecdotal, theoretical and hopefully thought-provoking. It is now time to move beyond high-level security strategies and focus on practical, actionable steps to protect real assets. Developing a comprehensive security vision is an important first step, as true cybersecurity resilience comes from translating that vision into measurable, repeatable processes that can adapt to changing conditions. This requires security leaders to bridge the gap between vision and execution, leveraging the support and buy-in from executive leadership. The foundation for this process was laid in earlier sections, where we discussed the importance of transforming security mindsets, communicating security as an enabler, and incorporating security into strategic planning. With this cultural and organizational groundwork in place, security leaders can now focus on breaking down the security vision into specific, time-bound objectives with clear ownership and accountability.

Translating security vision into actionable steps

Actionable steps require actionable tasks with explicit, measurable outcomes as well as clear checkpoints along the way. Rather than broad, ambiguous goals, security teams should define measurable targets such as 'deploying advanced endpoint detection and response (EDR) tools across 100 per cent of endpoints within the next six months' or 'reducing the mean time to detect and respond to endpoint threats from 30 days to seven days within the next year'. By establishing these types of concrete, time-bound milestones, security leaders can then work backwards to identify the necessary steps, resources and checkpoints to achieve them.

Agile methodology (traditionally applied to software development) is a very useful tool for nearly any project, even one as grand as cultivating a security culture in an organization. In Agile methodology, large, complex projects are broken down into smaller, more manageable 'epics' and 'user stories' – each with clearly defined, measurable outcomes. Think of the tenets of the security vision as the overarching 'epics' – the big-picture goals that the organization is working towards. To make meaningful progress, this epic needs to be broken down into a backlog of specific, measurable 'user stories'. A user story is a concise description of a specific functionality or capability that a user needs, written from the user's perspective and with clear, measurable acceptance criteria. The acceptance criteria for a user story define the specific conditions that must be met in order for the story to be considered complete and successful, providing clear, objective standards for evaluating whether the user's needs have been adequately addressed.

For example, let's say a risk assessment has identified the organization's endpoints as a major vulnerability, with a high risk of data breaches stemming from advanced threats targeting unprotected or poorly managed devices. This risk assessment would then inform the security vision and the specific user stories needed to address it. The vision could be something as simple and vague as 'improve endpoint security', but it begs the question: what does 'improve' mean? What is the metric used to measure improvement? This is where Agile methodology can be a useful tool. If we take 'Improve endpoint security' as an epic, it could have user stories such as:

- 'As a security analyst, I need to be able to detect and respond to advanced endpoint threats within seven days, in order to minimize the impact of security incidents and protect sensitive data.'

- 'As an IT administrator, I require 100 per cent coverage of advanced EDR tools across all endpoints, to enhance our threat detection and response capabilities and reduce the risk of successful attacks.'
- 'As a business leader, I need to reduce the risk of endpoint-based data breaches by 50 per cent within the next 12 months, to protect our customers, maintain regulatory compliance and safeguard the organization's reputation.'

Breaking down the overarching security vision (epic) into actionable steps requires crafting well-structured user stories. A good user story should have several key attributes:

- **Stakeholder-focused**: Each user story should be written from the perspective of a specific stakeholder – whether that's a security analyst, IT administrator, business leader or end-user. This helps ensure the story addresses a real, tangible need rather than an abstract requirement.
- **Measurable outcomes**: The user story should have a clear, measurable outcome that can be objectively evaluated. Phrases like 'reduce by X per cent', 'increase to Y' or 'detect/respond within Z days' provide concrete targets to work towards.
- **Reasonable scope**: User stories should be narrow in scope, addressing a single, well-defined need. Overly broad or complex stories can be difficult to implement and track. Breaking down larger goals into multiple, manageable user stories is often more effective.
- **Business alignment**: The user story should clearly articulate how its successful completion will benefit the organization, whether that's improving security, enabling innovation, reducing risk or supporting broader business objectives.

Closely tied to the measurable outcome, these user stories should then have well-defined 'acceptance criteria' which define the specific conditions that must be met for the user story to be considered complete. These criteria act as guardrails, ensuring the deliverable focuses on achieving the intended functionality. This could include metrics like percentage of endpoints covered, mean time to detect/respond and reduction in breach incidents. Crafting user stories that embody these key characteristics will lead to a robust and actionable backlog that translates the high-level vision into tangible, measurable progress. This, in turn, helps build buy-in and support from executive stakeholders who can see the direct business value of the security initiatives.

Breaking down the security vision in this way lets security leaders work with their teams to prioritize the most critical user stories, establish sprint-based delivery cycles, and track progress through Kanban boards – workflow management systems that use cards to represent work items and columns to depict the different stages of the work process – or other Agile project management tools. This provides a structured, iterative approach to security implementation, with clear milestones and opportunities for feedback and course correction along the way. Ultimately, the key is to avoid lofty, open-ended security goals, and instead focus on translating the vision into a series of concrete, time-bound objectives with clear ownership and accountability. Importantly, this process should involve close collaboration between security, IT and business stakeholders. As it has been discussed, security is no longer just an IT concern – it must be integrated into the fabric of the organization. Aligning security objectives with broader business goals and priorities will confirm that the implementation roadmap supports strategic growth and innovation.

Aligning security measures with strategic objectives

Engaging a diverse range of business stakeholders in the security decision-making process is crucial to ensuring that security measures align with the company's strategic objectives and risk tolerance. Often, the natural tendency is to focus solely on technical controls and compliance requirements, which may not necessarily address the unique needs or concerns of the organization at large. Soliciting input from stakeholders across different departments, such as finance, operations and marketing, offers security teams a more comprehensive understanding of the business landscape. Stakeholders can provide valuable insights into the company's strategic priorities, the impact of security measures on day-to-day operations, and the potential risks and challenges that may arise from a business perspective.

Conversely, when security measures are developed without considering the diverse needs and perspectives of the organization, they can be perceived as overly restrictive or cumbersome by end-users. This can lead to the adoption of workarounds, the proliferation of shadow IT, and a general lack of security buy-in across the organization which are all steps in the wrong direction. This, in turn, can undermine the effectiveness of the security programme and expose the company to greater risks. Instead, actively engaging business stakeholders, having a security team can lead to the development of security controls that strike a balance between technical requirements and the practical needs of the organization. This collaborative approach can foster a culture of security awareness and ownership, where employees understand the importance of security and are more likely to comply with established policies and procedures. Ultimately, the inclusion of diverse stakeholder perspectives in the security decision-making process is a critical step in ensuring that security measures are aligned with their strategic objectives and risk appetite, while also promoting a culture of security that is embraced organization-wide.

From the outside perspective (outside of the security function), when security is fully integrated into the broader strategic planning and decision-making processes, the benefits can be substantial. Aligning security objectives with the company's overarching business goals will demonstrate the direct, measurable value of security initiatives which further promotes the security function as an enabling one. Cross-functional collaboration also allows security teams to leverage the unique insights and expertise of their counterparts in other departments. IT administrators can provide critical technical context, operations leaders can share on-the-ground user perspectives, and business executives can offer strategic guidance on emerging risks and growth opportunities. Tapping into this collective intelligence will undoubtedly craft more holistic, effective implementation plans that address the organization's needs from multiple angles. Also, integrated security implementation fosters a stronger, more resilient security culture: when employees in all departments understand how their individual roles and responsibilities contribute to the overall security posture, they are more likely to embrace security best practices and actively participate in risk mitigation efforts. This 'security-aware' mindset creates a robust defence against evolving cyber threats, even ones yet to be identified.

So, how can security leaders go about establishing this cross-functional, collaborative approach to security implementation? It starts with breaking down the traditional silos and proactively engaging stakeholders from across the business.

Identifying key stakeholders

The first step is to identify the key stakeholders who need to be involved in the security implementation process. This typically includes representatives from IT, operations, legal/compliance, risk management and the executive leadership team. The IT team is responsible for the day-to-day management and maintenance of the technology infrastructure, including hardware, software and network systems. They can provide valuable insights into the technical feasibility and compatibility of proposed security controls, as well as the potential impact on system performance and user experience. IT representatives can also share their understanding of emerging threats, vulnerabilities and industry best practices, helping to inform the overall security strategy.

The operations team is responsible for the core business processes and workflows, ensuring the smooth and efficient delivery of products or services. They can offer insights into the practical implications of security measures for operational efficiency, identifying potential bottlenecks or disruptions that could impact productivity or customer experience. Operational stakeholders can also highlight the need for streamlined access controls, user-friendly security tools and seamless integration with existing business systems.

The legal and compliance team is responsible for ensuring that the organization adheres to relevant laws, regulations and industry standards, such as data privacy, cybersecurity and industry-specific requirements. They can provide guidance on the legal and regulatory implications of security decisions, helping to ensure that the security posture aligns with its legal and compliance obligations. Legal and compliance stakeholders can also help to identify potential risks and liabilities associated with security breaches or non-compliance, informing the overall risk management strategy.

The risk management team is responsible for identifying, assessing and mitigating the various risks facing the organization, including operational, financial and reputational risks. They have a holistic perspective on the organization's risk profile, helping to prioritize security investments and ensure that the security strategy is aligned with the overall risk appetite. Risk management stakeholders may also share insights into emerging threat landscapes, industry trends and best practices for risk mitigation, informing the development of more comprehensive security controls.

The executive leadership team, including the CEO, CIO and other C-suite members, is responsible for setting the strategic direction and ensuring the alignment of all business functions, providing high-level guidance on the strategic priorities, risk tolerance and resource allocation, helping to ensure that the security implementation roadmap supports the overall business objectives. Executive stakeholders play a key role in fostering a culture of security awareness and accountability across the organization by driving the adoption and implementation of security measures.

Establishing regular communication channels

Next, security teams should work to establish regular touchpoints and communication channels with these stakeholder groups; communication is key. This could take the form of monthly or quarterly security steering committee meetings, where leaders from different functions come together to review progress, identify emerging risks and align priorities. Alternatively, security teams may embed representatives within other departmental planning and decision-making processes to ensure security is considered at every stage. Importantly, these collaborative discussions should not be one-way lectures from the security team. Instead, they should be open, two-way dialogues where all participants feel empowered to share their insights, concerns and ideas. Security leaders must be prepared to listen, understand and adapt their implementation plans accordingly. An effective communication technique is to leverage the user story-driven approach discussed earlier by framing security objectives in terms of specific stakeholder needs and measurable outcomes to facilitate more productive, action-oriented conversations. Business leaders are more likely to engage with security initiatives that clearly articulate how they will benefit the organization, rather than abstract technical controls.

That said, establishing this collaborative security implementation process is just the first step. Sustaining cross-functional alignment and engagement over time requires ongoing effort and commitment from all stakeholders involved. One critical element is regular communication and feedback loops. Security teams should provide frequent updates on implementation progress, emerging threats and any course corrections or adjustments to the roadmap. This keeps all stakeholders informed and allows them to provide timely input and guidance. This open communication should be **perpetual** and **passive** so that it fills in the gaps between more formal meetings of the committee proposed above. Transparent and passive access to the most up-to-date progress on security projects is a great way to let the stakeholders choose their own level of engagement, as some will benefit from more frequent updates than others. Also, during the in-between times, security leaders should actively solicit feedback from their cross-functional partners when the opportunity arises, specifically on the effectiveness of the security initiatives and on any unintended impacts or pain points experienced by end-users. This feedback should be carefully documented and used to continuously refine the implementation approach. Security teams should also seek out informal opportunities to engage with stakeholders, such as attending departmental meetings, participating in project retrospectives, or even conducting 'lunch and learn' sessions to share security best practices and lessons learned. Maintaining a constant dialogue will establish that the implementation roadmap remains closely aligned with the organization's needs and priorities. It also helps to foster a greater sense of shared ownership and accountability for security across the business.

Establishing clear roles and processes

Establishing clear roles, responsibilities and decision-making processes is another key factor in sustaining cross-functional collaboration. While security teams may be responsible for the overall strategy and technical execution, other stakeholders should have defined responsibilities and decision rights within the implementation process. For example, the legal and compliance team may be responsible for reviewing security controls to ensure they meet regulatory requirements. The IT department may own the deployment and configuration of security tools. The business leadership team may have final approval on security investments and risk tolerance levels. This structured approach helps to ensure accountability, streamline decision-making and prevent conflicts or bottlenecks during the implementation phase. The security team can leverage the expertise and decision-making authority of their cross-functional partners by clearly delineating the roles and responsibilities of each stakeholder group, while also maintaining overall control and coordination of the security programme.

Effective collaboration is not a one-time event, but an ongoing, iterative process. As the organization's threat landscape, business objectives and technology ecosystem evolve over time, the security implementation roadmap must also adapt accordingly. This means regularly revisiting the collaborative planning and review processes, adjusting stakeholder involvement as needed, and being open to new ideas and perspectives. Security leaders should view their cross-functional partners not as obstacles to be overcome, but as valuable allies in the quest for a more secure and resilient organization.

The power of collaborative security implementation lies in its ability to transform security from a necessary cost centre into a strategic enabler of innovation, growth and competitive advantage. When security is fully integrated into the organization, it becomes a powerful tool for unlocking new opportunities, building customer trust and safeguarding the company's most valuable assets. So, for security leaders looking to translate their high-level vision into practical, measurable progress, the key is to look beyond the traditional IT silo and engage their cross-functional partners as strategic allies.

Secure software development practices

Even for organizations that are not in the technology sector, where technology is not the company's primary output, they will likely be developing software internally to support their core products and services. As a result, secure software development practices have become a critical area of focus for many, if not all, organizations. With more and more business-critical functions moving to custom-built or cloud-based applications, the attack surface for potential vulnerabilities has expanded exponentially. To address this challenge, security leaders (ideally backed by executive leadership), must work closely with development teams to embed security controls and testing throughout the software development lifecycle. This collaborative approach is essential to ensuring the security and integrity of the software being developed.

Secure coding training and guidelines for developers

One particularly significant aspect of the software development lifecycle is the support of the engineering function within the business, as a core competency of software engineers is problem-solving. I have often advocated for software engineers to be termed as 'developers' over 'programmers', as the latter implies that the individual is just 'following instructions'. A developer on the other hand suggests that this person is going to create something new, and in order to do that, they must understand the status quo and also the intended outcome. Armed with that information, the developer then plots a course to solve the problem, often with all of the trimmings. With that in mind, one thing I learned during my time as the Chief Technology Officer at a cybersecurity firm which was offering Security-as-a-Service to third parties, was that the best way to scale good security practices was to delegate as much day-to-day activities to the customer and even their end users.

For example, the company could be provided with all the network access and IP addresses for a customer's servers that require vulnerability scans. The company could devise some queuing and automation to support that, or provide the customer with a way to scan their own servers with the company's technology without the company's involvement. The customer could then be supplied with a report detailing the vulnerability scan results. It is doubtful that anyone would agree that the latter is a better solution; however, when you're operating a service, you want to delight your customers and make their lives easier. One of my principles as a security and technology leader is that if you're going to ask someone to do *more*, then you ought to provide them with tools to make it easier for them to do it. From my own experience, this yields higher cooperation and measurably better results. In context, if you want engineers to write more secure software, I posit that you must also give them the tools, training and the runway to do so.

Providing developers with comprehensive training on secure coding practices is a great first step, as it can help them identify and mitigate potential vulnerabilities during the coding process. This should include topics such as input validation, secure authentication and authorization, and the proper handling of sensitive data. Many larger (and especially regulated) organizations typically have standards and guidelines on how these things are implemented at the company. Even in the absence of standards, there are industry-wide best practices for these things which can easily be inspiration for implementation into your own technology stack.

INPUT SANITIZATION

When it comes to input validation, the techniques and best practices are largely well-known. Even if an organization is just getting started with implementing secure software development practices, they can leverage the common knowledge and experience of those who have come before them. One of the most fundamental and widely used input validation techniques is input sanitization. This involves removing or escaping any potentially malicious characters or code from user input before it is processed by the application. This helps to prevent injection attacks, such as SQL injection or cross-site scripting (XSS), where an attacker attempts to inject malicious code into the application's input fields. There are several common methods for input sanitization:

- **HTML encoding:** This involves replacing special characters, such as '<' and '>', with their HTML entity equivalents (e.g. '<' and

'>'). This ensures that any HTML tags or scripts included in the input are rendered as plain text, rather than being executed by the browser.

- **URL encoding:** This involves replacing special characters in a URL with a percent-encoded equivalent. This helps to prevent URL-based injection attacks, such as directory traversal or remote file inclusion.

- **SQL parameterization:** When working with databases, it's important to use parameterized queries rather than concatenating user input directly into SQL statements. This helps to prevent SQL injection attacks by separating the data from the SQL syntax.

- **Regular expressions:** Regular expressions can be used to validate the format and content of user input, ensuring that it matches a specific pattern or set of rules. This can be particularly useful for validating things like email addresses, phone numbers or other structured data.

INPUT TYPE

Another common input validation technique is input type validation. This involves ensuring that the user input matches the expected data type and format for the application's requirements. For example, if the application expects a numeric value, the input should be validated to ensure that it contains only digits and does not include any non-numeric characters. Common methods for input type validation include:

- **Data type checking:** This involves using language-specific data type checks (e.g. isInteger(), isFloat(), isString()) to ensure that the input matches the expected data type.

- **Range validation:** This involves checking that the input value falls within a specific numeric range, such as ensuring that a price value is between 0 and 1000.

- **Enumeration validation:** This involves checking that the input value is one of a predefined set of valid options, such as validating a user's resident country by selecting it from a picklist.

In addition to input sanitization and type validation, it's also important to consider input size and length validation. This involves ensuring that the input does not exceed the maximum size or length that the application can safely handle. Accepting overly large inputs can lead to issues such as buffer overflows, denial of service attacks or even application crashes. Techniques for input size and length validation may include:

- **Maximum length checks:** This involves setting a maximum length for input fields and validating that the user's input does not exceed this limit.

- **File size validation:** When accepting file uploads, it's important to validate the size of the uploaded file to ensure that it does not exceed the maximum size that the application can handle.

- **Array/collection size validation:** When working with collections of data, such as arrays or lists, it's important to validate the size of the collection to ensure that it does not exceed the maximum size that the application can safely process.

CONSIDERING INPUT VALIDATION IN CONTEXT

It's important to consider input validation in the context of the application's specific requirements and use cases. While the techniques mentioned above are widely used and well known, the specific implementation and application of these techniques may vary depending on the application's architecture, data model and security requirements. For example, in a financial application that processes sensitive user data, the input validation requirements may be more stringent than in a simple blog application that only accepts user comments. In the financial application, the input validation may need to include additional checks for sensitive data, such as credit card numbers or social security numbers, to ensure that this information is properly protected. Similarly, in a real-time, high-throughput application, the input validation may need to be optimized for performance, potentially using techniques such as asynchronous or parallel processing to ensure that the input validation does not become a bottleneck in the application's overall performance.

Another important aspect of input validation is the concept of 'defence in depth'. In context, this means implementing multiple layers of input validation, rather than relying on a single validation check. This helps to ensure that even if one validation check is bypassed or fails, there are additional safeguards in place to prevent malicious input from being processed by the application. One common approach to defence in depth in input validation is to perform validation at multiple points in the application's architecture, including:

- **Client-side validation:** Performing initial input validation on the client-side, such as in the user's web browser or mobile app, to catch obvious issues and provide immediate feedback to the user.

- **Server-side validation:** Performing more comprehensive input validation on the server-side, where the input is processed, to ensure that it meets the application's security requirements.

- **Database-level validation:** Implementing additional input validation checks at the database level, such as using database constraints or triggers, to ensure that only valid data is stored.

Overall, a layered approach to input validation can significantly reduce the risk of successful attacks, even if an attacker is able to bypass one of the validation checks.

WHITELISTING VS BLACKLISTING

Another form of input validation is the concept of 'whitelisting' versus 'blacklisting'. Whitelisting involves defining a specific set of allowed input values or formats and rejecting anything that does not match the whitelist. Blacklisting, on the other hand, involves defining a set of known malicious input patterns or values, and rejecting anything that matches the blacklist. Whitelisting is generally considered a more secure approach, as it is more proactive and less prone to missing new or evolving threats because the list of allowable values remains the same even as new permutations (threats) emerge.

Blacklisting, while easier to implement, can be more reactive and may miss new types of malicious input. For example, in the context of input sanitization, a whitelisting approach might involve replacing all non-alphanumeric characters in a user's input with a safe character, such as an underscore. A blacklisting approach, on the other hand, might involve removing specific known malicious characters, such as '<' and '>', but potentially miss other types of malicious input.

It's important to remember that input validation is not a one-size-fits-all solution, and the specific implementation will depend on the application's requirements, the type of input being processed, and the overall security posture of the organization. In some cases, a combination of whitelisting and blacklisting may be the most effective approach, with the whitelisting serving as the primary defence and the blacklisting providing an additional layer of protection. Regardless of the specific techniques used, the key to effective input validation is to stay up-to-date with the latest security best practices, continuously monitor for new threats and vulnerabilities, and be willing to adapt and evolve the input validation strategies as the application and the threat landscape change over time.

Automated security scanning and testing during development

Integrating security testing tools into the development pipeline is a crucial component of secure software development practices. Automating security scanning and testing throughout the development process can identify and address security issues early on, reducing the cost and complexity of remediation later in the project lifecycle. One of the primary benefits of automated security scanning and testing is the ability to shift security 'left' in the development process. Rather than waiting until the end of the development cycle to perform security assessments, automated tools can be integrated into the continuous integration (CI) and continuous deployment (CD) pipelines, allowing security checks to be performed as part of the regular build and deployment processes.

This shift-left approach has several key advantages. Running security scans and tests as part of the development workflow will have issues identified and addressed much earlier in the process, when they are typically faster and less expensive to fix. Integrating security testing into the development workflow also helps to raise security awareness among developers, encouraging them to consider security implications as they write code, rather than treating it as an afterthought. To check the output, automated security scanning and testing should be set up to run on a regular cadence, providing continuous monitoring of the application's security posture throughout the development lifecycle.

There are a wide range of automated security testing tools available, each with its own strengths and capabilities. Static Application Security Testing (SAST) tools analyse the application's source code to identify potential security vulnerabilities, such as input validation issues, insecure coding practices and the use of vulnerable libraries or frameworks. These tools can be integrated directly into the development environment, allowing developers to receive immediate feedback on security issues as they write code.

Dynamic Application Security Testing (DAST) tools analyse the running application, simulating real-world attacks to identify vulnerabilities that may not be evident from the source code alone. These tools can be integrated into the CI/CD pipeline to automatically test the application at various stages of the development process.

Software Composition Analysis (SCA) tools scan the application's dependencies and third-party libraries to identify known vulnerabilities or licence compliance issues which help development teams stay on top of security issues introduced through the use of external components.

As more organizations adopt Infrastructure as Code (IaC) practices, it's important to also incorporate security scanning into the IaC pipeline. Tools like Terraform, CloudFormation and Ansible can be scanned for security misconfigurations or vulnerabilities before the infrastructure is provisioned. For applications that utilize containerized deployment, it's crucial to scan container images for known vulnerabilities, misconfigurations and compliance issues before they are deployed to production.

When implementing automated security scanning and testing, it's important to consider the integration points within the development workflow. Ideally, these tools should be seamlessly integrated into the CI/CD pipeline, with the results of the security tests being fed back to the development team in a timely and actionable manner. This may involve integrating security testing tools directly into the developer's integrated development environment (IDE), so that they can receive immediate feedback on security issues as they write code.

Alternatively, the security tests can be configured to run as part of the automated build and deployment processes, with the results being surfaced in the team's project management or collaboration tools. These security testing tools and processes are absolutely not passive solutions and must also be kept up-to-date and aligned with the latest security best practices and threat landscapes. As new vulnerabilities and attack vectors emerge, the security testing suite should be updated accordingly to ensure that the application remains secure.

A major challenge when automating security testing is the potential for false positives, where the tools identify issues that are not actually security vulnerabilities. To address this, it's important to carefully configure the security testing tools and establish clear processes for triaging and validating the results. Incorporating human review and analysis into the process or leveraging machine learning and artificial intelligence to improve the accuracy of security testing are some great ways to approach this issue.

When implementing automated security testing, pay close attention to the need to balance security with developer productivity and the overall development lifecycle. While it's important to identify and address security issues early in the process, it's also crucial to ensure that the security testing does not become a bottleneck or create unnecessary friction in the development workflow. Adopting a risk-based approach to security testing is useful, where the depth and frequency of the security scans are tailored to the specific needs and risk profile of the application being developed. For example, a mission-critical financial application may require more extensive and frequent security testing than a simple marketing website. Prioritizing the security testing based on the application's risk profile results in the most critical security issues being identified and addressed, while still allowing the development team to maintain a productive and efficient workflow.

For companies which are subject to regulatory oversight, the legal and regulatory implications must also be considered when implementing security automation. Depending on the industry and the type of data being processed, there may be specific compliance requirements or standards that the organization must adhere to, such as HIPAA, PCI-DSS or GDPR. Aligning the automated security testing practices with these regulatory requirements will show that they are not only improving the security of their applications, but also demonstrating compliance with the relevant laws and regulations. This can be particularly important for organizations operating in highly regulated industries, where the consequences of security breaches or compliance failures can be severe.

The integration of automated security scanning and testing into the development process is a critical component of secure software development practices. Shifting security left and incorporating security testing into the CI/CD pipeline can identify and address security issues early in the development lifecycle, reducing the cost and complexity of remediation while also improving the overall security posture of their applications. However, it's important to strike a balance between security and productivity, and to ensure that the security testing practices are aligned with the risk profile and regulatory requirements of the organization.

Vulnerability management and patching processes

Vulnerability management and patching processes are also critical components of secure software development practices. Developers must work closely with security teams to proactively identify and address known vulnerabilities in the software they are creating, as well as in the underlying frameworks and libraries they are utilizing.

Effective vulnerability management begins with maintaining a comprehensive inventory of all software components, including their versions and known vulnerabilities. This inventory should be regularly updated to reflect the latest security advisories and patch releases from software vendors and open-source communities. This sounds like a daunting task, but when delegated out to application owners, each of them would only need to be responsible for their own inventory. Staying informed about the security landscape allows for teams to prioritize the remediation of high-risk vulnerabilities and ensure that their software remains resilient against emerging threats.

In addition to software development, the patching process is an important aspect of vulnerability management. Timely and consistent application of security updates is essential to mitigating the risks posed by known vulnerabilities. A well-defined patching strategy that aligns with security policies and procedures is a must-have for a security conscious technical team. This strategy should include clear guidelines for testing and deploying patches, as well as mechanisms for ensuring that all affected systems are updated in a timely manner. Patches are software updates released by vendors to address security vulnerabilities or bugs in their products. A key consideration in the patching process is the potential impact on the software's functionality and performance. Developers should carefully evaluate the changes introduced by a patch and assess its compatibility with the existing codebase. This may involve conducting thorough testing (e.g. integration testing, regression testing), both in isolated environments and in production-like settings, to check that the patch does not introduce any unintended consequences or regressions. Taking a proactive and measured approach to patching can minimize the risk of disrupting the software's operation and maintain a high level of reliability and availability.

Secure software development practices also emphasize the importance of proactive vulnerability detection and remediation by integrating security testing and analysis tools into the development lifecycle, such as static code analysis, dynamic application security testing and penetration testing. These tools can help identify and address vulnerabilities early in the development process, further reducing the cost and complexity of remediation efforts.

Even with the best intentions, things do happen (hopefully to a lesser degree), so clear processes for handling and responding to security incidents and vulnerability disclosures are essential. This involves establishing communication channels with security researchers, bug bounty programs and other external stakeholders who may uncover vulnerabilities in the software. A culture of transparency and collaboration can quickly address emerging threats and maintain the trust of users and customers.

Development teams can enhance the overall security posture of their software and mitigate the risks posed by known and emerging threats by adopting a holistic approach to vulnerability management and patching. This not only protects the software and its users but also helps to maintain the reputation and compliance of the organization with relevant security standards and regulations. Either way, vulnerability management and patching processes are essential components of secure software development practices. Proactively identifying and addressing vulnerabilities results in software that remains resilient and secure, even in the face of evolving cybersecurity threats.

Secure software deployment and configuration practices

When software is built securely and scanned, and the deployment environment is patched, deploying the software securely will further strengthen security posture. Secure software deployment and configuration practices ensure that software is established with appropriate access controls, logging and monitoring in place. It also involves maintaining secure configurations throughout the software's lifecycle, including during updates and upgrades.

A fundamental aspect of this process is access control. Development teams must be sure that only authorized personnel have the necessary permissions to access and manage the software deployment infrastructure. Using role-based access controls, multi-factor authentication and other security measures to prevent unauthorized access minimize the risk of data breaches or system compromises. Access to production systems should be monitored and audited on a regular basis, even for users with current authorized access.

Implementing secure communication channels, such as encrypted connections and secure protocols, will protect the transfer of software artefacts and configuration data during the deployment process which helps to mitigate the risk of eavesdropping, man-in-the-middle attacks, and other security threats that could compromise the integrity of the software or the underlying infrastructure.

Once the software is deployed, comprehensive logging and monitoring to capture and record all relevant events, including user actions, system changes and security-related incidents are essential. This data can be used for forensic analysis, incident response and compliance purposes, as well as to identify and address potential security vulnerabilities or misconfigurations. One of the key benefits of comprehensive logging and monitoring is the ability to establish a baseline of 'normal' activity within the system. Continuously reviewing the log data will identify patterns of user behaviour, system changes and other events that are typical and expected. This baseline can then be used to detect anomalies or deviations from the norm, which could be indicative of a security incident or an attempted attack.

For example, if the log data shows a sudden increase in failed login attempts, or a series of unauthorized access attempts to sensitive areas of the system, these could be early warning signs of a brute-force attack or an attempt to exploit a security vulnerability. Identifying these anomalies in a timely manner provides an opportunity to immediately investigate the issue, implement additional security controls and mitigate the potential threat before it can cause significant damage. Similarly, ongoing log analysis can help identify and address potential security vulnerabilities or misconfigurations that may have been overlooked during the initial deployment or configuration process. The concepts can be enabled by using effective monitoring solutions, such as security information and event management (SIEM) systems which detect and respond to security incidents in a timely manner. These tools can analyse log data, identify anomalies and trigger alerts when suspicious activities are detected, enabling the team to take appropriate action to mitigate the threat and prevent further damage.

In addition to deployment and monitoring, software needs to be deployed with the appropriate security configurations, including the implementation of secure default settings, the disabling of unnecessary features or services, and enforcement of secure coding practices. Even pre-deployment, maintaining secure configurations throughout the software's lifecycle is beneficial. This comes in the form of robust change management processes to ensure that any updates or upgrades to the software are thoroughly tested and validated before being deployed to production environments. Clear policies and procedures for managing software configurations, including the use of version control systems and configuration management tools to maintain a comprehensive record of all changes and modifications, are ways to enforce secure configuration management.

Monitoring and adapting security postures

Effective cybersecurity implementation requires continuous monitoring and adaptation. These concepts – especially the technical ones – will generate a tremendous amount of valuable data which can enrich security decisions and adapt postures to be able to quickly identify, investigate and respond to new risks. Harnessing this data often translates to adopting the use of security monitoring and analytics capabilities, such as security information and event management (SIEM) tools, user and entity behaviour analytics (UEBA), and extended detection and response (XDR) platforms. These solutions provide the visibility and contextual intelligence needed to detect and respond to advanced threats.

SIEM tools, for example, aggregate and analyse log data from various sources and application logs that will identify potential security incidents that may have gone unnoticed by individual security controls. This allows security teams to quickly detect and investigate potential threats and take appropriate action to mitigate the risks. UEBA solutions, on the other hand, focus on analysing user and entity behaviour to identify anomalies that could indicate a security breach or insider threat. These tools use machine learning and advanced analytics to establish a baseline of 'normal' behaviour, and then detect deviations that may be indicative of malicious activity, such as unauthorized access attempts, unusual data access patterns or suspicious user actions.

XDR platforms take a more holistic approach to threat detection and response, integrating data from multiple security tools and technologies, including SIEM, endpoint detection and response (EDR), and network security solutions. XDR platforms can provide a more comprehensive view of the security landscape, enabling security teams to detect and respond to complex, multi-stage attacks more effectively.

Just as importantly, security leaders must establish clear processes for reviewing security metrics, identifying emerging risks and rapidly adjusting security controls and processes as needed. This agile, data-driven approach to security management is essential for maintaining a strong, resilient security posture. Regular review and analysis of security metrics and KPIs by tracking and analysing data on security incidents, vulnerability management, user behaviour and the effectiveness of security controls will identify trends, patterns and areas for improvement. This information can then be used to inform strategic decision-making, prioritize security investments, and optimize security processes and controls using the communication strategies discussed in Chapter 6.

For example, analysing data on the time it takes to detect and respond to security incidents, opportunities can be identified to streamline the incident response processes, or inform the investment in additional tools and technologies to improve threat detection and investigation capabilities. Similarly, by tracking metrics on the prevalence and severity of known vulnerabilities, patching and remediation efforts can be prioritized and enable development teams to address underlying security weaknesses in the software they are building.

To further strengthen cross-functional collaboration, the security team may also consider establishing *shared* KPIs or success metrics that align with the organization's overall business objectives. For instance, the security team may work with the finance and risk management teams to develop KPIs that measure the financial impact of security investments, such as the return on investment (ROI) or the reduction in risk exposure. Alternatively, they may collaborate with the operations and IT teams to develop metrics that track the efficiency and user-friendliness of security controls, such as the time required to onboard new employees or the number of security-related incidents that disrupt business operations. Aligning security KPIs with broader business goals demonstrates the tangible value of security efforts and fosters a shared sense of ownership and accountability, which, in turn, can help to secure the necessary resources and support for ongoing security initiatives, and ensure that security remains a top priority.

Data and communication will go hand in hand with continuous improvement and adaptation, as the data informs the 'chores' which need to be done, such as updating security controls, implementing new technologies or revising security policies and procedures to address emerging threats. One way to foster this culture of continuous improvement is to establish a formal process for reviewing and updating the organization's security strategy and implementation plan on a regular basis. This could involve conducting periodic risk assessments, reviewing the effectiveness of existing security controls, and identifying new security requirements or priorities based on changes in the threat landscape, regulatory environment or business operations. Whatever the mechanism, it will allow for the security posture to remain aligned with evolving business needs and the changing threat environment. This process of continuous improvement should also extend to the security team itself, with a focus on developing the skills, knowledge and capabilities needed to effectively manage and respond to emerging security threats. For example, it could involve ongoing training and professional development opportunities for security personnel, as well as fostering a culture of continuous learning and knowledge sharing within the team.

One effective approach to fostering this culture of continuous improvement is to establish a dedicated security operations centre (SOC) or security incident and event management team. These specialized teams are responsible for monitoring, analysing and responding to security incidents and threats in real-time, and they play a critical role in identifying and addressing emerging security risks. Centralizing security monitoring and incident response capabilities is a great way to know that the necessary expertise, tools and processes to quickly detect, investigate and mitigate security incidents are present within the organization which can help to reduce the overall impact and cost of security breaches, and improve the ability to maintain business continuity and protect critical assets.

Conclusion

Effective cybersecurity is not just about having the right strategy – it's about translating that strategy into measurable, repeatable processes that can adapt to changing conditions. Remember that implementation is not a one-time event, but rather a continuous process of monitoring, adapting and improving. Investing in robust security monitoring and analytics capabilities, aligning security metrics with business objectives, and fostering a culture of continuous improvement, will lead to a security posture that is agile, responsive and resilient in the face of evolving security threats.

KEY TAKEAWAYS

- Try using user stories to make security initiatives more tangible and relevant.

- Software development is an easy place to implement security practices because it is technical, finite and a closed environment that offers integration points to definitively implement security tools and monitoring.

- Continuously evaluate and adjust your security approach using the metrics and telemetry available to you from the implemented tooling.

10

Metrics for security empowerment

Throughout this book, one of the common themes is measuring success. For most of the topics covered so far, I have included suggestions for how to measure the success of implementing new risk management initiatives or a new technology strategy. This chapter will cover those in more detail, but from the perspective of the board. If you've been a board member or have presented to a board, you'll know it is a data-driven discussion. The objective of board meetings is to get an overview of each domain and make strategic decisions based on the information at hand. The data in question should be at a very high level and must be in relevant context, which is a tricky job for a security leader (see Chapter 2). A security leader's goal is to present domain-specific data (often referred to as 'jargon' or requested to be 'in layperson terms'), but the metrics that drive those data are often deep and technical. This chapter will explore how to bridge that gap and translate technical security metrics into high-level, business-relevant data that the board can understand and act upon.

Common security metrics are available at the operational and tactical levels, such as vulnerability management metrics, incident response metrics and security awareness training metrics. The things that these metrics measure, how they are calculated and how they can provide insights into the overall security posture of the organization are an important first step. These lower-level security metrics can be aggregated and distilled into higher-level, strategic metrics that are meaningful to the board. Additional metrics regarding risk exposure, compliance and the return on investment (ROI) of security initiatives enrich the message and will add a welcome dimension to the more technical security metrics that will enrich the data resulting in a higher quality output that can then be mapped to the board's KPIs and decision-making criteria.

With data in hand, effective board presentation is essential. Doom and gloom is a very easy (and common) route that security people take, but consciously and subconsciously this is actually counter-productive. Data visualization, storytelling and aligning security metrics to the board's priorities and concerns will turn technical secu-rity data into valuable, board-level insights that drive strategic decision-making.

DEFINING KEY PERFORMANCE INDICATORS (KPIs) FOR SECURITY

A well-rounded security metrics programme should include both lagging and leading indicators. Lagging indicators, such as the number of successful breaches or the cost of data recovery, provide insights into past performance and the overall security posture. Leading indicators, such as the percentage of employees trained in security awareness or the time to patch critical vulnerabilities, help predict and proactively address emerging threats. Monitoring a balanced set of metrics provides a comprehensive understanding of their current state, identifies areas for improvement and demonstrates their ability to anticipate and mitigate risks before they materialize.

Vulnerability management

In alignment with the previous chapter, vulnerability management is a critical component of any comprehensive security programme. Proactively identifying, prioritizing and remediating vulnerabilities will always help reduce the risk of successful cyber-attacks on an organization. However, effectively communicating the progress and impact of vulnerability management efforts to the board can be a challenge, as the data on its own will mean very little to someone outside the security domain.

A fundamental metric for vulnerability management is the number of known vulnerabilities within a given IT environment that provides a high-level view of the overall attack surface and the potential risk exposure facing the organization. When presenting this metric to the board, it is essential for security leaders to provide context and analysis beyond just the raw numbers. For example, consider trends over time to examine how the number of known vulnerabilities has changed. See whether the organization is seeing a reduction, which could indicate that remediation efforts are effective. Additionally, look at the age distribution of the vulnerabilities, as older, unpatched vulnerabilities pose a greater risk than recently discovered ones. It is also important to understand which systems or applications contain the majority of the vulnerabilities and whether these are mission-critical assets or contain sensitive data. Comparing the organization's vulnerability count to industry benchmarks will also help the board understand the relative security posture. This additional context will help the board better interpret the significance of the vulnerability count and its implications for the organization's overall risk profile, which, in turn, can inform strategic decision-making and resource allocation to address the most pressing security concerns.

Another way to convey the effectiveness of vulnerability management is by using the percentage of vulnerabilities remediated within a target timeframe. This metric demonstrates the ability to identify and address vulnerabilities in a timely manner, reducing the window of opportunity for potential attackers. When presenting this metric, discuss the organization's defined remediation timeframe targets, which may vary based on the severity or risk level of the vulnerability, followed by the organization's progress in meeting these targets and highlighting the percentage of vulnerabilities that are being remediated within the specified timeframes. If the organization is falling short of its goals, be sure to identify the root causes, such as resource constraints, process inefficiencies or other factors impeding timely remediation. This level of detail will undoubtedly increase the board's understanding of the vulnerability management programme's maturity and identify areas for improvement.

The mean time to remediate critical vulnerabilities is another particularly important metric, as it focuses specifically on the organization's ability to address its most pressing security risks. When presenting this metric, first explain how critical vulnerabilities are defined within the organization. These are typically based on industry-standard vulnerability scoring systems like the Common Vulnerability Scoring System (CVSS). Following this, discuss the average time it takes to remediate these critical vulnerabilities, any challenges or root causes that are impacting remediation timelines, and the strategies being employed to accelerate the remediation of the most severe vulnerabilities. Highlighting the organization's performance in addressing its most critical vulnerabilities is a useful way to demonstrate the security programme's ability to mitigate the organization's most significant risks. Vulnerability risk score (often based on the CVSS) provides a quantitative assessment of the severity and potential impact of a vulnerability, which is useful for prioritizing remediation efforts and aligning security initiatives with the overall risk profile. When presenting vulnerability risk scores to the board, explain the CVSS score breakdown, including the different factors that contribute to the overall score, such as the vulnerability's exploitability and the potential for impact, as well as how the organization uses these risk scores to prioritize remediation, focusing resources on the vulnerabilities that pose the greatest threat to the business. Going even further, consider incorporating other risk-based metrics, such as the percentage of vulnerabilities with a 'high' or 'critical' risk score, or the percentage of vulnerabilities that are associated with known, active threats. These metrics can help the board understand the organization's exposure to the most significant security risks and the effectiveness of the vulnerability management programme in addressing them.

When presenting vulnerability management metrics to the board, it's important to not only provide the data but also to tell a compelling story. This means translating technical security jargon into business-relevant language and framing the metrics in the context of the organization's strategic objectives and risk tolerance. Security leaders should be prepared to answer questions, provide additional context, and demonstrate how the vulnerability management programme is contributing to the overall security posture and risk management strategy.

Data visualization is easily the most effective way to present vulnerability management metrics (and probably all metrics). Dashboards, charts and graphs can help the board quickly understand the key trends and insights, without getting bogged down in technical details. For example, a line chart showing the number of known vulnerabilities over time can illustrate whether the organization is making progress in reducing its attack surface. A stacked bar chart depicting the percentage of vulnerabilities remediated within different timeframes can highlight the efficiency of the remediation process. Either way, even if the numbers themselves do not mean much outside of the security team, humans can easily understand a graph; trending down is good, trending up is bad (sometimes the other way around). Even still, not all graphs are created equal. Be sure to keep the board's needs and preferences in mind. The visualizations should be clean, intuitive and focused on the most relevant metrics. Avoid overwhelming graphs with too much information or complex charts that require extensive explanation. Instead, prioritize the metrics that directly address the board's concerns about risk, compliance and the overall security of the organization. Be prepared to provide deeper dives into the vulnerability management programme when requested which may involve presenting detailed reports, analysis and recommendations on specific areas of concern. For example, the board may want to understand the approach to vulnerability prioritization, the effectiveness of remediation strategies or the impact of vulnerabilities on critical business systems, so come prepared! Being proactive to the board's information needs will build trust and credibility, demonstrating that the security programme is aligned with strategic objectives and risk management priorities.

Effectively communicating vulnerability management metrics to the board also means linking them to business outcomes and risk mitigation. Articulate how the vulnerability management programme is contributing to the overall security posture and the protection of its most valuable assets, which may involve quantifying the potential financial impact of unmitigated vulnerabilities, such as the cost of a data breach or the loss of customer trust, and comparing it to the investment in vulnerability management initiatives. Highlight how the vulnerability management programme supports the organization's compliance requirements and regulatory obligations. Demonstrating the direct connection between vulnerability management and the ability to meet the organization's legal and industry-specific security standards will only further strengthen the board's understanding of the programme's strategic importance.

As the organization's security needs and business priorities evolve, the relevant metrics may change. Prepare to adapt their reporting, ensuring that the board receives the most up-to-date and meaningful information to support their decision-making. Mastering the presentation and communication of vulnerability management metrics will definitively translate technical security data into business-relevant insights that resonate with the board. This, in turn, can help the organization make informed decisions, allocate resources more effectively and strengthen its overall security posture.

Incident response

Effective incident response, which has been mentioned throughout this book, is yet another important component of a comprehensive security strategy because it enables the rapid detection, containment and resolution of security incidents which minimize the impact on operations, protect assets and maintain stakeholder trust. Like all other KPIs, communicating the performance and value of an incident response programme to the board can be a challenge, as the metrics involved often require technical expertise to understand. However, they are highly valued for their ability to demonstrate the security programme's resilience and the organization's ability to manage security risks effectively.

One of the foundational incident response metrics is quite simply the number of security incidents detected and responded to. This metric provides a high-level view of the security threats facing the organization and the overall workload of the incident response team. When presenting this metric to the board, security leaders should not only share the raw number of incidents but also provide context and analysis to help the board interpret the significance of the data. For example, consider trends over time: examining whether the number of incidents is increasing, decreasing or remaining stable. This is a simple and impactful way to demonstrate the effectiveness of the organization's security controls. Categorize the incidents by type, such as malware infections, unauthorized access attempts or data breaches, to provide the board with a more nuanced understanding of security challenges.

Another important metric is the mean time to detect security incidents. Similar to vulnerability management, this metric measures the organization's ability to quickly identify and respond to potential threats, which is crucial for minimizing the impact and preventing further escalation. This metric explains the organization's target detection timeframes, based on industry best practices or internal risk tolerance, and compares the actual performance to these benchmarks. If the organization is struggling to meet its detection targets, be prepared to discuss the root causes, such as limitations in security monitoring capabilities, gaps in threat intelligence or a lack of automation and integration within the security ecosystem. Providing this level of detail will help your audience to better understand the organization's security maturity and the areas that require additional investment or optimization.

Beyond detection, the mean time to contain and resolve security incidents is another critical metric for incident response. This metric measures the organization's ability to quickly isolate and remediate security incidents, limiting the potential damage and restoring normal operations. When presenting this metric, security leaders should again reference the organization's target containment and resolution timeframes, and compare the actual performance to these benchmarks. As a rather easy to understand metric, if the organization is not meeting designated resolution targets, there will most likely be an inquisition into the reasons for this. This will require knowledge of the challenges faced, such as a lack of incident response playbooks, insufficient collaboration between security and IT teams, or limitations in the organization's ability to quickly mobilize resources and expertise.

The percentage of incidents resolved within target service-level agreements (SLAs) is one more important metric for demonstrating the reliability and consistency of the incident response programme that measures the organization's ability to adhere to its own incident response commitments, which can be critical for maintaining stakeholder trust and meeting regulatory or contractual obligations. An overview of what the SLAs are (which may vary depending on the severity or type of incident), then sharing the percentage of incidents that were resolved within those timeframes is a common way to share this information.

A visual that conveys the overall incident response trends since the last meeting will increase the board's understanding of the impact that incident response is having. Brevity at this level is important; however, the detailed information supporting the visual should always be readily available if needed.

Tying incident response to strategic initiatives will likely include quantifying the potential financial impact of security incidents, such as the cost of downtime, data breaches or regulatory fines, and comparing it to the investment in incident response capabilities. Additionally, highlighting how the incident response programme supports the business continuity and disaster recovery plans is a nice touch. It demonstrates the direct connection between effective incident response and the ability to maintain operations and recover from disruptions. This can further strengthen the board's understanding of the programme's strategic importance.

As business priorities evolve, so must the incident response metrics provided to the board. Prepare to adapt reporting to be sure that the board receives the most up-to-date and meaningful information to support their decision-making. For example, as the reliance on cloud-based services and remote work increases, the board may become more interested in metrics related to the detection and response to cloud-based threats or incidents involving remote employees. Staying attuned to the board's evolving information needs will ensure that the incident response metrics remain relevant and impactful.

Security awareness and training

As discussed in Chapter 8, the human element of security has become increasingly critical. Employees, who are often the first line of defence against cyber threats, play a vital role in the overall security posture of the organization. Security awareness and training programmes are designed to empower employees with the knowledge and skills to recognize and respond to security risks, ultimately strengthening the organization's resilience, which makes them a powerful data point when conveying a successful security programme.

The first port of call when considering metrics for security awareness and training is the percentage of employees who have completed the organization's security awareness training. This very obvious metric provides a clear indication of the programme's reach and the level of employee engagement. Whilst compulsory for most security frameworks, one should not assume that there is 100 per cent engagement across the business. Even a high percentage of engagement on its own does not dictate the efficacy of a training programme or especially an entire security effort. Enrich this figure by providing trends over time, examining whether the percentage of employees who have completed the training is increasing, decreasing or remaining stable. This will help the board understand the organization's commitment to security awareness and the effectiveness of the training programme in reaching its target audience. Perhaps also consider segmenting the data by employee role, department or location to identify any gaps or areas that require additional focus.

When training participation numbers are lower than desired, it is helpful to discuss the underlying reasons and what initiatives are in place to address them. Potential factors to consider may include the frequency and duration of the training, the relevance and accessibility of the content, or the incentives and reinforcement mechanisms used to encourage participation.

One of the most common and successful human-based attacks is phishing. Security awareness programmes will no doubt include a module on phishing, and many companies employ email banners to indicate *external* emails; even domains that appear to be internal may be off by a letter or two which makes this simple tool so effective. However, as attacks get more sophisticated, and phishing emails come from within, employee vigilance is still of critical importance. A comprehensive security programme will want to simulate phishing attacks to internal staff, in order to assess the employee base's ability to detect a malicious email. Measuring the simulated phishing click-through rate measures the percentage of employees who fall victim, providing valuable insights into the organization's susceptibility to social engineering threats. A very important precursor to presenting this data would be to first explain the organization's phishing testing programme, including the frequency of the tests, the sophistication of the simulated attacks and the benchmarks or targets that have been set for acceptable click-through rates. Reporting the click-through rate will demonstrate the effectiveness of their security awareness training in improving employee vigilance and reducing the organization's vulnerability to phishing-based attacks. On the flip side, consider presenting the percentage of employees who can *correctly* identify social engineering attempts which provides a more direct assessment of the organization's ability to recognize and respond to social engineering threats, which are often a significant vector for cyber-attacks.

Be sure to keep the information contextual and relevant. For example, as the organization's reliance on remote work increases, the board may become more interested in metrics related to the security awareness and training of remote employees, such as the completion rates of remote-specific training modules or the phishing click-through rates for remote workers. By staying attuned to the board's evolving information needs, security leaders can ensure that the security awareness and training metrics remain relevant and impactful.

Combining security and awareness training metrics with other security metrics (such as number of total incidents) could portray the relationship between investment in these trainings with the overall resiliency of the organization. It can be argued that an increase in cybersecurity awareness will drive down the number of security incidents, but this relationship will not be made on its own. Try to include metrics such as the percentage of incidents that were detected and

reported by employees, or metrics related to the vulnerability management programme, such as the percentage of employees who have
completed training on vulnerability identification and reporting.
Presenting security awareness and training metrics in this way can
help the board understand the interconnected nature of security initiatives and the importance of a comprehensive, risk-based approach
to security management. This, in turn, can strengthen the board's
confidence in the security programme and its ability to effectively
mitigate security risks. This data can even go as far as informing the
organization's broader workforce development and talent management strategies by demonstrating how security education and
empowerment contribute to the overall professional development
and engagement of employees. This strengthens the board's understanding of the programme's strategic value and its alignment with
broader business objectives.

Compliance

Many businesses today are regulated. And for those who aren't
directly regulated, they often find their target market to be regulated,
which means they must have an effective compliance programme in
place. Even for those who are not regulated or adjacent to a regulated
industry, setting the bar for good security is never a bad idea. In
general, failure to meet compliance obligations can result in significant financial penalties, reputational damage and operational
disruptions. As such, the board of directors is increasingly focused on
understanding the organization's security compliance posture and
the effectiveness of its compliance management programme. Security
leaders play a pivotal role in communicating compliance metrics to
the board, translating technical security data into business-relevant
insights that support strategic decision-making.

A useful metric in the realm of compliance is the percentage of
systems and applications that are in compliance with the organization's security policies. This metric is a low-hanging fruit which
provides a high-level assessment of the organization's ability to

enforce its security standards across its IT infrastructure, ensuring that critical assets are properly configured and protected. It would be useful to segment the data by asset type, business unit or risk level to identify any areas of non-compliance that may require additional attention or resources. Back this up with the organization's approach to policy enforcement, including the use of automated tools, the frequency of compliance audits, and the processes in place for remediating non-compliant systems or applications, should it be asked for. Factors such as the complexity of the security policies, the availability of resources for addressing compliance issues, or the level of employee awareness and involvement in the compliance programme can all contribute to the percentage of compliant systems and applications falling below the target level.

Another useful compliance metric is the number of compliance violations or audit findings. This metric provides a direct measure of the organization's ability to meet its regulatory and industry-specific security requirements, as well as the effectiveness of its internal controls and monitoring processes. For context, categorize the findings by type, such as configuration errors, access control weaknesses or missing security controls, to help the board understand the nature of the compliance challenges faced. Knowledge of how the organization addresses compliance violations, including the timelines for remediation, the resources allocated to the effort and the strategies employed to prevent similar issues from recurring in the future, provides important context to understand the organization's current adherence to compliance requirements.

Compliance implementation coverage provides a holistic view of the organization's overall compliance posture, indicating the extent to which the security programme is meeting its regulatory and industry-specific obligations. This data stems from the organization's compliance framework and will include the specific requirements that have been defined, the target levels of compliance and the processes in place for monitoring and reporting on compliance status. Share the percentage of requirements that are currently being met, highlighting any areas where the organization is falling short of its targets, as well as factors that impact that, such as the complexity of the regulatory landscape, the availability of resources for compliance management, or the need for better integration between the security programme and the organization's broader governance, risk and compliance initiatives. When compliance data is used in the context of the organization's broader governance, risk and compliance (GRC) framework, it demonstrates how the security compliance programme aligns with and supports the organization's overall GRC strategy. This can further solidify the board's understanding of the programme's strategic value and its contribution to long-term success.

Security operations

The security operations centre (SOC) is the heart and soul of an organization's security efforts. This is where the real-time monitoring, detection and response to security incidents happens. Ensuring the SOC is operating at peak efficiency is critical to protecting the business. That's why tracking key SOC metrics is so important.

Two of the most valuable metrics to monitor are the mean time to triage (MTTT) and the mean time to resolve (MTTR) security incidents. The MTTT measures how quickly the SOC team can analyse an alert, determine its severity, and decide on the appropriate response. A low MTTT means the team is highly skilled at quickly triaging threats and getting the ball rolling on remediation. The MTTR, on the other hand, tracks how long it takes to fully investigate an incident and implement a complete resolution. Reducing the MTTR is crucial for minimizing the impact of security events.

These metrics represent SOC performance, and by monitoring these metrics, you can identify areas where the SOC team may need additional training or process improvements to streamline their workflows. For example, if the MTTT is consistently high, it could indicate that analysts are struggling to quickly categorize and prioritize alerts. Digging into the data may reveal bottlenecks in the triage process, such as a lack of clear incident classification guidelines or insufficient collaboration between team members. Armed with this information, targeted interventions can be implemented to get the

MTTT back on track. Similarly, tracking the MTTR can shed light on the efficiency of incident response procedures. If it's taking too long to fully resolve security incidents, it may be a sign that the team lacks the necessary tools, resources or playbooks to execute a swift and effective response. Analysing the MTTR data can help you pinpoint the root causes of delays, whether it's a lack of automation, poor communication channels, or gaps in the team's technical skills.

When these metrics are ready to be reported up to the board, they provide clear, data-driven evidence of the SOC's operational efficiency. Demonstrating the SOC team's ability to quickly triage and resolve security events can reassure the board that security operations are running like a well-oiled machine. And if there are areas that need improvement, you can use the metrics to justify the resources and support required to address those gaps.

But the SOC is just one piece of the security operations puzzle. A close eye must also be kept on how security tools and technologies are being utilized and how effective they are at detecting and preventing threats. Security tool utilization is an important metric that reveals how well your organization is leveraging its security investments. Are the tools being used to their full potential? Are there areas where additional training or support is needed? Tracking utilization rates can help you identify opportunities to optimize your security stack. For example, let's say you've deployed a new security information and event management (SIEM) system, but the data shows that only a small fraction of your analysts are actively using the tool on a regular basis. This could indicate that the team needs more training on how to effectively leverage the SIEM's features and capabilities. Or it might suggest that the tool isn't well-integrated with your existing workflows, leading to low adoption. Addressing utilization challenges will keep security investments delivering the maximum return. Equally crucial is evaluating the actual effectiveness of those security tools. Are they accurately detecting threats? How many incidents are they preventing? Conducting regular testing and analysing real-world performance can give you valuable insights into which tools are delivering the greatest impact on your risk profile. Imagine you've implemented a new endpoint detection and response (EDR) solution to bolster defences against malware and other advanced threats. Running simulated attacks and analysing the EDR's detection and response capabilities can assess how well the tool is performing. If the testing reveals that the EDR is missing certain types of threats or generating a high volume of false positives, you'll know that it may not be the best fit for your environment. Armed with this data, you can make informed decisions about whether to optimize the tool's configuration, supplement it with additional security controls, or explore alternative solutions.

When presenting these security operations metrics to the board, it's important to strike the right balance. You want to provide enough technical detail to demonstrate your command of the subject matter, but you also need to translate the data into business-relevant terms that non-technical stakeholders can easily understand. A well-designed dashboard or scorecard can be an effective way to communicate the key metrics in a clear, visually compelling way. For example, instead of just listing the MTTT and MTTR values, align them in the context of your organization's overall security posture and risk profile. Say something like, 'Our mean time to triage security incidents has improved by 25 per cent over the past quarter, from an average of 30 minutes down to just 22 minutes. This means our SOC team is able to quickly identify and prioritize potential threats, reducing the window of exposure for the business. Similarly, our mean time to resolve security incidents has decreased by 18 per cent, from an average of 4 hours down to 3.3 hours. This faster response time helps us minimize the impact and cost of security events.' This frames the metrics in terms of their business impact which helps the board understand the real-world implications of security operations performance. They'll be able to see how improvements in efficiency and effectiveness directly translate to reduced risk and better protection for the organization.

The same principle applies to the security tool utilization and effectiveness metrics. Rather than just presenting raw numbers, contextualize the data to show how it supports the board's strategic priorities. For instance, 'Our security tool utilization data shows that 85 per cent of our analysts are actively using the new SIEM platform on a weekly basis, up from just 65 per cent six months ago. This increased adoption has enabled us to detect and respond to 28 per cent more security incidents in the last quarter, helping us stay ahead of emerging threats.' Ultimately, the security operations metrics being tracked and reported should directly support the board's strategic decision-making. A transparent, data-driven view into the efficiency and effectiveness of security operations will give the board the confidence that their security investments are paying off and that the organization is well-positioned to navigate the threat landscape.

Metrics aren't just for reporting. The real value comes from using the data to continuously improve security operations and drive better outcomes for the business. Analysing the trends and patterns in MTTT, MTTR, tool utilization and effectiveness metrics will identify areas for optimization, allocate resources more effectively and make informed decisions about future security investments. For example, if the MTTR for a particular type of security incident is consistently higher than the overall average, you can dig deeper to understand the root causes. Maybe incident response playbooks need to be updated, or perhaps the team lacks the necessary skills or tools to efficiently resolve those types of events. Addressing these gaps will drive down the MTTR and minimize the impact on the business. Similarly, if security tool utilization data reveals that certain tools are being under-utilized, steps can be taken to improve user adoption, such as providing additional training, streamlining integration with other systems, or even exploring alternative solutions that better fit the team's workflows and requirements.

Risk management

The name of the game in all of this is risk and risk management. Risk is the great equalizer when it comes to having broad discussions about the benefits of a strong cybersecurity programme. Those external to the security function might not understand the technical details of how a ransomware attack works, but they do understand it when you tell them that a successful ransomware attack could cost the company $5 million in ransom payments, lost productivity and recovery efforts. If I could pick any single thing to report on, it would be on risk management. Measuring and quantifying an organization's overall risk posture is a critical component of effective risk management. To recap, the enterprise risk score or risk index is a high-level metric that provides a holistic view of the organization's risk exposure. This metric aggregates various risk factors, such as the likelihood and impact of potential threats, the effectiveness of security controls, and the organization's vulnerability to those threats. The enterprise risk score is typically calculated using a risk assessment framework that considers both quantitative and qualitative data (see Chapter 4 for full details on risk). Quantitative data may include metrics such as the number of security incidents, the financial impact of those incidents, and the cost of implementing security measures. Qualitative data may include the organization's risk appetite, the maturity of its security processes, and the effectiveness of its risk management strategies.

Tracking the enterprise risk score over time will uncover trends, monitor the impact of risk mitigation efforts, and make data-driven decisions to improve the organization's overall risk posture. This metric is particularly valuable for board-level reporting, as it provides a concise and easily understandable representation of the organization's risk profile.

Mitigated risks are those that have been addressed through the implementation of security controls or other risk-reducing measures. Accepted risks are those that the organization has consciously decided to retain, either because the cost of mitigation outweighs the potential impact or because the risk is deemed to be within the organization's risk appetite. Monitoring the percentage of identified risks that have been mitigated or accepted can help demonstrate the progress made in reducing the organization's overall risk exposure. This metric is particularly useful for board-level reporting, as it provides a clear indication of the organization's risk management capabilities and the effectiveness of its security investments.

A term commonly found in the boardroom is 'return on investment', and security is no exception. The return on security investment (ROSI) metric is a critical tool for demonstrating the value of security investments to the board. This metric calculates the financial benefits of implementing security measures, such as the reduction in the cost of security incidents or the avoidance of potential losses. It is a metric that is as powerful as it is elusive, because most will consider that successful security measures mean no breaches, and therefore nothing has happened. Security investments are often treated like insurance: they are there *just in case* something goes wrong, and proving a negative is extremely difficult. This can get misconstrued, and the security budget could take a hit because nothing remarkable has happened (which is a good thing), which is why ROSI is such a powerful tool.

To calculate ROSI, first identify the costs associated with implementing a security measure, such as the purchase of hardware or software, the cost of personnel, and the ongoing maintenance and support expenses. Then estimate the potential benefits, such as the reduction in the frequency and severity of security incidents, the avoidance of regulatory fines or legal penalties, and the preservation of the organization's reputation and customer trust. The ROSI formula is typically expressed as:

$$ROSI = (AnnualizedBenefit - AnnualizedCost)/AnnualizedCost$$

where:

- Annualized Benefit is the estimated financial benefit of the security measure over the course of a year.

- Annualized Cost is the estimated cost of implementing and maintaining the security measure over the course of a year.

The ROSI demonstrates the financial value of security investments and justifies the allocation of resources to the board. This metric is particularly useful for comparing the relative value of different security initiatives and for prioritizing investments based on their potential return. When ROSI is combined with other factors, such as the organization's risk appetite, the potential impact of security incidents, and the strategic alignment of security initiatives with the organization's goals, the ROSI impact grows and becomes a valuable tool for demonstrating the financial benefits of security investments to the board.

KEY TAKEAWAYS

- To assess 'better' vs 'worse', or 'effective' vs 'ineffective', you must first find ways to measure things, tangible or otherwise.

- There are a wealth of metrics available at the technical level of security, but they must be adapted to be meaningful so that stakeholders can answer the rhetorical question of 'why do I care?'

- Applying technical metrics to business initiatives sounds daunting, but for a security leader who understands the metrics for what they are, it is an opportunity to demonstrate the value of their security efforts.

11

The future of security empowerment

Throughout this book I've deliberately drawn attention to methods and concepts that are meant to 'keep up with the evolving threat landscape', as a good cybersecurity programme (and culture) is one that can handle almost anything, come what may. Nobody knows what the future holds, so organizations must be prepared to adapt and evolve their security posture to stay ahead of the curve. The cybersecurity landscape is in a constant state of flux, with new challenges and opportunities emerging on the horizon. To ensure the protection of critical assets and maintain business continuity, embracing a proactive and comprehensive approach to cybersecurity is a must.

Evolving technologies and security challenges

This section will discuss evolving technologies that are shaping the future of cybersecurity and outline the strategies and best practices organizations can adopt to build a resilient and adaptable security framework.

Supply chain

In the current technological world, it feels like most software applications, cloud-based services and IT infrastructure components are provided through third-party vendors, rather than being self-developed or owned by the organization, and they all come with a subscription model. This shift towards a vendor-based model has been driven by factors like the increasing complexity of technology, the need for specialized expertise, and the cost-effectiveness of outsourcing these capabilities rather than building them in-house. The barrier to entry for new technology is getting lower every day, so larger and less agile organizations have been buying more off-the-shelf software and cloud-based services rather than developing their own custom software and IT infrastructure in-house. This means that in today's interconnected digital landscape, organizations are increasingly reliant on a complex web of software, hardware and service providers that make up their supply chain. This interdependence has introduced a new set of challenges, as high-profile supply chain attacks have demonstrated the devastating consequences of vulnerabilities in third-party components and services.

Adversaries have become adept at exploiting these vulnerabilities, using them as entry points to gain access to sensitive data and systems. The recent SolarWinds and Kaseya attacks are prime examples, where malicious actors were able to infiltrate the networks of numerous organizations by targeting their trusted software providers.

REAL-WORLD EXAMPLE

The SolarWinds supply chain attack was a devastating cyber intrusion that came to light in late 2020, exposing the significant risks posed by vulnerabilities in third-party software.[1] The attackers, believed to be the Russian state-sponsored hacking group APT29 or 'Cozy Bear', were able to compromise the build process of SolarWinds' Orion software, a widely used network monitoring and management platform. They skilfully inserted malicious code, known as 'sunburst', into a legitimate software update, allowing the malware to be distributed to thousands of SolarWinds customers.

The impact of the attack was widespread and far-reaching. Estimates suggest that up to 18,000 SolarWinds customers may have been affected, including numerous government agencies, such as the US Department of Homeland Security, the State Department and the Treasury Department, as well as major corporations like Microsoft, FireEye and Cisco.[2] The Sunburst malware was designed to be stealthy and difficult to detect, giving the attackers the ability to gain access to the networks of these organizations and potentially compromise sensitive data and systems.

The SolarWinds breach highlighted the critical importance of securing the software supply chain and the need for organizations to implement robust vendor risk management practices, conduct thorough due diligence, and establish secure communication and data exchange protocols with their supply chain partners. The incident sparked extensive investigations by US government agencies, cybersecurity firms and international partners, as they worked to identify the full scope of the attack, assess the damage, and implement measures to prevent similar supply chain attacks in the future.

REAL-WORLD EXAMPLE

The Kaseya supply chain attack, which occurred in July 2021, was another devastating incident that exposed the vulnerabilities inherent in software supply chains.[3] Similar to the SolarWinds breach, the attackers were able to compromise the software development and update processes of Kaseya, a provider of remote monitoring and management (RMM) tools used by managed service providers (MSPs) and small and medium-sized businesses. Attackers managed to insert malicious code into a legitimate Kaseya software update and were able to gain access to the networks of not only Kaseya's direct customers, but also the clients of the affected MSPs.

Thousands of organizations worldwide were impacted, and as many as 1.5 million systems were affected by the deployed ransomware.[4] The attack caused significant disruption, forcing many businesses to temporarily shut down their operations to contain the damage. The Kaseya incident has been attributed to the REvil ransomware group, a prolific cybercriminal organization with suspected ties to Russia, known for its sophisticated ransomware tactics and ability to target high-profile victims.

The Kaseya attack underscored the cascading effects that can occur when a software supply chain is compromised, with the impact felt not only by Kaseya's direct customers, but also by the clients of the affected MSPs. The incident prompted renewed calls for improved software supply chain security practices, including the need for better visibility into the components and dependencies used in software products, as well as the importance of robust incident response and business continuity planning. The global investigation into the Kaseya attack, led by law enforcement agencies and cybersecurity firms, has resulted in steps to disrupt the operations of the REvil group, further highlighting the critical importance of addressing the evolving threat landscape and the need for a comprehensive and collaborative approach to supply chain security.

To mitigate these risks, organizations must implement a comprehensive approach to securing their software supply chain. This begins with strong vendor risk management practices that involve thoroughly vetting and assessing the security posture of all third-party providers. Conducting due diligence is vital, as organizations need to have a clear understanding of the security controls, policies and procedures in place at their supply chain partners. This includes evaluating the provider's access controls, patch management processes, incident response plans and overall security culture. Additionally, establishing secure communication and data exchange protocols with their supply chain partners will help with the flow of information.

One way to secure the software supply chain is to implement software composition analysis (SCA) tools. These tools help organizations identify and manage the open-source and third-party components used in their software, allowing them to detect and address vulnerabilities in a timely manner. SCA tools enable security teams to quickly identify and remediate any known vulnerabilities by maintaining a comprehensive inventory of the software components used throughout the organization. This is particularly important in today's fast-paced software development environment, where new vulnerabilities are constantly being discovered.

Robust access controls are another useful component of supply chain security. Organizations should ensure that only authorized personnel have access to sensitive systems and data, and that access privileges are regularly reviewed and updated, so that only the right people have the right level of access at the right time.

One emerging approach to supply chain security is the use of blockchain technology. Blockchain-based solutions can help to create a secure, transparent and tamper-resistant record of all transactions and interactions within the supply chain. This can help to improve traceability, reduce the risk of fraud, and enhance overall supply chain resilience.

However, even with these solutions in place, organizations must remain vigilant and proactive in their approach to securing the software supply chain. Activities such as the adoption of new technologies, the implementation of robust policies and procedures, and the fostering of a strong security culture throughout the organization and its supply chain partners are crucial.

Cloud

Although widely considered as part of the supply chain, the cloud is still a technology that continues to evolve. Years ago, the large cloud providers were convincing everyone that 'cloud is the new normal', and this sentiment is not far from the truth in most cases today. Even still, cloud can present ongoing challenges for some organizations. While cloud computing has become the predominant model, certain organizations, especially those with legacy systems, security/compliance concerns, limited IT expertise or budget constraints, may still struggle to fully embrace and optimize cloud-based infrastructure and services. Not every organization has the resources to afford and manage their own on-premises data centres, making cloud adoption a necessary step. However, the technical, financial and organizational changes required to transition to the cloud can still be a significant hurdle for some enterprises. The cloud has undoubtedly been a game-changer and enabled a deep ownership of applications in the enterprise. DevOps practices call it 'you build it, you run it'. Unsurprisingly, when engineers are now responsible for the production operations for the applications they build, they build applications that fail a whole lot less.

The challenge with identity and access management (IAM) in the cloud stems from the fact that application owners are now responsible for managing the infrastructure-level components and configurations that were previously handled by a dedicated IT team. This shift in responsibility can be daunting, as IAM is a complex and often obscure topic that is best handled by security specialists. The policy of least privilege, a fundamental security principle, becomes especially crucial in the cloud environment. This principle states that users, programs or processes should have only the minimum permissions necessary to perform their intended functions. Adhering to this principle helps minimize the potential damage that can be caused by unauthorized or malicious actors, as they would have limited access to sensitive resources.

However, for application owners, the policy of least privilege can be a double-edged sword. Their primary focus is on ensuring that their applications function correctly, and if permissions get in the way of that, the easy solution is to relax the permissions until the desired outcome is achieved. This approach, while expedient, can lead to a violation of the policy of least privilege and expose the organization to unnecessary security risks.

The complexity of managing and securing their cloud environments is a close second to IAM challenges. As businesses adopt a multi-cloud strategy, where they utilize services from multiple cloud providers, the task of maintaining consistent security policies and controls becomes increasingly complex. To overcome this challenge, cloud governance frameworks end up being rather useful, as well as tools that can help manage cloud resources effectively. This may include the use of cloud management platforms that provide a centralized view of the organization's cloud infrastructure and enable the enforcement of consistent security policies across multiple cloud environments.

Expansion of Internet of Things (IoT) security

The growth of the Internet of Things (IoT) has introduced a vast array of connected devices into homes, businesses and industrial settings. While these IoT systems offer numerous benefits in terms of automation, efficiency and data-driven insights, they also introduce significant security risks that must be addressed. Vulnerabilities in IoT devices can be exploited by cyber attackers to gain unauthorized access, disrupt operations or compromise sensitive data.

One of the primary security challenges with IoT is the sheer number and diversity of connected devices. Unlike traditional IT systems, which are typically managed by dedicated IT teams, IoT devices are often deployed and maintained by non-technical personnel, such as facility managers or homeowners. This can lead to a lack of consistent security practices, such as regular firmware updates or the use of strong passwords. Additionally, many IoT devices are designed with limited computational resources, making it difficult to implement robust security measures directly on the devices themselves. To mitigate these risks, a comprehensive approach to IoT security is needed, focusing on several key areas:

- **Device authentication:** Ensuring the authenticity of IoT devices is crucial to prevent unauthorized access and the introduction of rogue devices onto the network. This can be achieved through the use of secure, cryptographic-based authentication mechanisms, such as digital certificates or pre-shared keys. Verifying the identity of each device before granting it access to the network can significantly reduce the risk of unauthorized access and the potential for device-based attacks.

- **Secure firmware updates**: IoT devices often have long operational lifespans, during which time vulnerabilities may be discovered and need to be patched. Implementing a secure firmware update process is essential to ensure that IoT devices can be kept up-to-date with the latest security fixes. This may involve the use of digital signatures, encrypted update packages and secure communication channels to ensure the integrity and confidentiality of the update process.

- **Network monitoring and segmentation**: Comprehensive network monitoring and segmentation are critical for detecting and mitigating IoT-related security threats. Continuously monitoring network traffic and device behaviour can quickly identify and respond to anomalies, such as unusual data patterns or suspicious communication attempts. Additionally, network segmentation, which involves logically separating IoT devices from other network resources, can help to contain the impact of a successful attack and prevent the lateral movement of threats across the network.

- **Data protection**: IoT devices often collect and transmit sensitive data, such as personal information, operational data or industrial control system parameters. Ensuring the confidentiality, integrity and availability of this data is essential to protect against data breaches and the potential for disruption or manipulation of critical systems. This may involve the use of encryption, access controls and secure data storage and transmission protocols.

In addition to these technical measures, there is a significant human element of IoT security due to their ease of setup and utility. For example, it might seem innocuous for someone to offer some 'free smart plugs they had lying around' when it is mentioned that one of the people in the office tends to forget to turn off the space heater at night, but without knowing the origins or security characteristics of that device, it may actually be leaking information. This education might require comprehensive training and awareness programmes for employees, contractors and end-users to ensure they understand their role in maintaining the security of IoT products and systems. Additionally, clear policies and procedures for the management and oversight of IoT devices, including guidelines for device procurement, deployment and retirement, are all pillars of a good IoT security programme.

As the IoT ecosystem continues to grow, the importance of robust security measures will only increase. Having a comprehensive IoT security strategy that addresses device authentication, firmware updates, network monitoring and segmentation, and data protection, means that organizations can significantly reduce the risk of cyber threats and ensure the safe and reliable operation of their IoT systems. However, it is important to note that the IoT security landscape is constantly evolving, and organizations must remain vigilant and adaptable in their approach. Continuous monitoring, threat intelligence gathering and the implementation of new security technologies and best practices will be essential to staying ahead of new cyber threats targeting IoT systems.

AI/ML

The rapid advancement of artificial intelligence (AI) and machine learning (ML) technologies has ushered in a new era of both incredible potential and significant security risks. As these powerful tools become more widely adopted across industries and even our day-to-day lives, adversaries are increasingly seeking to exploit them for malicious ends.

One of the primary security challenges posed by AI/ML is the threat of adversarial attacks. Researchers have demonstrated that AI models can be 'fooled' by carefully crafted inputs designed to cause the model to misclassify or behave in unintended ways. For example, adding imperceptible perturbations to an image can cause a state-of-the-art image recognition model to confidently misidentify the contents. Adversaries could leverage such techniques to bypass security controls, evade detection or even cause physical harm in the real world. Imagine a self-driving car that is tricked into misinterpreting a stop sign, or a malware detection system that fails to identify a malicious payload. The potential for abuse is vast and growing.

Another major concern is the potential for AI/ML to be used to automate and scale up cyber-attacks. Malicious actors could develop AI-powered tools to scan for vulnerabilities, launch distributed denial-of-service (DDoS) attacks, or even generate convincing phishing emails and deepfake videos. The ability to rapidly iterate and optimize these attacks could make them far more difficult to defend against. The rapid increase of deepfake technology in particular poses a serious threat to security and trust. Highly realistic fake videos and audio can be used to impersonate public figures, spread disinformation or even commit financial fraud.

Compounding these challenges is the inherent nature of many AI/ML models. The complex, non-linear relationships learned by these systems can make it difficult to understand how they arrive at their outputs, let alone audit or verify their behaviour. This opacity can hamper efforts to detect and mitigate malicious use cases. Unlike traditional software programs, which are built using explicit, rule-based logic, most modern AI systems rely on complex neural network architectures that learn patterns from vast amounts of training data. During the training process, these neural networks adjust millions or even billions of internal parameters, forging intricate connections and representations that allow them to recognize patterns and make predictions. However, the specific reasoning behind these learned representations is often opaque, even to the researchers and engineers who create the models. This is because the training process is fundamentally different from human learning. Rather than consciously encoding rules and logic, AI models discover their own implicit, non-linear relationships within the data. The end result is a highly capable system, but one that can be difficult to interpret, explain or audit. The deeper and more complex the model, the more challenging it becomes to understand the reasoning behind its outputs. This opacity can be particularly problematic when it comes to security and safety-critical applications. If an AI system makes a decision that leads to unintended or harmful consequences, it may be difficult to pinpoint the root cause or ensure that the issue has been fully resolved.

To address these emerging security threats, a multi-pronged approach is required. First and foremost, researchers and developers must prioritize the security and depth of AI/ML systems from the ground up. This means incorporating adversarial training, anomaly detection and other techniques to harden models against malicious inputs and behaviours. Adversarial training, for example, involves exposing models to carefully crafted adversarial examples during the training process, helping them learn to recognize and resist such attacks. Anomaly detection, on the other hand, can be used to identify and flag unusual or suspicious model outputs that may indicate malicious activity.

Additionally, organizations must also invest in comprehensive security monitoring and incident response capabilities tailored to the unique challenges of AI/ML. This could involve developing specialized threat intelligence, deploying AI-powered security tools, and training personnel to recognize and respond to AI-related attacks.

One promising area of focus is the development of 'explainable AI' (XAI) systems that aim to provide greater transparency and interpretability. XAI techniques, such as feature importance analysis and model visualization, can shed light on the inner workings of AI/ML models, allowing for better understanding and control. This, in turn, can enhance trust, enable more effective risk management, and support the development of robust, secure AI systems.

Another approach is the development of AI security frameworks that provide a structured way to assess and manage the risks associated with AI/ML systems. These frameworks can help identify potential vulnerabilities, implement appropriate safeguards, and monitor emerging threats. The National Institute of Standards and Technology (NIST), for example, has published a draft AI Risk Management Framework that outlines a comprehensive set of guidelines and best practices for AI security and governance. This includes recommendations for risk assessment, model testing and incident response planning. Similarly, the IEEE has developed the Ethically Aligned Design (EAD) framework that provides guidance on the responsible development and deployment of autonomous and intelligent systems. Incorporating ethical principles and security considerations into the design process can help ensure that AI/ML technologies are aligned with societal values and interests.

Policymakers and regulators play a critical role in shaping the responsible development and deployment of AI/ML technologies. The European Union's AI Act, which entered into force on 1 August 2024, has established a comprehensive regulatory framework for AI, including risk-based rules for high-risk applications, transparency requirements, and governance structures. Since February 2025, bans on AI systems posing unacceptable risks (e.g. social scoring) are already in effect,[5] with phased enforcement continuing through 2027. Similarly, the US has institutionalized its AI strategy through the National AI Initiative Office, launched under the 2020 National AI Initiative Act to coordinate research, policymaking, and public–private collaboration.[6] These frameworks aim to balance innovation with safeguards, promoting best practices and responsible AI development globally.

As AI/ML continues to evolve and become ubiquitous, the need for vigilance and innovation in cybersecurity will only grow. With the right strategies and investments, we can stay one step ahead of the adversaries and build a more secure and resilient digital future. Key to this effort will be the development of robust, secure and trustworthy AI/ML systems that can withstand the scrutiny of adversaries and the demands of mission-critical applications.

Edge computing security

The rapid increase in the global mobile device count has significant implications for the rollout and adoption of 5G networks and edge computing. With 18.2 billion devices expected to be in use by 2025,[7] 5G infrastructure and edge network capabilities will need to be able to support and connect this massive number of devices seamlessly.

Edge computing refers to the practice of processing and analysing data closer to the source of data generation, rather than in a centralized data centre or cloud. This distributed computing model aims to reduce latency, improve responsiveness, and minimize the bandwidth required for data transmission. The sheer scale of the 5G network and distributed edge computing required to serve this many mobile endpoints introduces new challenges around capacity, coverage, data processing and security that network providers and edge computing operators will have to carefully navigate.

At the core of the 5G revolution is the promise of faster speeds, lower latency and greater connectivity. 5G networks aim to enable a wide range of new applications by leveraging advanced radio technologies and network architectures from autonomous vehicles to remote healthcare. However, with these capabilities come significant security risks.

One of the primary concerns is the expanded attack surface created by 5G. The increased number of connected devices, the increase in the number of network access points, and the complexity of 5G infrastructure all provide more opportunities for malicious actors to gain unauthorized access and wreak havoc. Adversaries could exploit vulnerabilities in 5G network components, such as base stations or core network elements, to launch distributed denial-of-service (DDoS) attacks, intercept sensitive data, or even disrupt critical infrastructure.

The transition to 5G will also require the integration of a wide range of technologies, including virtualization, software-defined networking and cloud computing. This convergence of systems and platforms can introduce new points of failure and increase the risk of cascading failures or cross-domain attacks. The scale and interconnectedness of 5G networks make them an attractive target for sophisticated cyber threats.

Compounding these challenges is the global nature of 5G deployment. As nations and organizations around the world race to build out their 5G networks, the potential for supply chain vulnerabilities and geopolitical tensions to undermine security grows exponentially. Adversaries could target the global 5G supply chain to inject malware, compromise hardware or disrupt critical components. The complexity and interdependence of these supply chains make them inherently difficult to secure, requiring a coordinated, international effort to mitigate the risks.

Edge computing introduces its own set of security concerns. The paradigm shift to distributing computing resources and data across a vast network of edge devices can create new attack vectors and increase the potential for data breaches. Edge devices, such as IoT sensors, surveillance cameras and industrial controllers, often have limited computational power and security capabilities, making them vulnerable to exploitation.

Yet another challenge compounding this domain is that the volume of data generated and processed at the edge can overwhelm traditional security monitoring and incident response approaches. Detecting and responding to threats in this highly distributed, dynamic environment requires new tools and techniques that can operate at scale and adapt to rapidly changing conditions.

Looking ahead, the continued evolution of these technologies will likely introduce even more complex security challenges. As 5G networks become more advanced and edge computing becomes more pervasive, the potential attack surface will only continue to grow. Edge computing security will benefit from strong identity and access management controls, data encryption both in transit and at rest, and real-time analysis of device telemetry. Traditional perimeter-based defences become less effective in distributed edge architecture, so be sceptical of network connections coming from edge devices ('zero trust' is discussed later in this chapter). Maintaining tight integration and visibility between edge devices and their control planes is an easy way to centralize security operations.

Quantum computing

The rapid advancement of quantum computing technology poses a significant threat to the security of our digital infrastructure. As quantum computers become more powerful and accessible, they have the potential to break many of the cryptographic algorithms that underpin the security of our online communications, financial transactions and sensitive data.

To understand this challenge is to understand the unique way that quantum computers operate. Traditional computers, based on classical physics, process information using binary bits that can exist in a state of either 0 or 1. Quantum computers, on the other hand, utilize quantum bits, or 'qubits', that can exist in a superposition of both

0 and 1 simultaneously. This allows quantum computers to perform certain computations exponentially faster than classical computers, particularly when it comes to factoring large numbers and solving discrete logarithm problems.

The implications of this quantum computing advantage are far-reaching. Many of the cryptographic algorithms that we rely on today, such as RSA and Elliptic Curve Cryptography (ECC), derive their security from the difficulty of factoring large numbers or solving discrete logarithm problems. RSA encryption is based on the difficulty of factoring large numbers, specifically the product of two large prime numbers. Factoring large numbers is an extremely computationally intensive task for classical computers, making it infeasible for attackers to reverse the encryption and recover the original plaintext.

Similarly, ECC is based on the difficulty of solving the discrete logarithm problem on elliptic curves. The discrete logarithm problem involves finding the exponent x, given a base g and a result g^x. On elliptic curves, this problem becomes exponentially harder to solve as the curve size increases, and the computational complexity of solving the discrete logarithm problem on elliptic curves is the foundation of ECC's security.

The security of these algorithms relies on the fact that there are no known efficient algorithms for factoring large numbers or solving the discrete logarithm problem on classical computers. This means that an attacker would need an impractically large amount of time and computational resources to break the encryption. However, quantum computers have the potential to solve these problems much more efficiently, using algorithms like Shor's algorithm. Shor's algorithm is a quantum algorithm that can efficiently solve the integer factorization problem and the discrete logarithm problem on a quantum computer. Specifically, Shor's algorithm allows a quantum computer to factor large integers and solve the discrete logarithm problem much faster than classical computers.

This is why the advent of large-scale quantum computing poses a significant threat to the security of these widely used cryptographic algorithms, as quantum computers could potentially break RSA and ECC encryption in a matter of seconds, rendering them obsolete for protecting sensitive information.

This threat is not just theoretical – it is a very real and pressing concern for governments, businesses and individuals around the world. As quantum computing technology continues to advance, the risk of a 'quantum apocalypse' – where all of our current cryptographic standards become obsolete – is becoming increasingly tangible.

The potential consequences of such a scenario are dire. Sensitive government and military communications could be compromised, financial transactions could be hijacked, and personal data could be stolen on a massive scale. The economic and social impact of a quantum-driven security breach could be catastrophic, with far-reaching implications for national security, economic stability and individual privacy.

In response to this threat, governments and industry leaders are working to develop new, quantum-resistant cryptographic algorithms that can withstand the power of quantum computers. This process, known as 'post-quantum cryptography', involves the creation of new encryption methods that are based on mathematical problems that are believed to be resistant to quantum attacks.

One approach is the use of lattice-based cryptography, which relies on the difficulty of solving certain lattice problems. A lattice problem is a type of mathematical problem that is believed to be resistant to attacks by quantum computers, making it a promising foundation for post-quantum cryptography. In the context of cryptography, a lattice is a discrete subgroup of a Euclidean space that is generated by a set of linearly independent vectors. Lattice problems involve finding solutions to various optimization and decision problems related to these lattice structures.

In addition to lattice-based cryptography, researchers are exploring several other approaches for developing quantum-resistant cryptographic algorithms. One such approach is hash-based cryptography, which uses cryptographic hash functions as the foundation for its security. Hash functions are believed to be resistant to quantum attacks, as they do not rely on the difficulty of factoring large numbers or solving discrete logarithm problems.

Another alternative is code-based cryptography, which uses error-correcting codes as the basis for its security. The security of code-based cryptography relies on the difficulty of decoding a random linear code, which is believed to be a computationally hard problem for both classical and quantum computers.

Multivariate cryptography is a third approach, which uses systems of multivariate polynomial equations as the foundation for its security. The security of multivariate cryptography relies on the difficulty of solving systems of nonlinear polynomial equations, which is believed to be a hard problem for both classical and quantum computers.

These alternative approaches to post-quantum cryptography offer different mathematical foundations and security properties compared to lattice-based cryptography. Through the exploration of a diverse range of quantum-resistant cryptographic techniques, researchers and policymakers hope to develop a robust and versatile set of tools for protecting against the threat of quantum computing. The development and standardization of these post-quantum cryptographic algorithms is an active area of research and collaboration within the global cybersecurity community, as governments and industry work to prepare for the potential advent of large-scale quantum computing. Such efforts are currently being tested and evaluated by organizations such as the National Institute of Standards and Technology (NIST) in the United States, with the goal of establishing new standards for quantum-resistant encryption.

In addition to these technical efforts, there is also a growing recognition of the need for broader policy and regulatory responses to the quantum computing threat. This includes the development of new standards and guidelines for the use of cryptographic algorithms, as well as the implementation of robust incident response and recovery plans in the event of a quantum-driven security breach. Somewhat recently, the European Union has produced the Quantum Flagship initiative. Launched in 2018, the Quantum Flagship is a 1 billion euro research and innovation programme that aims to accelerate the development of quantum technologies, including quantum computing and quantum-resistant cryptography.[8] The initiative brings together researchers, industry leaders and policymakers from across Europe to collaborate on the development of new quantum-based solutions and to address the security challenges posed by quantum computing.

Similar efforts are underway in other parts of the world, including the United States, where the National Quantum Initiative Act was signed into law, also in 2018.[9] This legislation provides funding and support for quantum research and development, with a particular focus on the development of quantum-resistant cryptography and other quantum-based security solutions.

Even still, the threat of quantum computing extends far beyond the realm of cybersecurity, highlighting the breadth of this issue. As quantum computers become more powerful, they could have significant benefits for other areas of technology and industry, such as materials science, drug discovery, logistics, supply chain management and financial modelling. However, the ability of quantum computers to perform complex simulations and optimizations could also be used to manipulate financial markets, disrupt critical infrastructure, and undermine economic stability.

This is a challenge that will require a comprehensive, cross-cutting response that addresses the potential impacts of quantum computing across a wide range of industries and applications. To meet this challenge, governments, industry leaders and the broader scientific community will need to work together to develop a coordinated, global strategy for addressing the quantum computing threat. This will require significant investments in research and development, the establishment of new standards and guidelines, and the implementation of robust incident response and recovery plans.

Insider threat

One of the most concerning threats facing any organization comes from within – the insider threat. Organizations are becoming more distributed and, with remote work becoming more common, the risk of malicious insiders or negligent employees compromising security is on the rise.

Insider threats can take many forms, from disgruntled employees seeking to sabotage the organization, to careless workers inadvertently exposing sensitive data, to malicious actors exploiting their privileged access for personal gain. These threats can be particularly insidious, as insiders often have intimate knowledge of an organization's systems, processes and vulnerabilities, making them well-equipped to bypass security measures and cause significant damage.

When employees work remotely, they often access sensitive information and systems from personal devices and networks that may not have the same level of security controls as the organization's on-premises infrastructure. This can make it easier for malicious actors to gain unauthorized access to critical data and systems. Additionally, the lack of physical oversight and the blurring of work–life boundaries can make it more difficult to detect and respond to insider threats in a timely manner.

Another factor contributing to the insider threat challenge is the increasing complexity of modern technology ecosystems. As organizations adopt a growing array of cloud-based applications, collaboration tools and IoT devices, the attack surface expands, creating more potential entry points for malicious insiders. Keeping track of user access privileges, monitoring activity across disparate systems, and ensuring consistent security practices can be a daunting task for many organizations.

Many of the risk mitigation strategies mentioned throughout this book apply here, such as strong identity and access management, as well as user and entity behaviour analytics, and incident response. Some companies go as far as employee monitoring and surveillance technologies. While this approach raises ethical and privacy concerns, it can be a necessary measure in certain high-risk environments, such as those dealing with sensitive national security or financial information. However, the implementation of such technologies should be balanced with the need to maintain employee trust and morale. Overly intrusive monitoring can lead to resentment and a breakdown in the employer–employee relationship that can ultimately undermine the organization's security posture. What's more, in many jurisdictions, there are strict laws and regulations governing the collection, storage and use of employee data, and organizations must ensure that their security practices comply with these requirements.

Skills gap

One of the most pressing challenges facing organizations is the growing skills gap in the field of cybersecurity. As the threat landscape becomes increasingly complex and the adoption of new technologies accelerates, there is a critical shortage of cybersecurity professionals with the necessary expertise to keep up and implement effective security measures. The cybersecurity skills gap is a global phenomenon, with organizations across industries struggling to find and retain qualified personnel. According to a report by ISC2, the global cybersecurity workforce needs to grow by 65 per cent to effectively defend organizations against the growing number of cyber threats.[10] This shortage of skilled cybersecurity professionals is a significant concern, as it leaves organizations vulnerable to a wide range of attacks, from data breaches and ransomware to sophisticated nation-state-sponsored cyber espionage.

The rapid pace of technological change is a significant driver of the cybersecurity skills gap. Embracing new technologies, such as cloud computing, the Internet of Things (IoT) and artificial intelligence (AI), expands the attack surface, and the skills required to secure these environments become increasingly specialized and in-demand. For example, the shift to cloud-based infrastructure has created a need for professionals with expertise in cloud security, including the ability to configure and manage cloud access controls, data encryption and incident response procedures. Similarly, the proliferation of IoT devices has introduced new vulnerabilities that require specialized knowledge of embedded systems, network protocols and device-level security.

Furthermore, the growing reliance on AI and machine learning in cybersecurity solutions has created a need for professionals who can not only understand the underlying algorithms and models but also assess the potential risks and ethical implications of these technologies.

Advancement of threats contributes to the gap as well. Cybercriminals, nation-state actors and other malicious entities are constantly developing new and more sophisticated attack methods, requiring cybersecurity professionals to continuously update their knowledge and skills to stay ahead of the curve.

This dynamic threat landscape demands that cybersecurity professionals possess a diverse range of skills, including technical expertise in areas such as network security, incident response and threat intelligence, as well as broader business acumen and strategic thinking to align security measures with organizational goals and risk management strategies.

The challenge of finding and retaining qualified cybersecurity talent is further exacerbated by the highly competitive job market. As the demand for cybersecurity professionals outpaces the supply, organizations are often forced to offer higher salaries and more attractive benefits to attract and retain the best talent, putting a strain on their budgets and resources.

To resist this global shortage in the short term, organizations can focus on upskilling and reskilling their existing workforce, providing comprehensive training and development programmes to help employees acquire the necessary skills to meet the evolving security challenges using initiatives such as hands-on workshops, online courses and certifications that cover the latest security technologies, threat intelligence and incident response best practices.

In the long term, organizations must work collaboratively with educational institutions, government agencies and industry associations to address the root causes of the cybersecurity skills gap with initiatives such as curriculum development, internship and apprenticeship programmes, outreach and awareness campaigns, and continuous professional development.

Emerging trends in cybersecurity

Evolving technologies and their security challenges overlap with emerging cybersecurity trends.

Increased use of artificial intelligence and machine learning

Artificial intelligence (AI) and machine learning (ML) have become indispensable tools in the realm of cybersecurity, revolutionizing the way organizations detect, respond and mitigate threats. These advanced technologies are being leveraged for a wide range of security-related tasks, from threat detection and vulnerability analysis to automated incident response, enabling security teams to keep pace with the ever-evolving landscape of cyber threats.

One of the primary ways in which AI and ML are transforming cybersecurity is through enhanced threat detection capabilities. Traditional security systems often rely on rule-based approaches that can be limited in their ability to identify novel or sophisticated threats. AI-powered systems, on the other hand, can analyse vast amounts of data from various sources, including network traffic, user behaviour and security logs, to identify patterns and anomalies that may indicate the presence of a cyber threat.

These systems can continuously learn and adapt, becoming more effective at detecting and preventing attacks over time just by leveraging machine learning algorithms. For example, AI-based intrusion detection systems can analyse network traffic in real-time, identifying suspicious activity and alerting security teams to potential breaches. These systems can detect complex, multi-stage attacks that may have gone unnoticed by traditional security tools, enabling organizations to respond more quickly and effectively. Additionally, AI-powered user and entity behaviour analytics (UEBA) can identify anomalies in user behaviour, such as unusual login patterns or data access activities that could be indicative of a compromised account or insider threat.

Another area where AI and ML are making a significant impact is in the realm of vulnerability analysis and management. Cybersecurity professionals are often tasked with identifying and addressing vulnerabilities in an organization's IT infrastructure, a process that can be time-consuming and resource-intensive. AI-powered vulnerability scanning tools can automate this process, continuously monitoring systems and applications for known vulnerabilities, and prioritizing remediation efforts based on factors such as the severity of the vulnerability and the potential impact on the organization.

AI and ML are also revolutionizing the way organizations respond to security incidents. Automated incident response systems can leverage machine learning algorithms to analyse security alerts, correlate data from multiple sources, and initiate appropriate response actions, such as quarantining infected devices or blocking malicious traffic. This not only reduces the time and effort required to respond to security incidents but also ensures a more consistent and effective response, as the system can make decisions based on pre-defined protocols and historical data.

In addition to these operational benefits, AI and ML are also transforming the way organizations approach cybersecurity strategy and decision-making. Easily analysing vast amounts of security data can provide valuable insights and recommendations to security teams, enabling them to make more informed, data-driven decisions. For example, AI-powered threat intelligence platforms can aggregate and analyse data from various sources, including open-source intelligence, dark web forums and security research, to provide organizations with a comprehensive understanding of the threat landscape and the latest attack trends.

AI and ML are being used to enhance the efficiency and effectiveness of security operations centres (SOCs) by automating repetitive tasks, such as alert triage and incident investigation. AI-powered SOC tools can free up security analysts to focus on more complex and strategic tasks, such as threat hunting and incident response planning. Additionally, these technologies can help SOCs to identify and prioritize the most critical security events, ensuring that limited resources are allocated to the most pressing threats.

There is no doubt that integration of AI and ML into the realm of cybersecurity has been a game-changer. These advanced technologies are being leveraged for a wide range of security-related tasks, from threat detection and vulnerability analysis to automated incident response, enabling security teams to keep pace with the ever-evolving landscape of cyber threats. However, the integration of AI and ML into cybersecurity is not without its challenges.

One of the primary concerns is the potential for bias and inaccuracy in the underlying data and algorithms used by these technologies. If the training data or the machine learning models are biased or incomplete, the resulting security decisions and recommendations may be flawed or even harmful. To mitigate these risks, organizations must carefully evaluate the data and algorithms used by their AI and ML-powered security solutions and ensure that they are regularly tested and validated.

Another challenge is the need for skilled personnel to effectively leverage these technologies. Implementing and maintaining AI and ML-powered security solutions requires a deep understanding of both cybersecurity and data science principles. Organizations must invest in training and upskilling their security teams to ensure that they can effectively utilize these technologies and interpret the insights they provide. Despite these challenges, the adoption of AI and ML in cybersecurity is only expected to accelerate in the coming years. As these technologies continue to evolve and become more sophisticated, they will play an increasingly crucial role in helping organizations to stay ahead of emerging threats. Automating security processes, enhancing threat detection and response capabilities, and providing valuable insights and recommendations will become indispensable tools in the arsenal of modern cybersecurity professionals.

Rise of cloud-based security solutions

As organizations continue to migrate their infrastructure and data to the cloud, the demand for cloud-native security tools and services has grown exponentially.

One of the primary advantages of cloud-based security solutions is their ability to scale up or down as an organization's cloud footprint evolves. Traditional on-premises security tools can often struggle to keep pace with the rapid growth and dynamic nature of cloud environments, leading to gaps in coverage and increased management overhead. Cloud-native security solutions, on the other hand, are designed to seamlessly scale with the organization, ensuring that security measures remain effective and efficient as the cloud infrastructure expands or contracts.

Cloud-based security solutions also offer a high degree of flexibility, allowing organizations to tailor their security posture to their specific needs. Rather than being locked into a one-size-fits-all approach, cloud-native security tools can be easily configured and customized to address the unique security challenges faced by each organization. This flexibility extends to the deployment and management of these solutions, as they can often be provisioned and maintained through a centralized cloud-based platform, reducing the burden on in-house IT and security teams.

Additionally, another key benefit of cloud-based security solutions is their cost-efficiency. Leveraging the scalability and on-demand nature of cloud computing avoids the upfront capital expenditures and ongoing maintenance costs associated with traditional on-premises security infrastructure. Cloud-native security tools are typically offered on a subscription-based model to scale security measures up or down as needed and only pay for the resources consumed. This can result in significant cost savings, particularly for organizations with fluctuating or unpredictable security requirements.

One of the defining features of cloud-native security solutions is their integration with other cloud platforms and services. These solutions are designed to work in harmony with the underlying cloud infrastructure, providing centralized visibility, control and incident response capabilities across the entire cloud ecosystem. This integration allows security teams to monitor and manage security controls, threat detection and incident response from a single, unified interface, streamlining the security management process and reducing the risk of blind spots or siloed security data. For example, cloud-native security tools can be integrated with cloud-based IAMI services to enforce granular access controls and monitor user activity across their cloud resources. Similarly, these solutions can be integrated with cloud-based logging and monitoring services, allowing security teams to analyse security events and detect anomalies in real-time, and initiate automated response actions to mitigate threats.

In addition to their technical capabilities, cloud-based security solutions often benefit from the scale and expertise of the cloud service providers that offer them. These providers typically have access to vast amounts of security data and threat intelligence that they can leverage to continuously improve the detection and prevention capabilities of their cloud-native security tools. This results in a more robust and up-to-date security posture with the advantage of the provider's ongoing research and development efforts gained.

As discussed earlier in the chapter, some organizations may find the adoption of cloud-based security solutions challenging, citing concerns regarding the potential for data privacy and compliance issues, as organizations must ensure that their cloud-based security tools and processes adhere to relevant data protection regulations and industry standards. To mitigate these risks, organizations must carefully evaluate the security and compliance features of their cloud-native security solutions, as well as the data handling practices of their cloud service providers. Just like AI and ML solutions, there will be the need for skilled personnel to effectively leverage these tools and services.

Adoption of zero trust security models

The traditional network perimeter, once the cornerstone of enterprise security, is rapidly becoming obsolete. As organizations embrace the transformative power of remote work, cloud computing and the proliferation of connected devices, the once-defined boundaries that protected corporate assets have become increasingly porous. In response to this shift, the adoption of zero trust security models has emerged as a critical strategy for organizations seeking to enhance their cybersecurity posture.

Zero trust security models are founded on the principle of continuous verification, rather than relying solely on perimeter-based defences. This approach assumes that no user or device can be inherently trusted, regardless of their location or network connection. Instead, every access request is scrutinized, and access is granted only after a thorough verification process. This concept would have helped Sony in 2014 (see Chapter 1).

A key advantage of zero trust security is its ability to adapt. Traditional security models often relied on static perimeter defences, such as firewalls and VPNs, which could become outdated and vulnerable with every new threat that emerges. In contrast, zero trust security employs a dynamic, risk-based approach that continuously evaluates and adjusts access controls based on a variety of factors, including user identity, device posture, location and behaviour. Implementing zero trust principles can enhance access controls and minimize the risk of unauthorized access. Instead of granting blanket access to users and devices based on their network location, zero trust security requires users and devices to authenticate and authorize themselves for each access request. This approach helps to mitigate the risk of credential theft, lateral movement and other advanced threats that can exploit traditional perimeter-based defences.

Zero trust security models also enable organizations to better protect their critical assets, even as the traditional network perimeter continues to dissolve. With the rise of cloud computing and remote work, sensitive data and applications are no longer confined within the physical boundaries of the organization like they used to be. Implementation of robust identity and access management (IAM) solutions is an essential component of a zero trust security strategy. These tools enable organizations to centrally manage user identities, enforce granular access controls, and monitor user activities across the entire IT ecosystem. IAM solutions help to ensure that only authorized individuals can access the resources they need, when they need them, by leveraging multi-factor authentication, risk-based access policies and continuous monitoring.

In addition to IAM, zero trust security models often incorporate other security technologies, such as network segmentation, endpoint security and data protection solutions. A layered approach to security can create a more resilient and adaptable defence against evolving threats.

One of the key drivers behind the rise of zero trust security is the need to address the growing threat of ransomware. Ransomware attacks have become increasingly sophisticated, targeting organizations of all sizes and across various industries. Zero trust principles can reduce the risk of successful ransomware attacks by limiting the lateral movement of threat actors, enforcing granular access controls, and quickly detecting and responding to suspicious activities.

Another important aspect of zero trust security is its ability to support the growing trend of remote work. As the Covid-19 pandemic has demonstrated, the traditional office-centric model of work is rapidly evolving, with more employees working from home or on the go. Zero trust security models are well-suited to this new reality, as they can provide secure access to corporate resources regardless of the user's location or device.

Zero trust security models can also bring operational benefits to organizations by centralizing identity and access management. One key aspect of this is the ability to effectively manage the 'joiners, movers and leavers' within the organization. The 'joiners, movers and leavers' concept refers to the ongoing changes in an organization's workforce, where new employees are joining, existing employees are changing roles or locations, and others are leaving the organization. Effectively managing these changes is critical for maintaining a secure and efficient IT ecosystem.

In a traditional security model, managing these workforce changes can be a complex and time-consuming process. When a new employee joins the organization, IT teams must provision access to the necessary systems and applications, often manually configuring permissions and access rights. As employees move to different roles or locations, their access privileges must be updated accordingly, which can be a laborious task. And when an employee leaves the organization, their access must be promptly revoked to prevent unauthorized access to sensitive data or systems. However, with a zero trust security model and a centralized identity and access management (IAM) solution, organizations can streamline these processes and improve overall visibility and control.

When a new employee joins the organization, the IAM system can automatically provision their access based on their role, department or other predefined criteria, ensuring that new employees can quickly and securely access the resources they need to be productive, without the need for manual intervention by IT teams.

As employees change roles or locations within the organization, the IAM system can automatically update their access privileges, ensuring that they maintain the appropriate level of access to perform their new responsibilities. This reduces the administrative burden on IT teams and helps to minimize the risk of over-privileged access or unauthorized access to sensitive resources.

When an employee leaves the organization, the IAM system can automatically revoke their access to all corporate resources, including cloud-based applications, on-premises systems and physical access to facilities. This helps to ensure that former employees cannot retain access to sensitive data or systems, reducing the risk of data breaches or other security incidents.

Centralizing identity and access management within a zero trust security model can streamline these 'joiners, movers and leavers' processes, reducing the administrative burden on IT teams and improving overall visibility and control over their IT ecosystem. This not only enhances the organization's security posture but also enables more efficient and effective IT operations, ultimately contributing to the overall operational benefits of a zero trust security approach.

As the corporate technology landscape continues to transform, the adoption of zero trust security will become a crucial strategy for organizations seeking to safeguard their data, applications and critical infrastructure. Through the continuous verification of users and devices and adapting their security measures to the evolving needs of the business, organizations can enhance their overall cybersecurity posture and better protect their critical assets.

The ongoing journey: a future-proof security strategy

Risk is the nucleus of the entire world of cybersecurity. Risk is embedded into our own subconscious and is assessed constantly by autonomous brain functions that sometimes manifest into consciousness in the form of things like the 'fight or flight' response. To 'future-proof' your security strategy, your strategy must be able to decisively and constantly evaluate risk. This means knowing the company's critical assets, potential threats and vulnerabilities first, supported by strategies such as flexible and scalable security architecture, a zero trust security model, security automation and orchestration, incident response and disaster recovery plan, a culture of security awareness and collaboration, and continuously monitoring and adapting the security strategy. A risk-based approach ensures that security resources are allocated efficiently, with the most pressing risks receiving the highest priority, and also allows for the adaptation of security measures as the threat landscape evolves, regularly reviewing and updating the risk assessment to address emerging threats and changing business needs.

As technology continues to advance and business requirements shift, organizations must ensure that their security infrastructure is designed to be flexible and scalable. This means creating a modular security architecture that can easily integrate new technologies and security solutions as needed. Leveraging cloud-based security services and platforms will benefit from the inherent scalability and adaptability of the cloud and can scale up or down as needs evolve, providing a cost-effective and agile approach to security.

Cloud or not, the technological solutions deployed must be carefully selected, integrated and maintained to provide comprehensive protection. This includes implementing a layered security approach, with multiple security controls working in harmony to detect, prevent and respond to security incidents.

However, effective cybersecurity is not just about implementing the latest security technologies; it requires a holistic approach that encompasses people, processes and technology. This means that organizations must also consider the human element, the organizational policies and procedures, and the technological solutions in a cohesive and integrated manner. Investing in security awareness training for all employees is a critical component of this holistic approach. Educating employees on security best practices, recognizing and reporting suspicious activities, and understanding their role in maintaining a secure environment will create a strong human firewall against cyber threats.

Equally important is the development and enforcement of comprehensive security policies and procedures. These guidelines should cover areas such as access controls, data management, incident response and acceptable use of company resources. Regular review and updates to these policies are necessary to ensure they remain relevant and effective in the face of evolving threats and business requirements.

Effective cybersecurity also requires a diverse and skilled team of professionals, each with their unique expertise and perspectives. Building a security team that encompasses a range of backgrounds, skills and experiences can enhance the organization's ability to identify, mitigate and respond to security threats. Attracting and retaining top talent in the cybersecurity field can be a challenge, as the demand for skilled professionals continues to outpace the supply. To address this, organizations should invest in comprehensive training and development programmes, offering opportunities for continuous learning and skill enhancement. Additionally, organizations should consider building partnerships with educational institutions, industry associations and government agencies to access a broader pool of talent and stay informed about the latest trends and best practices in cybersecurity.

Diversity within the security team is also crucial, as it can foster a culture of innovation, collaboration and problem-solving. Bringing together individuals with diverse backgrounds, experiences and perspectives will enhance the ability to anticipate and respond to a wide range of security challenges.

The security team should also be empowered to collaborate closely with other departments, such as IT, legal and compliance, to ensure a holistic and coordinated approach to security management. This cross-functional collaboration can help identify and address potential blind spots, as well as ensure that the security strategy is aligned with the organization's overall business objectives.

A culture of continuous improvement, where security processes and controls are regularly reviewed and refined, will ensure that the security strategy remains agile and adaptable. Activities for continuous improvement involve conducting post-incident reviews to identify lessons learned, implementing feedback loops to gather input from stakeholders, and continuously benchmarking the organization's security posture against industry standards and best practices.

Remember that cybersecurity is not a solo endeavour; it requires collaboration and coordination within a broader ecosystem of partners and stakeholders. By fostering strong relationships with industry peers, security vendors, government agencies and other relevant organizations, companies can leverage collective intelligence, share best practices and access a wider range of resources and expertise. Participation in industry associations, information-sharing initiatives and threat intelligence-sharing platforms can be particularly valuable in this regard. These collaborative efforts can help organizations keep informed about emerging threats, access timely and relevant security information, and coordinate response efforts in the event of a large-scale cyber incident.

However, at the heart of this strategy lies the critical importance of people. Fostering a culture of security awareness and collaboration, cultivating a diverse and skilled security team, and investing in continuous learning and improvement are essential elements that cannot be overlooked. Employees play a vital role in maintaining a strong security posture. Educating and empowering them to be active participants in the security process creates a headwind against cyber threats. Encouraging a security-minded mindset and providing opportunities for ongoing training and development can help ensure that all members of the organization are equipped to identify, report and respond to security incidents.

As the cybersecurity landscape continues to evolve, organizations that prioritize the development and implementation of a comprehensive, adaptable and forward-looking security strategy, with a strong emphasis on the human element, will be better equipped to navigate the challenges of the digital age and protect their critical assets, reputation and long-term success.

KEY TAKEAWAYS

- Security is an arms race, with malicious actors and defenders both rapidly advancing their technologies – organizations must continuously adapt their security measures to keep up with nascent threats.

- AI is here to stay and is a valuable tool in the security toolbox due to its ability to go very deep and very wide when it comes to assessing information.

- Cloud is also a useful tool to handle vast amounts of data quickly, due to its distributed nature (but watch out for costs).

- Never trust anything, from anywhere on the network; ensure atomic authorization for each request.

Notes

1 Dan Goodin. SolarWinds hackers have a clever way to bypass multifactor authentication, Ars Technica, 15 December 2020. https://arstechnica.com/information-technology/2020/12/solarwinds-hackers-have-a-clever-way-to-bypass-multi-factor-authentication/ (archived at https://perma.cc/7KSR-NT47)

2 Lawrence Abrams. The SolarWinds cyberattack: The hack, the victims, and what we know, BleepingComputer, 19 December 2020. www.bleepingcomputer.com/news/security/the-solarwinds-cyberattack-the-hack-the-victims-and-what-we-know/ (archived at https://perma.cc/FYX5-EVP4)

3 National Counterintelligence and Security Centre. Kaseya VAS supply chain ransomware attack, 10 August 2021. www.odni.gov/files/NCSC/documents/SafeguardingOurFuture/KaseyaVSASupplyChainRansomwareAttack.pdf (archived at https://perma.cc/TA36-HR7R)

4 National Counterintelligence and Security Centre. Kaseya VAS supply chain ransomware attack, 10 August 2021. www.odni.gov/files/NCSC/documents/SafeguardingOurFuture/KaseyaVSASupplyChainRansomwareAttack.pdf (archived at https://perma.cc/TA36-HR7R)

5 European Union. Open data and AI: An update on the AI Act, 24 January 2025. https://data.europa.eu/en/news-events/news/open-data-and-ai-update-ai-act (archived at https://perma.cc/5Q5Z-H34Q)

6 The White House. The White House launches the National Artificial Intelligence Initiative Office, 12 January 2021. https://trumpwhitehouse.archives.gov/briefings-statements/white-house-launches-national-artificial-intelligence-initiative-office/

7 Federica Laricchia. Number of mobile devices worldwide 2019-2025. Statista, 10 March 2023. www.statista.com/statistics/245501/multiple-mobile-device-ownership-worldwide/ (archived at https://perma.cc/XD7Y-9HY7)

8 Quantum Technology. 2019. https://qt.eu/ (archived at https://perma.cc/8S2G-VQTJ).

9 Lamar Smith. H.R.6227 – 115th Congress (2017–2018): National Quantum Initiative Act. 2018. www.congress.gov/bill/115th-congress/house-bill/6227 (archived at https://perma.cc/SF6B-CASL)

10 ISC2 Cybersecurity workforce study sheds new light on global talent demand amid a lingering pandemic, ISC2, 25 October 2021. www.isc2.org/Insights/2021/10/ISC2-Cybersecurity-Workforce-Study-Sheds-New-Light-on-Global-Talent-Demand (archived at https://perma.cc/UK2N-VFHF)

12

Conclusion

The primitives of security haven't changed over time. Although technology and threats are evolving at lightning speed, this has not prompted a novel concept on how to deal with them. During my time leading the technology effort of a cybersecurity SaaS provider, I learned that the best way to address a forever-growing backlog of threats and vulnerabilities was to pass along as much mitigation effort to the end users as possible – after all, there are more of them than there are of cybersecurity experts. That is symbolic of the purpose of this book, which is to create a culture of security, where it is everyone's responsibility. To create this security culture, people have to feel connected to it.

Rethinking security culture

Cybersecurity is often perceived as a 'dark art', a domain that requires specialized knowledge and expertise to navigate. This perception stems from the fact that understanding vulnerabilities and how they can be exploited necessitates a certain level of technical proficiency. However, the benefits of a robust security culture are readily apparent to all members of an organization. The challenge lies in bridging the gap between the specialized knowledge of cybersecurity professionals and the broader understanding of the rest of the organization. Silos and cliques can easily form within the security domain, creating a disconnect that hinders the organization's overall security posture. Overcoming this requires a cultural shift that democratizes the specialist knowledge and makes it relatable to everyone.

Achieving this cultural shift is a skill in itself, one that demands a delicate balance of technical expertise and effective communication. Traditionally, soft skills and technical or security skills have been viewed as mutually exclusive, with individuals often excelling in one area while lacking in the other. However, the modern cybersecurity landscape requires professionals who can seamlessly blend these two domains. The ability to translate complex technical concepts into easily understandable terms is crucial. Security professionals must be able to convey the importance of security measures, the potential consequences of vulnerabilities, and the steps required to mitigate risks in a way that resonates with non-technical stakeholders. This involves not only a deep understanding of the technical aspects but also a keen awareness of the organization's culture, communication styles and the varying levels of technical proficiency among employees. Fostering this bridge between the security team and the rest of the organization creates a stronger security culture. When everyone in the organization understands the importance of cybersecurity and their role in maintaining it, the overall security posture becomes more robust and resilient.

Democratizing specialized knowledge and encouraging cross-functional collaboration will break down silos, promote knowledge sharing, and introduce a more inclusive and innovative environment. Employees from diverse backgrounds and skill sets can contribute to the organization's security efforts, leading to more comprehensive and effective solutions.

Ultimately, the 'dark art' of cybersecurity can be demystified through the strategic application of soft skills and the deliberate effort to make specialized knowledge accessible to all. By embracing this cultural transformation, organizations can empower their employees, strengthen their security defences, and position themselves for long-term success.

Security and innovation

The relationship between security and innovation has often been a complex and challenging one. Traditionally, the primary focus of security professionals has been on risk mitigation and the prevention of threats, which can sometimes come at the expense of innovation and agility. This dilemma has been a persistent challenge for organizations, as they strive to balance the need for robust security measures with the desire to foster a culture of innovation and adaptability.

The traditional security mindset has often been characterized by a risk-averse approach, where the primary objective is to erect barriers and implement rigid controls to safeguard against potential threats. While this approach may be effective in the short term, it can inadvertently stifle the very innovation that organizations need to thrive in an ever-changing business landscape.

Innovative ideas and new technologies can sometimes be perceived as introducing additional vulnerabilities or disrupting established security protocols – taking on more risk. Security teams may be hesitant to embrace these changes, fearing the potential risks they may pose. This reluctance can create a culture of resistance, where security and innovation are seen as mutually exclusive, rather than complementary. The consequences of this traditional security dilemma can be far-reaching as organizations may miss out on opportunities to leverage innovative technologies, streamline processes or develop new products and services that could give them a competitive edge. Additionally, a rigid security posture can frustrate employees, who may feel that their creative ideas are being stifled, leading to disengagement and a loss of talent.

However, the narrative is shifting, and forward-thinking organizations are recognizing that security can actually be a driver of innovation, rather than a hindrance. Adopting a more holistic and proactive approach to security can unlock new opportunities for growth and transformation.

A key aspect of this shift is the recognition that security should not be viewed as a standalone function, but rather as an integral part of the overall business strategy. Security professionals are increasingly being called upon to collaborate with other departments, such as product development, IT and operations, to identify and address security challenges in a way that enables, rather than constrains, innovation. This collaborative approach allows security teams to gain a deeper understanding of the organization's strategic objectives and the evolving needs of its customers and stakeholders. Armed with this knowledge, they can work alongside their colleagues to design security solutions that are not only robust but also flexible and adaptable, allowing the organization to respond quickly to changing market conditions and emerging threats.

Security can also serve as a catalyst for innovation by driving the development of new technologies and processes that enhance the organization's overall resilience. For example, the rise of cloud computing and the increasing adoption of remote work have necessitated the development of innovative security solutions that enable secure access to data and resources from anywhere, at any time. Organizations can leverage security as a competitive advantage by embracing this mindset and using it to drive innovation, improve customer experiences, and enhance overall business agility. This shift requires a cultural transformation, where security is seen as an enabler of innovation, rather than a barrier to it.

Embracing risk for strategic growth

As the business landscape continues to evolve at a rapid pace, organizations see the need to adopt a more nuanced and strategic approach to risk management with a paradigm that embraces risk as a necessary component of strategic growth, rather than simply trying to eliminate it altogether. This shift in mindset requires a fundamental change in the way organizations view and approach risk. Instead of seeing risk as something to be avoided at all costs, organizations are now recognizing that calculated risk-taking can be a key driver of innovation, competitive advantage and long-term success.

Embracing risk for strategic growth requires a diverse approach that combines a deep understanding of the organization's risk profile, a willingness to experiment and innovate, and a robust framework for managing and mitigating those risks. One key strategy is to create a culture of risk-taking and experimentation within the organization. This involves empowering employees to explore new ideas, test hypotheses, and take calculated risks without fear of failure which can lead to the development of new avenues for growth and competitive differentiation.

Another important strategy is to develop a comprehensive risk management framework that enables the organization to identify, assess and mitigate potential risks in a proactive and systematic manner. This may involve leveraging data analytics, scenario planning and other risk assessment tools to gain a deeper understanding of the organization's risk landscape and the potential impact of various risk factors. Additionally, organizations can explore strategies for transferring or sharing risk, such as through the use of insurance, partnerships or other risk-sharing mechanisms. Diversifying their risk exposure frees up resources to invest in more strategic initiatives while still maintaining a robust security posture.

Effective risk management requires a careful balance between risk-taking and security investments. Potential risks must be carefully evaluated, and organizations should make informed decisions about where to allocate their resources by prioritizing investments in security measures that directly support their strategic objectives. They should also explore opportunities to leverage innovative technologies and processes that can enhance both security and agility, while carefully weighing the potential rewards associated with various initiatives. For example, an organization may choose to invest in cloud-based security solutions that provide scalable and flexible protection, rather than relying on traditional on-premises infrastructure. This approach can not only enhance the organization's security posture but also enable it to respond more quickly to changing market conditions and customer needs.

Similarly, organizations may explore the use of automation and artificial intelligence to streamline security processes, freeing up resources that can be redirected towards more strategic initiatives. Striking the right balance between risk and security investments will position an organization for long-term success.

Embracing risk for strategic growth is not a simple or straightforward process, but it is a necessary one for organizations that aspire to thrive. A culture of risk-taking and innovation, developing robust risk management frameworks, and carefully balancing security investments, will yield new opportunities for growth and competitive advantage, while still maintaining a strong security posture.

Cultivating a security-driven organization

To cultivate a truly security-driven organization, it is essential to promote security awareness and engagement among all employees, not just the security team. This requires a concerted effort to educate and empower the workforce, ensuring that everyone understands the importance of security and their individual role in maintaining it.

Comprehensive security training programmes equip their employees with the knowledge and skills needed to identify and respond to potential threats by teaching them how to recognize phishing attempts, handle sensitive data securely, and report suspicious activities. Additionally, organizations can encourage a security-first mindset by recognizing and rewarding employees who demonstrate exemplary security practices.

On the technical side, cultivating a security-driven organization means the seamless integration of security into the organization's development lifecycles. This means shifting from a reactive, bolt-on approach to security, where it is addressed as an afterthought, to a proactive, embedded approach where security considerations are baked into every stage of the development process. Incorporating security requirements and best practices into the design, development and deployment of new products, services and systems significantly reduces the risk of vulnerabilities and minimizes the potential for costly security breaches. This approach also fosters a collaborative mindset between security teams and their counterparts in product development, IT and other relevant departments, ensuring that security is not just an afterthought but a fundamental part of the organization's innovation and growth strategies.

Cultivating a security-driven organization requires a holistic and strategic approach that goes beyond traditional security measures. It involves building a security-aware workforce, integrating security into development lifecycles, and ultimately, positioning security as a key driver of innovation and competitive advantage.

Leadership's role in security empowerment

The role of leadership cannot be overstated in the pursuit of cultivating a security-driven organization. Effective security empowerment begins with securing the buy-in and commitment of the executive team. Without this critical foundation, efforts to integrate security into the fabric of the organization are likely to falter.

Executive leaders play a pivotal role in setting the tone and establishing the strategic priorities for the entire organization. When they demonstrate a clear understanding of the importance of security and actively champion security initiatives, it sends a powerful message to the rest of the workforce. This top-down approach helps to break down the perception of security as a necessary evil and instead positions it as a strategic imperative that is essential to the organization's long-term success. Executive buy-in provides the necessary resources, both financial and human, to support the implementation and ongoing maintenance of robust security measures. It also empowers security teams to collaborate more effectively with other departments, fostering a culture of shared responsibility and collective ownership of security-related risks and challenges.

Beyond securing executive buy-in, effective security empowerment requires the seamless integration of security considerations into the organization's strategic planning processes. This means that security is not relegated to a standalone function, but rather is woven into the fabric of the organization's overall business strategy. Incorporating security into the strategic planning process means that security objectives are aligned with the organization's broader goals and priorities. This, in turn, helps to prioritize security investments, allocate resources more effectively, and ensure that security initiatives are directly supporting the organization's long-term growth and success. This integrated approach to security planning also encourages cross-functional collaboration, as security teams work closely with their counterparts in areas such as product development, operations and finance to identify and address potential security risks and opportunities. This collaborative mindset helps to break down silos, foster a shared understanding of security challenges, and ultimately, strengthen the organization's overall security posture.

Effective security empowerment also requires clear and consistent communication from organizational leaders. This involves not only articulating the importance of security to the workforce but also translating complex security concepts into easily understandable terms that resonate with employees at all levels of the organization. As such, leaders must be able to effectively communicate the potential consequences of security breaches, the benefits of strong security measures, and the role that each employee plays in maintaining the organization's security. This communication should be tailored to the specific needs and concerns of different stakeholder groups, ensuring that the message is relevant and actionable. Be sure to actively seek feedback and input from employees, encouraging them to share their concerns, ideas and experiences related to security. This open dialogue helps to build trust, foster a culture of security awareness, and empower employees to take an active role in the organization's security efforts.

Organizational leaders can drive the transformation towards a security-driven organization by embracing their role as security champions. Through executive buy-in, the integration of security into strategic planning, and effective communication, leaders can empower their workforce, align security initiatives with business objectives, and ultimately, position the organization for long-term success in an increasingly complex and volatile business landscape.

Strategies for effective risk management

Establishing a risk assessment framework that enables organizations to continuously monitor their digital environment, identify potential vulnerabilities, and evaluate the likelihood and potential impact of various risk scenarios is vital to effective risk management. Things like leveraging advanced analytics, threat intelligence and industry benchmarking to gain a deeper understanding of the organization's risk profile and the evolving threat landscape will aid in that pursuit.

Start by prioritizing the most critical risks and understanding their interdependencies to develop targeted mitigation strategies and allocate resources more effectively. The proactive approach to risk management helps to ensure that the organization is prepared to respond to emerging threats and minimize the potential for costly disruptions.

Even with the most comprehensive risk management strategies in place, be prepared to respond effectively to security incidents and data breaches when they occur. Effective incident response planning is a crucial component of a robust risk management framework, as it enables the organization to contain the damage, restore operations, and learn from the experience. The plan should be tested regularly to be sure that all relevant stakeholders, including IT, security, legal and communications teams, are aligned and prepared to execute their respective roles. Establish clear communication protocols, define escalation procedures, and ensure that the necessary tools and resources are in place to facilitate a timely and coordinated response. This process should be followed by a thorough review and analysis to identify the root causes of the incident, assess the effectiveness of the response, and implement necessary improvements. This continuous improvement mindset helps to strengthen the organization's overall resilience and better prepare it for future challenges.

It is more necessary today than ever to have a more adaptive and agile approach to risk management, as the digital world is expanding so quickly. Traditional risk management strategies that rely on static, one-size-fits-all solutions are often ill-equipped to handle the rapid pace of change and the complexity of modern digital risks. Adaptive risk management strategies involve the development of flexible, scalable and responsive frameworks that can evolve alongside the organization's changing needs and the evolving threat landscape. Scenario planning, stress testing and other dynamic risk assessment techniques help anticipate and prepare for a range of potential disruptions. Additionally, adaptive risk management strategies should leverage the power of emerging technologies, such as artificial intelligence and machine learning, to enhance the organization's ability to detect, analyse and respond to risks in real-time.

Automating certain risk management processes and leveraging predictive analytics frees up resources to focus on more strategic, proactive risk mitigation efforts.

Effective risk management is heavily dependent on the ability to collect, analyse and leverage data to inform its decision-making processes. Organizations can gain deeper insights into their risk profiles, identify emerging trends, and make more informed, data-driven decisions by harnessing the power of data and analytics. Implementing advanced data management and analytics platforms that enable the organization to aggregate and analyse data from a variety of sources, including internal systems, external threat intelligence and industry benchmarks, are useful ways to identify potential blind spots and proactively address emerging threats. The effective use of this data can also support efforts to optimize risk management strategies and investments. Through the tracking of performance and effectiveness of various risk mitigation measures, organizations can identify areas for improvement, reallocate resources and continuously refine their approach to ensure that it remains aligned with their strategic objectives.

Effective risk management combines proactive risk identification, adaptive response strategies and the strategic use of data and analytics. Organizations can enhance their overall resilience and minimize the potential for costly disruptions by embracing these strategies.

Human factors in security

It is essential to recognize that security is not solely a technical challenge, but also a deeply human one. The decisions and behaviours of individuals within the organization can have a profound impact on the effectiveness of security measures, often in ways that are not immediately apparent. At the heart of this human factor in security is the psychology of decision-making. Individuals, whether they are employees, customers or other stakeholders, often make security-related decisions based on a complex interplay of cognitive biases, emotional responses and situational factors, rather than purely rational considerations.

For example, the phenomenon of 'security fatigue' can lead individuals to become desensitized to security warnings or to bypass security protocols in the interest of convenience. Similarly, the 'illusion of control' can cause individuals to overestimate their ability to mitigate security risks, leading to complacency and a false sense of security. Understanding these psychological factors is significant in the development of more effective security strategies that account for the human element and empower individuals to make informed, security-conscious decisions.

The rise of remote and hybrid work arrangements has further amplified the importance of the human factor in security. As organizations adapt to the challenges of a distributed workforce, they must grapple with the increased risk of security breaches and data leaks that can arise from the decentralization of work environments. In a distributed work setting, employees may be operating in less controlled environments, with potentially weaker security measures and a greater reliance on personal devices and home networks. This can make them more vulnerable to social engineering attacks, phishing scams and other security threats that exploit the human element. Also, the lack of face-to-face interaction and the blurring of work–life boundaries can make it more difficult for organizations to foster a strong security culture and ensure consistent adherence to security protocols. Employees may feel less connected to the organization's security objectives, leading to a greater risk of security incidents.

To mitigate these risks, organizations must invest in comprehensive security training and awareness programmes that are tailored to the needs of a distributed workforce. This may include the use of interactive simulations, gamification and other engaging approaches to help employees develop the necessary security skills and mindsets.

When security incidents do occur, the human factor can amplify their impact, creating a ripple effect that extends far beyond the immediate technical or financial consequences. The emotional and psychological toll of a security breach can be significant, leading to feelings of fear, anxiety and loss of trust among employees and customers. This can have a detrimental impact on morale, productivity and the organization's reputation, ultimately undermining its long-term resilience and competitiveness. The human response to security incidents can also shape the organization's ability to recover and learn from the experience. Individuals may be reluctant to report or acknowledge security breaches due to fear of blame or reputational damage, hindering the organization's ability to investigate the incident, identify root causes, and implement effective remediation measures.

Organizations can combat this effect by fostering a culture of transparency, accountability and continuous learning, where security incidents are viewed as opportunities for growth and improvement, rather than sources of shame or blame. This requires strong leadership, clear communication and the establishment of robust incident response and crisis management protocols.

Ultimately, the human factor in security represents a persistent challenge that organizations must continually address and evolve their strategies to overcome. A human-centric approach to security can empower employees, customers and other stakeholders to become active participants in the security process, rather than passive recipients of security measures. This involves cultivating a security-driven culture, providing comprehensive training and support, and leveraging behavioural insights to design more effective security interventions. The ability to effectively manage the human factor in security will be a key differentiator, enabling them to build resilience, maintain trust and position themselves for long-term success in an interconnected business environment.

Practical implementation: from theory to action

Developing a comprehensive security strategy is a critical first step, but the true test of its effectiveness lies in the organization's ability to translate this vision into practical, actionable steps. This process of implementation is where the rubber meets the road, as organizations must navigate the complexities of aligning security objectives with the realities of their operations, resources and organizational culture.

The key to successful implementation lies in the development of a detailed, phased action plan that outlines the specific initiatives, timelines and responsibilities required to bring the security strategy to life. This plan should be grounded in a thorough understanding of the organization's current security posture, its unique challenges, and the needs of its various stakeholders. Breaking down the security strategy into manageable, measurable milestones will effectively allocate resources, track progress and course-correct as needed. This approach also helps to build momentum and demonstrate the tangible benefits of the security programme, which can be crucial in securing ongoing support and buy-in from leadership and the broader organization.

Integrating secure software development practices into the organization's development lifecycle plays an important role in mitigating the risks posed by vulnerabilities, cyber threats and other security challenges. Adopting secure coding practices, implementing automated security testing tools and establishing strong vulnerability management processes are all worth their weight. Shifting security 'left' in the development process can identify and address potential issues earlier, reducing the time and cost associated with remediation. Also consider the security implications of their technology choices, favouring solutions that have been designed with security in mind and that offer robust security features and capabilities, such as the use of secure coding frameworks, the implementation of encryption and access controls, and the integration of security monitoring and incident response capabilities.

Effective security implementation is not a one-time event, but rather an ongoing process of monitoring, evaluation and adaptation. As the threat landscape and the organization's own needs and priorities evolve, the security programme must be able to adapt and respond accordingly. This requires complete security monitoring and analytics capabilities, which enable the organization to continuously assess the effectiveness of its security measures, identify emerging threats, and make data-driven decisions about where to allocate resources and focus its efforts.

Also, by leveraging advanced technologies such as security information and event management (SIEM) systems, security orchestration and automated response (SOAR) platforms, and threat intelligence feeds, organizations can gain a more comprehensive and real-time understanding of their security posture. This, in turn, allows them to quickly identify and address vulnerabilities, respond to incidents, and make informed adjustments to their security strategies. The process of monitoring and adaptation must also be embedded into the broader governance and risk management frameworks, ensuring that security considerations are consistently factored into decision-making processes and that the security programme remains aligned with business objectives and risk tolerance.

Practical implementation of a security strategy is a complex and multifaceted endeavour, requiring a combination of strategic planning, technical expertise and organizational agility. Translating the security vision into actionable steps, integrating secure software development practices, and continuously monitoring and adapting the security posture will bridge the gap between theory and practice.

Measuring success

Defining the right key performance indicators (KPIs) can provide valuable insights into the effectiveness of an organization's security programme, inform decision-making, and demonstrate the value of security investments to stakeholders. However, identifying the appropriate KPIs for security can be a complex and nuanced task, as security encompasses a wide range of technical, operational and human factors. Traditional security metrics, such as the number of security incidents or the percentage of systems patched, may provide a limited view of the organization's overall security posture and fail to capture the broader strategic impact of security initiatives.

To develop a more comprehensive and meaningful set of security KPIs, consider a balanced approach that encompasses both quantitative and qualitative measures. This may include operational metrics, such as incident response time and vulnerability remediation rate;

risk management metrics, like risk exposure score and percentage of identified risks mitigated; organizational impact metrics, including cost savings from avoided security incidents and improvement in customer trust; as well as behavioural and cultural metrics, such as employee security awareness and adoption rate of security best practices.

Aligning these KPIs with the organization's strategic security objectives and the broader business goals means having a more holistic understanding of the security programme's effectiveness and its impact on the overall organization. The process of defining and tracking security KPIs should be an iterative one, with regular reviews and adjustments to ensure that the metrics remain relevant and responsive.

Successful measurement of security empowerment requires a balanced, data-driven approach that combines technical, operational and strategic considerations. The establishment of a comprehensive KPI framework can not only enhance their security posture but also position security as a strategic enabler of business growth and resilience.

Embracing security empowerment

The time has come for leaders to take bold and decisive action, moving beyond the traditional, reactive approach to security and instead cultivating a security-driven culture that positions security as a strategic enabler of growth and innovation. This call to action begins with a fundamental shift in mindset – one that recognizes security as an integral part of the organization's overall business strategy. Aligning security objectives with the organization's broader goals and priorities can unlock new opportunities to leverage security as a competitive advantage, driving innovation, enhancing customer trust and securing the long-term success of the enterprise.

At the heart of this security empowerment lies the need to foster a culture of security awareness and engagement among all employees, from the C-suite to the frontline. This requires a concerted effort to educate, empower and embolden the workforce, equipping them with the knowledge, skills and tools necessary to identify, mitigate and respond to security threats. This call to action also demands a holistic, adaptive approach to risk management, one that embraces calculated risk-taking and leverages the power of data and analytics to anticipate and respond to emerging threats. A flexible, scalable security framework that can evolve alongside the organization's changing needs will position said organization for long-term resilience and agility.

The path to security empowerment requires steadfast commitment from organizational leaders, who must champion security initiatives, allocate the necessary resources, and foster a culture of collaboration and continuous improvement which will unlock the full potential of their security programmes, driving innovation, enhancing customer trust, and securing their place as leaders in the digital age. Organizational leaders must be willing to lead by example, demonstrating their own commitment to security best practices and actively participating in security awareness and training programmes because modelling the desired security-first behaviours and mindset will inspire and empower their employees to become active participants in the security process. Security empowerment can not only safeguard a company's assets and reputation but also position themselves for sustained growth and competitive advantage.

Organizations face a barrage of constantly evolving security threats, from sophisticated cyber-attacks and data breaches to the growing risk of insider threats and supply chain vulnerabilities. The rapid pace of technological change, the volume of connected devices, and the increasing sophistication of threat actors have all contributed to a security landscape that is more complex and dynamic than ever before.

The increasing reliance on remote and hybrid work models, accelerated by the Covid-19 pandemic, has introduced new security risks, as employees access sensitive data and systems from a variety of devices and locations, often outside the traditional corporate perimeter. As such, organizations must now have a proactive, comprehensive approach to security that goes beyond traditional perimeter-based defences and reactive incident response.

Aligning security as part of the wider business strategy begins with a deep understanding of the organization's risk profile, its critical assets, and the potential impact of security breaches on its operations, reputation and financial performance. Armed with this knowledge, leaders can then develop a security strategy that is tailored to the organization's unique needs and challenges, ensuring that security initiatives are closely linked to the organization's broader objectives, and identify opportunities to leverage security as a competitive advantage.

INDEX

Looking for another book?

Explore our award-winning
books from global business
experts in Risk and
Compliance

Scan the code to browse

www.koganpage.com/risk-compliance

More from Kogan Page

ISBN: 9781398614284

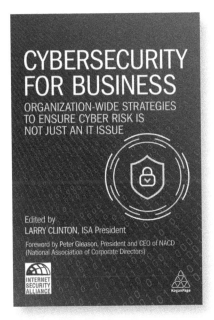

ISBN: 9781398606142

ISBN: 9781398613492

ISBN: 9780749496951

www.koganpage.com

From 4 December 2025 the EU Responsible Person (GPSR) is:
eucomply oÜ, Pärnu mnt. 139b – 14, 11317 Tallinn, Estonia
www.eucompliancepartner.com